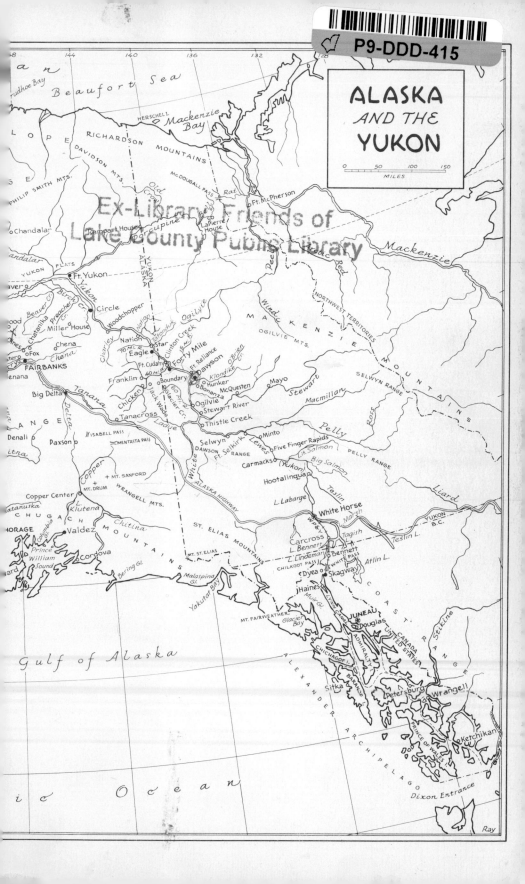

ALASKA
AND THE
YUKON

0   50   100   150
MILES

148 144 140 136 132 128

Beaufort Sea

Prudhoe Bay
HERSCHELL I.
Mackenzie Bay

RICHARDSON MOUNTAINS

DAVIDSON MTS.

McDOUGALL PASS
Rat R.
Ft. McPherson

PHILIP SMITH MTS.

Chandalar

Rampart House
Porcupine
LaPierre House

Mackenzie

Chandalar
YUKON FLATS
Ft. Yukon
Beaver Cr.

Yukon
Averd

Birch Cr.
Circle
Woodchopper
Nation
Charley

Peel R.
Red R.

NORTHWEST TERRITORIES

MACKENZIE

OGILVIE MTS.

wood
Chatanika
Miller House
Chena
Preacher Cr.

Nation
Klondike
Eagle
Star
Clinton Creek
Forty Mile
Ft. Reliance
O'Brien Cr.

Ogilvie

FAIRBANKS
Fox
Chena

To Mi. R.
To Mi. R.
Ft. Cudahy
Dawson

SELWYN RANGE

MOUNTAINS

Nenana
Franklin
Boundary
40 Mi.
Klondike
Hunker
Bonanza
McQuesten
Mayo

Big Delta
Chicken
Jack Wade
Glacier Cr.
Ogilvie
Stewart River
Thistle Creek
Stewart
Macmillan

Tanana
Delta
Tanacross
Ladue

White
ROSS

Denali
ISABELL PASS
Selwyn
Dawson
Minto
Pelly

Paxson
MENTASTA PASS
Ft. Selkirk
Lewes
Five Finger Rapids
PELLY RANGE

itna
RANGE
Carmacks
Lt. Salmon
Big Salmon

Copper
MT. SANFORD
Yukon

Liard

Copper Center
MT. DRUM
WRANGELL MTS.
Hootalinqua

Matanuska
L. Klutena
CHUGACH

ANCHORAGE
Valdez
Chitina
MOUNTAINS

ALASKA HIGHWAY
L. Labarge
L. Laberge
Teslin
YUKON
B.C.

Columbia Gl.
Prince William Sound
Cordova

ST. ELIAS MOUNTAINS
White Horse
Marsh
Teslin L.

Bering Gl.
MT. ST. ELIAS
Carcross
L. Bennett
Tagish
Atlin L.

Malaspina Gl.
Yakutat Bay
L. Lindeman
CHILKOOT PASS
Bennett
WHITE PASS

MT. FAIRWEATHER
Dyea
Skagway

Glacier Bay
Haines
Muir Gl.
LYNN CANAL

Gulf of Alaska
JUNEAU
Douglas

CANADA
UNITED STATES

CHICHAGOF I.
ADMIRALTY I.

COAST

STIKINE R.

RANGE

ic Ocean

Sitka
BARANOF I.

Petersburg
Wrangell

ALEXANDER ARCHIPELAGO

PRINCE OF WALES I.
Ketchikan

Dixon Entrance

Ray

THE ALASKA

GOLD RUSH

David Wharton

THE ALASKA
GOLD RUSH

Indiana University Press

Bloomington and London

Published in Canada by Fitzhenry & Whiteside Limited,
Don Mills, Ontario

Library of Congress catalog card number: 72-75394

ISBN: 0-253-10061-5

Manufactured in the United States of America

SECOND PRINTING 1972

CONTENTS

ILLUSTRATIONS

PREFACE

THIS IS NOT ANOTHER STORY OF THE KLONDIKE. The Klondike strike was just one of many that constituted the last stampede. This is the history of all the major strikes that together formed the gold rush to Alaska and the Yukon, the events leading to those strikes, and the routes that led to the gold fields. But it is not a history in the sense of being a factual chronology of events; it is history in the sense of presenting events in their emotional context. It is an attempt to show the breadth and diversity of this final gold rush, the country as it was, and the life as it was lived along the streams and in the towns of the North at the end of the nineteenth century.

I first became acquainted with Alaska, and more particularly the Yukon, in 1964. In that year, the Sierra Club dispatched an expedition to study what effects the damming of the Yukon at Rampart might have on the ecology of the Yukon River valley. The study group, of which I was a member, traveled by boat from the Canadian border to Tanana, stopping at Eagle, Circle, Fort Yukon, Beaver, and Rampart, as well as camping at many sites in between these towns. Subsequent reading about the Yukon, the towns along the river, and the stampedes to the gold fields which opened up the interior of Alaska, while informative, revealed that the authors of these books did not seem to be writing of the Yukon I had seen or the towns that are there today. Descriptions of the gold rush seemed equally lacking in true perspective. They did not show the country as it is or as it must have been. The accounts were either dryly factual, lacking in human warmth, or overdramatized, losing authenticity. Dangers were magnified, hardships exaggerated, the glitter of gold made too brilliant. To resolve for myself these different views, I decided to follow the most popular of the routes to the gold fields, from Dyea over the Chilkoot Pass and down the Yukon, as had the stampeders in the nineteenth century.

Accordingly, in 1968 three of us with backpacks left Skagway, hiked across the low spur of hills to Dyea, up the Dyea Trail to the Chilkoot Pass. We crossed over the Chilkoot, as did thousands of stampeders in 1897, 1898, and 1899. We dropped to Crater Lake, where the Yukon starts, hiked on to Lake Lindeman, where they built their boats and rafts to start the trip down the Yukon, and on to Lake Bennett, where the stampeders who crossed the Chilkoot joined with those who crossed over the White Pass from Skagway. We went on to Whitehorse, where a flatboat awaited us. We drifted downriver to Lake Labarge, down the Thirty Mile River with its wrecks of steamboats, past Hootalinqua, Little Salmon, Big Salmon, past the abandoned town of Minto, Fort Selkirk, Stewart Island, Indian River, to Dawson. We camped and fished and panned for gold and browsed through every deserted cabin and empty village along the way. We worked an old digging on Bonanza Creek and then continued to Fort Reliance, Forty Mile, Eagle, and repeated that portion of the river between Eagle and Circle, so as to visit the old mining camps of Star City, Nation, Seventy Mile, Slaven's Camp, and Woodchopper.

Knowing by this time that Dawson and the Klondike were but a fraction of the gold rush, we went on to Fairbanks, camping on the Tanana and visiting the nearby gold camps. I flew to Kotzebue and Nome, the site of one of the most exciting of the stampedes. I drove to Valdez, where gold was being mined before the discovery on the Bonanza.

I combed the Bancroft Library of the University of California at Berkeley, the libraries of the University of Washington at Seattle and the University of Alaska, and the Alaska Historical Library at Juneau, as well as the museums at Dawson, Stewart Island, and Eagle, for old letters, diaries, and manuscripts. Wherever possible I talked with the people who had lived in the country all their lives and with the few who were living in the gold country at the turn of the century. These letters, diaries, manuscripts, and interviews do not always produce facts. More often they reflect opinions and impressions as important as facts in arriving at the truth. Truth is an amalgam of fact and opinion and impression. Truth is color as well as outline. Truth is flesh as well as bones. It is by these precepts that I have sought to present the truth.

Except for passing references, two comparatively minor stampedes to the Koyukuk and the Kuskokwim countries, which did not influence the development of the last stampede, are omitted from this book. Also omitted is the Juneau gold strike which occurred sixteen years before the Klondike, since it involved quartz gold and big mining combines rather than placer gold and individuals, the key ingredients of the Alaska gold rush.

I acknowledge with gratitude the permission granted to me by Dora E. McLean Simpson to quote from her thesis, "Early Newspapers on the Upper Yukon Watershed"; C. W. Snedden to quote from the *Daily News-Miner*; O. T. Hampton to quote from *Jessen's Daily*; Paul McCarthy, University of Alaska Archivist and Curator of Manuscripts, to quote from "The Pioneer Days in Alaska" by George Pilz and from the manuscript collections of Major General Farnsworth and Frank Buteau; Volney Richmond, Jr., of the Northern Commercial Company to quote from Mr. Gerstle's letter to Moses Lorenz; Charles Scribner's Sons to quote from Hudson Stuck's *Voyages on the Yukon and Its Tributaries*; The Caxton Printers, Ltd., of Caldwell, Idaho, to quote from *Yukon Voyage* by Walter R. Curtin; and Mrs. Ellen W. Lawrence for permission to use material written by John Lawrence about Stewart Island.

Additionally, never has it been more essential to acknowledge the assistance of the people of an entire area. The people of the Yukon and Alaska are the most generous, the friendliest people in the world. With hardly an exception, they gave of their time, their private papers, their memories, which have helped make this book possible. Among so many, a few must be mentioned specifically. In the order of the towns visited, there was George Rapuzzi of Skagway, who took time off from final preparation for a prospecting trip to talk at length about the early days of Skagway. There was the whole Burian family of Stewart Island—Rudolf Burian and his wife Yvonne, who let me read John D. Lawrence's account of early days at Stewart Island, and the daughter, Linda,

who had an especial interest and knowledge concerning the history
of the island, and the elder son, Robin, who showed us how to pan
for gold on the Bonanza. In Dawson there are Don McDonnell,
and Taffy, and Syd and many pleasant hours yarning at the firehouse and at Syd's bar. Bob Burkhart, who gave us a joint of moose
and showed us where he was born in Forty Mile. In Eagle, Barney
and Borghild Hansen with anecdotes and history served up with
coffee and cake. Attractive Mary Warren in Circle City, whose
mother was one of the first residents of the community. Frank
Miller at Miller House between Circle and Fairbanks. Fairbanks
Clara Hickman Rust, whose knowledge of early Fairbanks is solid
and real. Charming, mercurial Eva McGowan. Helen Callahan,
whose life is the history of the Yukon. Her grandfather was Russian. Her father discovered gold on Preacher Creek. She was baptized by Archdeacon McDonald, schooled by Bishop Bompas at
Forty Mile, lived in Circle, worked for Archdeacon Hudson Stuck
at Fort Yukon, and was related to McQuesten and Mayo. To know
this delightful person is to love her. Fabian Carey, trapper, scholar,
conversationalist, whose knowledge of Alaska is drawn from the
intimate depths of the forests and lonely winter trap lines. Bill
Berry, who knows more about the Yukon steamboats than any
man living. The entire staff of the library at the University of
Alaska and Dr. W. R. Cashen, who placed his office at my disposal.
And, of course, firsthand experience of the Yukon would not have
been possible without Steve Spengler, ex-marine, school principal,
and riverman, who provided our boat and the skill to keep it in the
proper channel, whose love of wilderness contributed so much
to my own understanding. And Paul Lien, as full of information
as only a trained reporter can be and as hospitable as an Arctic
summer day is long. In Nome there is Carrie McLain, who came to
Nome in 1905 and wouldn't live anywhere else; and pretty Laura
Johnsen, a taxi driver, whose grandfather crossed from Siberia on
the ice, was shanghaied out of Sitka to die in London, who gladly
talked of earlier days between taxi calls and cups of coffee. The
Board of Trade saloon with its old newspaper-festooned walls. Billy
Quitch is in Valdez, the grand old man of the town, typical
Alaskaner, independent, self-reliant, hospitable. In Juneau, Phyllis
Nottingham, Historical Librarian. And Robert D. Monroe, Chief,
Special Collections Division, University of Washington Libraries,

was most helpful, especially in giving me access to all their old photographs of Alaska and the Yukon.

Especial mention must be made of Bettie Thomas, who bar-hopped Whitehorse, Carmacks, Dawson, and Valdez before my arrival, digging up stories and names of people to see, and prepared a map of the trip. And my own Toby Wharton, who assisted in the bar-hopping, helped with the lengthy research required at the University of Alaska, and stayed home in 1969 to see the manuscript through its final typing, while I returned to Alaska. And Dr. Arnold Fletcher and Bruce MacKenzie, whose critical readings of the early manuscript were most helpful.

ALONE WITHOUT HELP
THIS COURAGEOUS GIRL
RAN A GRUB TENT
NEAR LOG CABIN
DURING THE GOLD RUSH
OF 1897-1898
SHE FED AND LODGED
THE WILDEST
GOLD CRAZED MEN
GENERATIONS
SHALL SURELY KNOW
THIS INSPIRING SPIRIT
MURDERED OCT. 27.
1902

1

The Last Stampede

HE GENERALLY ACCEPTED DATE for the beginning of the Alaska gold rush is 1897. Although significant gold strikes had been made for over a decade before, this year marked the beginning of the great rush of men to the Far North which was to constitute the final gold rush of the nineteenth century, the last stampede.

Gold had been discovered in California in 1848, then in British Columbia, South Africa, Australia, and New Zealand before it was found in Alaska and the Yukon Territory of Canada. For half a century men and women swept back and forth across the globe in search of sudden wealth. Each new strike had its important consequences. But in this half-century of gold discovery, the Alaska rush holds a special place in the imagination of the world. It was the final example of the individual existing as an individual, succeeding by his own efforts, neither exploiting nor being exploited by anyone. The remoteness of the country lying along the Arctic Circle and the unknown hazards of the Far North against which men were willing to gamble their lives in search of wealth gave to the Alaska gold rush a romantic significance.

In 1897 Alaska was still generally unknown. It was the mysterious North. Nearly two and a half centuries passed after Columbus' voyage of discovery before Europeans knew of Alaska. In 1741 Vitus Bering, a Dane in the service of Russia, first sighted the coast of Alaska. However, it was not until near the end of the century that Russian control of Alaska was expressed in definite action. The Russian-American Company was granted a charter to govern and exploit all the resources of an area one-fifth the size of the present United States, excluding Alaska. With such extensive authority, the Russian-American Company did little but develop fur trading along the coast and among the island chains. Russians did explore the Yukon and Kuskokwim to a limited extent. They discovered coal deposits and knew of the likelihood of gold. A Russian mining engineer, Peter Doroshin, who spent five years prospecting for gold and coal, reported color everywhere he dug along the Kenai River. In 1865 the Russian Minister to Washington reported to his government that the prospects for gold in Alaska were good. He stated that he had been informed by a California geologist that there must be gold in Alaska since the geologic coast formation is the same as that of other parts of the Northwest where gold had been found.[1] However, the Russian-American Company did not have the resources to search for gold. It remained principally a fur trading company until it was liquidated in 1867 with the sale of Alaska.

The true reasons for the sale of Alaska are clouded in political intrigue. It is probably safe to assume that the Russian-American Company was opposed to the sale. The Russian government was not anxious to sell. Nor was the American government overly desirous to make the purchase. The United States Senate ratified the treaty by only a single vote. And yet the sale and the purchase were made. Russia may have felt that the growing United States might seize Alaska eventually as it had seized California, and it was better to sell it than to lose it to conquest. Or it may have felt its position in Alaska was untenable, and that it would be better to have a friendly United States in Alaska rather than the British, whom they had small reason to like or trust after the Crimean War. On the American side there was sympathy for Russia, which had supported the Union during the Civil War. Russia was in economic difficulties at the time, and the payment of the purchase price may have been considered as economic assistance to a friendly ally.[2]

Whatever the political truth of the sale, the United States was not totally unaware of the economic potential of Alaska. American trading ships and whalers knew Alaskan waters well. The

Western Union Telegraph Company had made a survey from Canada to the Bering Strait preparatory to installing a telegraph line from the United States to Europe via Siberia. Daniel B. Libby, a member of the survey party, found gold in 1865 while digging post holes near what is now Nome. The *New York Times*, in an article on the merits of the purchase, commented favorably on the prospects of gold in the territory.[3]

The Americans, unlike the Russians, thought first of gold, not the fur trade, and the history of gold in Alaska properly starts with the American acquisition of the country. Shortly after the purchase in 1867, the *Alaska Herald*, published in San Francisco, carried an article stating that gold is found on the main peninsula of Alaska and on the peninsula east of Cook's Inlet. "The Indian women wear necklaces of gold and nuggets picked up from the surface."[4]

American soldiers found gold near Sitka soon after the transfer of the former Russian capital. A few years later Arthur Harper, an American prospector, found gold along the tributaries of the Yukon. George Holt crossed the Chilkoot Pass in 1878 and returned from the Yukon with nuggets. In 1880 the first rich strike was made. That year Fred Harris and Joe Juneau found gold in Silverbow Basin, a mile and a half inland from the present capital of Alaska.[5] A hundred and fifty million dollars worth of gold were to be produced in this region before technical difficulties forced the closing of the mines. The Juneau strike, however, was sixteen years before the Klondike and not properly a part of the Alaska gold rush.

In the meantime, men were pushing north, crossing the Coast Range and filtering into the Yukon basin. The Russians earlier had penetrated the lower Yukon and the British the upper Yukon. Neither, however, had been interested in opening the country. They preferred to keep it closed to any influence that might interfere with the fur trade with the Indians. The American traders who came with the purchase of Alaska were a different breed. They did not have the traditions of the Hudson's Bay Company and the Russian-American Company behind them, with a single-minded orientation toward furs. The first American traders on the upper Yukon were as much prospectors as traders. They traded for a living and prospected for the love of the search. When miners found their way into the interior from the coast, they were welcomed, not resented. The American trading posts quickly adjusted to the potential offered by the presence of prospectors. In addition to Indian trading goods, traders began stocking mining equipment and food for the prospectors, making it possible for these men to remain in the interior longer and prospect more extensively. With more extensive prospecting, new gold fields were found, new strikes made. As the trickle of prospectors increased, the trading posts became stores for miners and grew into communities. Strikes increased and stampedes began.

For sixteen years an ever-increasing number of men worked the tributaries of the Yukon—the Pelly, the Teslin, Big Salmon, Sixty Mile, Stewart, Indian, Forty Mile, Birch Creek, Rampart, rivers, streams, creeks, and pups, as the smaller creeks were known. Everywhere was some gold, and stampedes were chronic. In 1884 there was a small stampede to the Stewart River. Two years later there was a more important stampede to the Forty Mile, and in 1893 a major stampede to Birch Creek. In 1896 George Washington Carmack, an American who had gone *siwash*—taken an Indian wife and adopted the Indian way of life—filed claims on Rabbit Creek, soon renamed the Bonanza, and the stampede which followed emptied every mining camp on the Yukon. In this year gold was also being mined in the Nome area. Two years later the Copper River country out of Valdez had its own stampede of several thousand miners. Men from the Yukon crossed over to the Tanana River, and in 1902 the final big strike produced Fairbanks.

The Alaska gold rush was not a single strike, it was a congeries of strikes. It was Stewart River, Forty Mile, Circle, Nome, Valdez, and Fairbanks, as well as Dawson. And much of it was not in Alaska but in Canada. Men did not care. They were going to Alaska or the Yukon, or thought they were, for neither name was definitive in the emotional context of the gold rush. Yukon, however, is both a river and a Canadian province. As a river, it starts in British Columbia about eighteen miles from the American coastal port, Skagway. It flows north six hundred miles through British Columbia and Yukon Territory to where the Klondike River enters. There it turns west and north, crossing into Alaska about one hundred miles downriver. For another thirteen hundred miles it is the main river of Alaska, serpentining through the center of the state before emptying into the Bering Sea. As a political unit, it is the Yukon Territory, Canada's westernmost province. And it was here that the first strikes were made on the Stewart

River, the Forty Mile River, and finally on the Klondike. The Klondike is a tributary of the Yukon River in the Yukon Territory, and Dawson, located where the Klondike enters the Yukon River, was the first capital of the Yukon Territory.

If the names Alaska and Yukon were ambiguous in 1897, what they symbolized was not. They stood for gold and the country where it was being found in unbelievable quantities. More confusion existed over the best route to reach this gold country. Transportation companies, town boosters, sharpsters, all pushed their favorite routes. Edmonton merchants promoted the Edmonton route across Canada. Seattle outfitters favored Skagway and Dyea with the White Pass and Chilkoot Pass to the Yukon River as the shortest route. Others advised Valdez and the Copper River trail known as the all-American route. Operators of the Yukon River steamers could point to the advantages of an all-water route with no cross-country hardships. Despite glowing promises, no route was simple or easy. Each tried men with its own tests. Each seemed to have a demoniac character of its own which marked the lives of those who followed it. The Chilkoot Pass is the most famous because so many crossed it, great photographers like E. A. Hegg caught its drama of men meeting nature's grimmest challenge, and Jack London, Rex Beach, and Joaquin Miller passed this way and wrote about it. The Valdez route was worse and made more terrifying by the reportorial flair of Captain Abercrombie, who wrote of thousands pitted hopelessly against the vast glacier, dying, going mad, blinded by the snow, starving, and finally turning back defeated to rot with scurvy on the beaches.[6]

The all-water route via St. Michael and the Yukon River seemed the simplest. But those attempting to avoid the hardships of the Chilkoot or Valdez routes found the ease of steamer travel all the way a special hardship in itself. St. Michael, where travelers transferred from ocean steamer to riverboat, was twice as far from Seattle as Skagway or Valdez. The riverboats ran only in the summer. They made frequent refueling stops. Boilers blew up. The thin hulls proved fragile to the slightest shock. Shifting channels, sandbars, mud-flats, and sunken snags were constant threats. And worst of all, the winter freeze. When the river froze, all traffic stopped. The river steamers pulled into side streams, sloughs, or sheltered channels and waited out the winter. For six to seven months, the impatient stampeder who elected the all-water route would have to sit in idleness, knowing that thousands of others were pouring into the Klondike. With nothing to occupy his hands or his mind, the stranded traveler would imagine rich strikes being made by others where his claim might have been. He could see luckier men scooping up the free gold, stuffing huge nuggets into moosehide pokes and heading out. He could see the steady stream of men from the Chilkoot spreading out over the gold country, staking every vacant piece of ground. He cursed the day he had listened to the hawkers of steamer travel.

The worst route was probably the Edmonton route, the all-Canadian route, promoted and advertised by the Edmonton merchants.[7] On the map, it was simple—take a train to Edmonton and from there a well-marked trail led to the Yukon. The trail, however, was nonexistent. The map did not show and brochures did not tell of the muskeg, the bogs, the willow thickets, the spruce forests so thick a man could wander for days without knowing his direction, the rivers in flood, the rock-sharp ravines that could not be crossed. Only one in a thousand of those who left Edmonton ever reached Dawson and for them it took two years.

The history of this last gold rush involves these routes, the towns marking the routes, and the towns to which the routes led. But, more importantly, it is the story of the individuals who followed the routes, made the strikes, and constituted the towns. The routes were difficult or dangerous only in relation to the people who followed them. Strikes, obviously, were the result of individual hard work or luck. Communities were only the composites of the men and women who formed them—Americans, Japanese, Canadians, Italians, Arabs, and Scandinavians. Some were frontiersmen, others were farmers, sailors, clerks, bookkeepers, teachers, or businessmen. There were poets—Joaquin Miller was sent to Dawson by the *San Francisco Examiner;* there were writers—Jack London and Rex Beach spent time in the gold camps. There were ruffians, vagabonds, and scoundrels. Skagway, the gateway to the gold fields of the upper Yukon, was for a time run by Jefferson Randolph "Soapy" Smith, the most colorful of all con men and probably the most adroit of all gangsters and crooks in the history of the country. Fairbanks was

Hard work was the rule for women as well as men. Mary's hotel was located at Number 20 Below on Bonanza. Like Mrs. Lowe, many women took in laundry or told fortunes. (E. A. HEGG)

founded by an ex-convict from Seattle who made a fortune in
the process of building the city and then absconded with the
funds of his own bank, leaving Fairbanks financially destitute
for several years. Nome was the scene of one of the most blatant
uses of official position to perpetrate fraud and corruption in
the history of the United States. There were also men of probity
and highest moral character. Father William H. Judge was in
the original stampede from Forty Mile to the Klondike. He was
not in search of gold. His concern was with the physical and
moral health of the miners. He drove himself to an early death
organizing, building, and staffing the first hospital in Dawson.

There were women on the trails, making strikes, and forming
a part of the towns. Not just dance-hall girls—there were those—
but wives dragging sleds with their husbands and single women
come to make their fortunes. These women, like the men of the
stampede, were individualists. They went across the Chilkoot, up
the Yukon, over the Valdez Glacier with the men. They panned
for gold, dug and rocked and sluiced. There were women running restaurants and hotels and buying stock and shares in
mines and other businesses. Wherever there was a stampede
there were women: on the beaches of Nome, on the Koyukuk
above the Arctic Circle, along the headwaters of the Forty Mile
River, on the Copper River. They put up tents and shacks and
retailed food or told fortunes or took in laundry. To these
women, as to the men, the Yukon was not a river, not a country
or territory; it was a romantic pulse beat, a myth come true.

This myth is known by different names: Bonanza, Klondike, Dawson, Yukon, Alaska, Far North, the Call of the Wild.
Charlie Chaplin portrayed it simply as *The Gold Rush*. But to
the sourdoughs, the experienced prospectors who had learned
to live frugally on bacon and sourdough bread, it was all summed
up in *stampede*. To them this was a more descriptive word than
rush, implying not just the motion of a rush, but a headlong,
heedless, mass movement of men like frightened cattle thunder-
ing before a rising storm. It seemed more properly descriptive of
the frenzied pouring of men into the North country, thoughtless
of what lay ahead. Even before the big strikes on the Klondike
and the Seward Peninsula, stampede was a sourdough expression
for the sudden flow of men from creek to creek. Each report of
a rich find, each rumor of a new gold field would start a stam-

pede. The gold glittered more brightly in other creeks. To prospectors bored with shoveling muck on the same claim day after day, the excitement of a stampede was the elixir of life. They would quit their cabins, abandon claims yielding a steady five dollars a day. They would pack their few belongings, throw a jar of sourdough starter and basic foodstuffs into a gunnysack, and slog miles across country, hoping this would be the big strike. If the reality proved less than the reports, it did not matter. There would always be a new stampede; and when they died, they would go to the great placer streams in the sky where flake gold would glitter on the gravel bars and nuggets the size of bird eggs could be scooped up by the handfuls.

But they were wrong. The stampedes could not go on forever. The stampede to Alaska and the Yukon was the last stampede. There would never be another like it. The world was growing too small. Today, with instant communications, no rich find could remain secret for long. A discovery in the Arctic, in central Africa, or New Guinea would be reported around the world in a matter of days. A year elapsed before verifiable reports of the Klondike strike reached the outside world. With the sophisticated transportation now available, *cheechakos*, the Yukon term for newcomers, could reach a strike before it was developed. After learning of the strike, it took the cheechakos a year before they could reach Dawson. The sourdoughs who discovered the gold after years of lonely work and disappointments had two years to thaw fortunes from the frozen gravel beds before having to share the river benches with those who had contributed nothing to the discoveries of gold. Today corporations and investment capital would move in immediately to seize the initiative from individuals. On the Klondike nearly four years passed before the financial centers of New York and London took over the exploitation of the gold streams, when huge hydraulics and dredges moved in to displace the individual effort of miners, and a crew of six operating a machine could do the work of a thousand prospectors.

In this age of big government and big business, when an entire generation is expressing revulsion toward the swaddling trappings of the "establishment," the independent individualism that marked the last stampede has a singular appeal. With the dredges and hydraulics, the end of that era of individualism was signaled, an era commencing with the discovery of America and reaching its apogee with the pioneering of the West. Its final flowering was in the Yukon and Alaska during the final years of the nineteenth century, when initiative and the daring ability to live with oneself under primitive conditions were determining weights in the balance of life.

After buying Alaska from Russia in 1867, the American government showed little interest in its newly acquired territory. The Canadian government had similar unconcern for the neighboring Yukon Territory. From the Bering Sea to the headwaters of the Yukon River there was not a single representative of law or government until the last decade of the nineteenth century. Except for a few trading posts, there were no business interests. The "establishment" was outside. Inside—inside the vast interior of Alaska and the Yukon watershed—was the individual, independent, self-reliant, responsible to none. The first prospectors had no place where they might replenish their supplies, replace a broken axe, or acquire additional ammunition for a rifle upon which they depended for food. The few trading posts along the rivers were stocked for trade with Indians, not miners. When winter came, these early prospectors built cabins. Isolated from all but their own resources, they chopped wood, shot caribou, moose, bear, and geese. They netted fish. They trapped grouse, porcupines, rabbits, and squirrels. With such shelter and food, men survived the long winter nights when the sun might come up at ten and set at one and temperatures dropped to fifty, sixty, and even seventy below zero. There were no police, marshals, or other government officials in the land. There was no law except that made by the miners as needed and enforced as necessary. Men dressed to keep warm in the winter and cool in the summer or for protection against mosquitos, wild roses, devil's club, nettles, and underbrush. They were bearded or clean-shaven by choice. Neither race nor previous social condition was of any consequence to an individual's ability to survive, and survival was the primary test of worth.

With the influx of tens of thousands of people at the peak of the stampede, government officials finally arrived—marshals, military personnel, Mounties, judges, customs officials. Some of the exuberance of individualism was curbed, but until the end of the nineteenth century and the gradual takeover by investment capital, true individualism, the ability to survive by one's own ability and to be judged by one's own worth, characterized the last stampede.

The paradox of this period is that though it is almost contemporary, it is as myth ridden as ancient history. It occurred within the life span of living people, but the glitter of the gold has so bedazzled those given to memoirs that the truth is only dimly revealed through a shimmer of nostalgia. The difficulty of access to the Yukon, the remoteness of Alaska were taken as an open license to prevaricate. Stories having only the vaguest relationship to fact are told and retold as truth. Were prices outrageously high? At times, yes. More often, considering the difficulty of transportation, they were surprisingly low. Room and lodging were a tenth of what they are today in Alaska. Bitter, freezing winters? There were blizzards. There were recorded temperatures below minus seventy Fahrenheit. Some men did freeze on the trail, but men also went around in shirt sleeves in January and young men wrote home that it was more comfortable than doing winter chores on the farm. Starvation? Men did go hungry. Some got scurvy. Others feasted on moose meat, grouse, and berry pies in their moss-chinked cabins. Lonely, remote? There were those who sought solitude and found it. Others formed literary societies, visited each other's cabins, had dances and games with the Indian girls. The spruce forests could be gloomy during the sunless winter days, but there were the summer months when the light never faded from the skies and the vast horizons exposed a man to himself, giving him a new understanding of life and beauty.

An ironic feature of the last stampede, showing that the individualism of the era was not a national trait, is that every major stampede was started by men who were foreigners to the country where they made their strikes. The important Canadian strikes along the Forty Mile and Klondike rivers were made by Americans. Circle City in Alaska resulted from a find made by a Russian half-breed. The Nome gold fields were discovered by Scandinavians. The rich Fairbanks gold fields were developed from claims filed by an Italian, and news of the strike was carried to Dawson by a Japanese. Even the Juneau mines of earlier years and not a part of the Alaska gold rush resulted from the combined efforts of a German, a Frenchman, and an Irishman. However, all the prospectors had one thing in common. Each was part of this last flourishing of individualism. No corporate structures, no massive financing backed their search for gold. Only their unformed dreams and love of an uncluttered life supported them in what they endured.

The chapter sequence of this history of the Alaska gold rush may cause some confusion. Since gold was discovered all over Alaska and along the Yukon almost simultaneously, it is necessary to make an arbitrary choice in presenting the stories of the different areas and towns. The trading posts along the upper Yukon River made possible the lesser gold discoveries which led to the major stampedes, so the opening of the Yukon seems a natural starting point. The first prospectors reached the Yukon via the Chilkoot Pass. When the Klondike strike was made, most of the stampeders to the area landed at Skagway and crossed the Chilkoot Pass, so the book next treats Skagway and the Dyea Trail. The chapters then follow the Yukon downstream, beginning with the first gold settlement nearest its source, Stewart Island. The next gold fields on this geographic route are around Dawson, then Forty Mile, Eagle, and Circle. The book then jumps across Alaska to Nome, which was later than Forty Mile or Circle but almost simultaneous with Dawson. Although not as important to the gold rush as Dawson and Nome, Valdez, which comes next, was being pioneered about the same time. The following chapter considers the last of the big gold strikes near Fairbanks.

Gold, however, is where you find it, and it was being found everywhere. Many small communities started and died within a year. Others survived. Chicken, Star City, Nation, Seventy Mile, Fort Yukon, Beaver, Rampart, Tanana, Coldfoot, Bettles, Ruby, Livengood—these and others came and went with the flow of the stampedes. They do not represent major strikes, but they are part of the last stampede. To ignore them is to ignore how widespread was the Alaska gold rush. For this reason a penultimate chapter is devoted to these towns.

2

The Yukon

HE YUKON HAS BECOME SYNONYMOUS with the Alaska gold rush. Although as many stampeders went to the Seward Peninsula, the Kuskokwim and Koyukuk rivers, the Valdez and Copper River country, and the Tanana River valley as to the Yukon, its name would symbolize a golden era. The rich placer discoveries along the tributaries of the upper Yukon River pulled men from Europe, Asia, Africa, Australia, and from every state in the Union.

Although it is not known when men first reached the Yukon, historians, archaeologists, and anthropologists have theorized that Asian peoples, seeking new sources of food, may have crossed a land bridge where the sea now forms the Bering Strait. Indian legends tell of migrations when distant ancestors of the Indians on a continent to the west fled before the onslaughts of more warlike tribes.[1] Seeking safety for their women and peace for their children, they crossed the sea to *Al-ay-ek-sa*, the great land.[2]

Spreading along the bleak coastline, these migrants discovered the *Kwikpak* or "mighty river," the name by which the Yukon was known to the Indians of the lower river and to the Russians. From old mounds found along the river, from shards and pieces of weapons, it is possible to reconstruct a migration following the spawning salmon into the interior, where the Indians learned the seasonal movements of the caribou herds, learned where the moose and the bear fed, where the ducks and geese came each summer in sun-eclipsing clouds. Tracing the spread of the Atha-

bascan language, some believe the warlike Tlingits of southeast
Alaska came this way and the Indians of eastern Canada and the
Navahos and the Apaches. When descendants of the early refu-
gees reached the unsilted headwaters of the Kwikpak, it was no
longer the "mighty river." It was small and the waters clear
instead of muddy. To them it became the Yukon, the "clear
waters."

The first recorded history of the Yukon dates back but a
century and a half. During the 1830's the Russians explored the
lower reaches of the river, and in 1842 the Russian-American
Company established a post at Nulato. This was to be their
farthest permanent penetration of the Yukon and is roughly halfway from the coast to the northernmost point on the Yukon,
where in 1847 the Hudson's Bay Company opened a trading post
called Fort Yukon.

Nulato was destroyed by the Indians several times before it
was fortified and made impregnable to Indian attack. The last
and most thorough destruction was in the spring of 1851. Vasili
Derzhavin was the Russian-American Company trader in charge
of the post at the time. As a guest during the preceding winter, he
had a young English naval officer, Lieutenant J. J. Barnard, who
had been detached from the H.M.S. *Enterprise* and sent inland
to inquire of the Indians if they had any knowledge of Sir John
Franklin. Sir John with his entire party had disappeared while on
a vain search for the Northwest Passage.

The Russians were noted for their openhanded hospitality,
and Vasili Derzhavin was no exception. He extended his guest
all facilities available for entertainment at the isolated post.
Among the facilities were two young Indian girls, daughters of
the neighboring chief. The chief called on Derzhavin to protest
the holding of his daughters and to demand some recompense
for depriving him of their services. Although hospitable to their
guests, the Russian-American Company officials were equally
noted for their high-handed treatment of the indigenous people
of the country. In this respect, Derzhavin was again no exception. He told the chief he was keeping one of the daughters for
his own use, and since he had a guest who needed entertainment,
he could not allow the other to return to the chief. If the chief
would come back after the guest departed, perhaps then they
could discuss releasing one of the girls.

The chief left without satisfaction and returned to his village to ponder the cavalier manner in which he had been treated. The taking of his daughters was not a serious matter, nor was the use to which they were being subjected, but it was highly improper that the trader did not compensate the chief for the loss of his daughters. It was a slight which caused the chief to lose face. There was but one recourse. During the night, he returned to the post with all his men and without warning attacked. No one was spared. Barnard and Vasili Derzhavin were both killed and the buildings razed.

Neither the Russians nor the British were familiar with more than a segment of the Yukon. The river was unmapped, unexplored, unknown.[3] The Russians knew only the first eight hundred miles from the mouth of this river they called the Kwikpak. As far as they knew, the Yukon was another river. The Hudson's Bay Company men, who knew of the Yukon only by hearsay before the 1840's, also considered the Kwikpak and the Yukon different rivers. They thought the Yukon was an extension of the Colville River, which empties into the Arctic Ocean. But whether the Yukon was part of the Colville or part of the Kwikpak was not as important as was the potential for fur trade along the river, whatever its name.

Within a year of each other, two traders of the Hudson's Bay Company reached the Yukon. In 1844 James Bell pushed west from the mouth of the Peel River. He blazed the Rat River portage to the Porcupine River and followed the Porcupine to the Yukon. The following year, Robert Campbell reached the Yukon five hundred miles upriver from the Porcupine. Here two rivers joined to form what Campbell considered the beginning of the Yukon. The branch flowing in from the east he called the Pelly; the other, the Lewes, a name which still appears on some maps. Neither man followed up his discovery with a settlement for several years. Bell was much too busy with his post on the Peel River to concern himself with the Yukon other than to keep in mind that it was a likely site for a trading post. It was not until 1846 that he had a chance to do anything about establishing a post there, and then only indirectly. Late in the summer of that year an assistant arrived who was to make possible the opening of a post on the Yukon. This assistant was Alexander Hunter Murray, who had married only six weeks earlier and brought his bride down the Mackenzie River to the Peel for their honey-moon.

During the winter of 1846–47 Bell and Murray went over and over the plans for the new post. Bell told Murray in detail the route he had taken, the types of Indians he had met, and the site he had chosen for a post where the Porcupine enters the Yukon. In the spring of 1847, the long winter's logistical planning completed, Murray left his bride and set out for the Yukon. Upon reaching the site selected by James Bell three years earlier, he established Fort Yukon, the westernmost post of the Hudson's Bay Company.

The next year Campbell returned to the Yukon and at the confluence of the Pelly and the Lewes built Fort Selkirk. The site proved unsatisfactory, so a year later he moved the post across the river to the present location of Selkirk. Campbell was the first white man to explore any part of the upper Yukon. After establishing a post, he descended the river by canoe five hundred miles to Fort Yukon, proving to his own satisfaction, at any rate, that the Yukon and the Kwikpak were the same river.

However, Fort Selkirk was not long-lived. It was destroyed by the Chilkoot Indians[4] in 1852 and the site abandoned for thirty years. Whereas Nulato had been the victim of a cultural clash resulting from Russian disregard for Indian customs, trading rivalry doomed Fort Selkirk. The Chilkoot Indians from the coast considered the upper Yukon their rightful preserve. Twice a year they packed over the Chilkoot Pass to the interior and traded for furs which they sold to the white traders upon their return. They allowed no white men to pass through their territory to the Yukon, and they permitted no Yukon Indians to come out to the coast. Fort Selkirk and the Hudson's Bay Company posed a threat to their monopoly which they met in a direct and Indian manner. They sacked the post and razed the buildings. With no supplies and no trade goods, Campbell had no alternative but to leave the Yukon, which he did. Although he wanted to return and rebuild the post, the Hudson's Bay Company decided against him. The upper Yukon was left to the Indians until the coming of the Americans.

Although the Russians had explored the lower Yukon or the Kwikpak, as they knew it, and Campbell the upper Yukon between Fort Yukon and Fort Selkirk, it was not explored as a single river until 1867. In that year Frank Ketchum and Mike Labarge, two employees of the Western Union Telegraph Company, traveled from the mouth of the river on the Norton Sound to Fort Selkirk. This was still some five hundred miles short of the headwaters. In 1883 Lieutenant Frederick Schwatka led an expedition across the Chilkoot Pass to Crater Lake, where the first waters of the Yukon gather from the melting snow of the encircling Coast Mountains. From there, he mapped the river as far as Fort Yukon and then on down the river to its northern mouth, though he assumed his exploration ended at Fort Selkirk.[5] He and his expedition were the first to follow the Yukon in its entirety.

By this time the men who were to make the final contribution to opening the Yukon country to white settlement were already there and had set in motion the train of events that were to lead to the great gold discoveries of the interior. When Schwatka made his survey, McQuesten, Harper, and Al Mayo had been on the Yukon for ten years. Joseph Ladue, who founded Dawson, reached the Yukon in 1882. These were the men who made the last stampede possible, who opened the first trading posts and provided the supplies to make it possible for the prospectors and the miners to stay in this remote country and search for the gold that would bring thousands to the Yukon. These were the men who started every town on the Yukon between Selkirk and Nulato.[6] Of the four, McQuesten had the greatest significance in the development of the upper Yukon. To the old sourdoughs, he was the father of the Yukon, the most trusted and respected man on the river, and the most popular. He first reached the Yukon in 1873.

As the California gold rush petered out, the men who could never get the gold fever out of their blood gradually moved north. As the old gold diggings were either overmanned or stripped clean or bought up by big combines, they sought new mineralized areas similar to those of the Sierra Nevada. They prospected Oregon, Washington, and Idaho. They pushed north into British Columbia, into the Caribou country. They went up the Stikine River out of Wrangell, where in 1861 over four hundred Americans stampeded into Russian America and just over the border into British Columbia to the considerable alarm of the Russians in Sitka. The Russians had seen what happened to the Mexican

control of California when the dynamic Americans flooded that
territory, and they feared that Russian America under the impact
of a gold stampede might follow the same route. This may have
hastened the Russian decision to sell what they controlled so
tenuously.

Leroy Napoleon "Jack" McQuesten, Captain Al Mayo, and
McKrieff[7] were among these prospectors. According to Mc-
Questen's own account, they were in the Caribou country of
British Columbia when they heard of the American purchase of
Russian America and decided to see for themselves what the
country was like. It took them nearly two years to make the trip
to the Yukon.

To the men of those days, there were no time schedules. There
were no hours or days or months or years against which life had
to be projected. There was winter, when travel was difficult or
impossible. There were the months between the break-up in the
spring and the freeze-up in the fall when traveling was easier. To
McQuesten there was no TV program which could not be
missed, no sporting event that had to be seen, no specific days
that had to be celebrated at a special place, no economic status
he must achieve, no corporate promotion that must be attained
by a given age to avoid failure. He lived by his own ability to
supply himself with food and clothing. When he took to the
river, he built a boat. When he stopped for the winter, he made
a log cabin. He shot caribou or moose or bear, and he had food.
With the furs and skins, he replenished his winter clothing and
made mukluks. He cut trees and he had heating and cooking fuel.

At the end of the first summer when McQuesten and Mayo
and McKrieff felt they had gone as far as possible before freeze-up,
they built a cabin at the confluence of the Liard and the Fort
Nelson rivers. They killed a fat bear and a couple of moose. They
made snowshoes and built a sleigh so they could trap during the
winter.

Three men from the Hudson's Bay Company arrived and built
a cabin nearby. McQuesten wrote, "They were very friendly and
we passed the evenings very pleasantly visiting each other." But
McQuesten knew, and it was no secret, the Canadians were there
to keep an eye on the American interlopers in the Hudson's Bay
territory. One of the Company men had been in the Yukon for
several years and had been at Fort Yukon when American troops

took possession of that post. According to him, Fort Yukon was a veritable trapper's and prospector's paradise. He recalled seeing one of the American officers wash out a jar of dirt near the post from which he got a teaspoon full of something yellow. The officer had thrown it away, remarking that it would not do to let men see it, as they would all desert if they thought there was gold in the country. The Hudson's Bay man said that he was not a miner and had never seen gold, but from the way the American officer acted, he figured that's what it was. "And as for trapping," the Hudson's Bay man added, "why men caught silver fox near the water hole just about every night and killed marten inside the fort with clubs." Even though McQuesten knew the purpose of this gratuitous advice was to get the possible American competition out of the Hudson's Bay Company territory, it was the kind of report he and Mayo and McKrieff liked to hear. It confirmed them in their decision to reach the Yukon.

With the spring, a second party arrived. Arthur Harper, Fred Hart, Finch, and Gestler (no first names are given for Finch and Gestler) had spent the winter sledding their provisions to the Liard. Upon learning what McQuesten had heard about Fort Yukon, they also determined to head for the post. McKrieff joined the Harper party, as McQuesten and Mayo had to make a detour to the Great Slave Lake for personal business. After completing their nearly one-thousand-mile detour, McQuesten and Mayo followed the Harper party down the Mackenzie to the Peel River.[8] They must have traveled over two thousand miles that summer to reach Fort Yukon by August 15, 1873. Not only traveled that distance, but constructed their means of transportation. They started by canoe, which they abandoned at the headwaters of the Peel. After portaging to the Porcupine, they made a raft to float to LaPierre House,[9] where they built a boat for the last stage of the trip.

Fort Yukon could not have been much, a primitive trading post run by Moses Mercier with two clerks in the employ of the Alaska Commercial Company. But to men who had been prospecting and trapping in the back country for years, it was the epitome of civilization. McQuesten wrote later, "Some of us had not had such good living in ten years."

While McQuesten and Mayo tried their luck at trapping in the vicinity of the lower Ramparts that winter, Harper and the other men went up the Yukon beyond the area where Circle City was to be built, beyond Eagle, the Forty Mile country, and the Klondike, to the White River; and there for the first time, as far as written evidence is available, men prospected for gold on the upper Yukon. They found gold on all the tributaries of the White River, but nothing worth working.

The next year, 1874, McQuesten and Mayo accepted employment with the Alaska Commercial Company and went into the upper Yukon. They selected as a location for their post a high riverbank well above the flood level some five miles downriver from the Trundeck, which was McQuesten's attempt to write the Indian name for the river that the stampeders would call the Klondike. There they felled trees and built a log trading post called Fort Reliance. This post was to make possible the opening of the upper Yukon to prospectors. The town of Forty Mile and Forty Mile River would be so named because they were forty miles from Fort Reliance. To prospectors and miners who were to depend on Fort Reliance for supplies, the distance to the post was the most important factor in life. To a man poling a boat upriver or breaking snow for a sled in the winter, each mile to Fort Reliance was a distance to be cursed and to be counted. "Where did you say this gold was found?" "Forty miles from Fort Reliance," or "Sixty miles from Fort Reliance." Except for the short-lived post at Fort Selkirk, this was the first trading post on the upper Yukon and the most important.

In 1875 Harper joined McQuesten and Mayo in the fur business, and the Alaska Commercial Company had a shake-up in management. With the arrival of a new agent at St. Michael, the old policy of direct company control of trading posts was changed. The posts were turned over to the individual traders on percentage. Harper, Mayo, and McQuesten were assigned all the upper Yukon territory. McQuesten himself took over the post at Fort Yukon while Harper and Mayo went to Fort Reliance, where they continued to operate for the next three years. But Harper was a prospector. To him, gold was the sole reality in life. He could never concentrate on trading. It was a spare-time occupation when he could not be out prospecting. He found gold in good quantities on the Sixty Mile and then lost the location. Spring floods wash away known gravel bars, destroy landmarks, change the face of rivers. He prospected the Klondike, the Forty

Mile, and the Tanana. He roamed thousands of miles by foot, by boat, and by sled. Everywhere, he found gold, but he was a prospector more than he was a miner. He was always looking for a new location. The business of running a trading post was an unwelcome restriction; so when trouble developed with the Indians at Fort Reliance, he and Mayo decided to quit the station.

With Fort Reliance abandoned, McQuesten, who had been operating Fort Yukon and then the Tanana Station, decided to return to the upper Yukon in 1878. On his way up the Yukon, he stopped off at Charley Camp. Here he learned that three Indian women had died at Fort Reliance from eating poison found in the trading post. The Chief of the Charley Indians told McQuesten: "Indians there no good. They angry for white man. White man poison women. No good. Better white man not return Fort Reliance. Better stay Charley Camp." But McQuesten suspected the chief was not so much concerned for the white man's safety as for the convenience of having a trading post at Charley Camp. Besides, the Indians had stolen many trade goods from Mayo and Harper, and McQuesten was not the man to abandon a post without attempting to recoup the losses. So he continued.

When he neared the familiar post, he fired in the air to arouse the populace. The Indians swarmed to the bank, yelling and prancing, the men firing their guns wildly. There was no evidence of hostility; instead, they were obviously glad to see him back.

Catsah, the chief of the Indians, had taken charge of all stolen goods and received furs in exchange. These he turned over to McQuesten. As for the poisoning, there was no serious complaint. McQuesten explained that Harper had mixed arsenic with flour to kill mice. It had been in the locked store out of the way of children. Older people should have known better, and if they broke into the trading post and were killed eating poison, it was their own fault. Catsah agreed with this reasoning, except for the case of one sixteen-year-old girl who had died from the poison. Although blind, she had been a great help to her mother. According to the dead girl's father, this was a serious loss, and for this reason, he had taken a dog belonging to the trading post to replace the girl. If McQuesten would pay for the girl, the dog would be returned. McQuesten, after giving the proposal due thought, called Catsah to the store. He agreed that the loss of the girl deserved special consideration. He could understand how the father must feel. Under the circumstances, it seemed only fair that the father should keep the dog. It was, McQuesten felt, a cheap price for peace. The Indian, hoping for trade goods, may have been disappointed, but at least he got something. A principle was recognized, and his sense of propriety was satisfied.

It was this kind of empathy that made it possible for the early American traders to get along with the Indians without serious trouble. McQuesten appreciated that what might seem irrational to him could be entirely reasonable within the framework of Indian social customs. Whereas Derzhavin or other Russian traders might have rejected the Indian father's claim to special consideration for the death of his daughter as ridiculous, Mc-Questen understood that his value judgments should not be paramount when dealing with the Indians.

That fall McQuesten went prospecting on the Sixty Mile to see if he could locate the place where Harper reported such a good show of color. He found gold on all the bars, but in small quantities. This was the year Holt, the first white man to cross the Chilkoot Pass, reached the headwaters of the Yukon and returned to Juneau with nuggets that were to drive men north in ever-increasing numbers.

The next year Ed Bean and the Rathe brothers tried to follow Holt's route and were turned back by the Chilkoot Indians. They went to Sitka and sought help, and in 1880 returned with the U. S. cutter, *Jamestown*. A few rounds fired from a cannon convinced the Indians that their monopoly on the Chilkoot Pass might more properly be shared with the white men who spoke with the voice of an avalanche.[10]

In the next seven years nearly one hundred people crossed over the Chilkoot Pass to the headwaters of the Yukon—the trickle that led to the flood, the trailblazers for the stampede to follow. There were the Whistling King, Cannibal Ike, Shoemaker Brown, Missionary Chapman, Seslie the Poisoner, Butter Frank, Caribou Steele, Russian Paul, Slim Jim Winn, and Dutch Kate Wilson, the first white woman to enter the Yukon on her own.

In 1882 eight men worked the Pelly River, rocking on the bars and averaging $8 a day. Joe Laduo came in this year with three partners and was introduced to the Sixty Mile country by Mc-Questen, who joined the prospectors there until it got too cold, and they all returned to Fort Reliance for the winter. Seven more miners arrived at Fort Reliance and went into winter quarters. Ed Schefflin, a successful miner from Arizona, arrived on the lower Yukon with his own steamer, the *New Racket,* and wintered at the Tanana Station after prospecting in the Tanana–Rampart area.

During the next four years there was a steady if not dramatic influx of prospectors to the Yukon. New posts were opened at Fort Selkirk, on Stewart River, and on Forty Mile. A good strike was made on the Stewart and a bigger one on the Forty Mile. The Yukon was open. The last stampede had started.

In these early years corruption, greed, and profiteering had not yet seized the country. Even the principal outside commercial interest in the Yukon showed a humanistic concern for the individual. The Alaska Commercial Company as successor to the Russian-American Company had a virtual monopoly on the trade and commerce along the river. With little competition, with no source of supply for the miners except the company trading posts, it could have charged what the traffic would bear. Instead, on May 7, 1886, Lewis Gerstle, President of the company, wrote Moses Lorenz, chief agent for the Yukon country:

Dear Sir: We have been informed that a large number of miners have already started to the Yukon and Stewart River mines, and it is probable that many others will be attracted to that section of the Territory in consequence of the supposed existence of rich diggings in the district. Considering that the Company's station at St. Michael is the nearest source of supply, an extra amount of groceries and provisions has been sent to meet the possible demands likely to be made upon you during the coming winter.

It must not be understood, however, that the shipment referred to is made for the purpose of realizing profits beyond the regular schedule of prices heretofore established. Our object is to simply avoid any possible suffering which the large increase of population insufficiently provided with articles of food, might occasion. Hence you are directed to store these supplies as a reserve to meet the probable contingency herein indicated, and in that case to dispose of the same to actual consumers only and in such quantities as will enable you to relieve the wants and necessities of each and every person that may have occasion to ask for it.

In this connection we deem it particularly necessary to say to you that traders in the employ of the company, or such others as draw their supplies from the stores of the company, doing business on their own account, must not be permitted to charge excessive profits, otherwise all business relations with such parties must cease, as the company cannot permit itself to be made an instrument of oppression toward anyone that they may come in contact with.

It is useless to add that in case of absolute poverty or want the person or persons placed in that unfortunate position should be promptly furnished with the means of subsistence without pay, simply reporting such facts at your earliest convenience to the home office.

Asking your strict compliance with the foregoing instructions, which we hope will be carried out with due discretion on your part, I am, etc. etc. Yours Truly, Lewis Gerstle, President.[11]

But even Gerstle could not anticipate the size of the stampede, could not dare stock an inventory adequate to satisfy the demands of the tens of thousands who were to pour into the interior a decade later. Nor could his admonition prevent subsequent gouging in the face of excessive demands. Dawson is reported by some to have been on starvation rations in the winter of 1897–98. Others deny this. Certainly Circle City suffered that winter, as well as Valdez, where thousands had gathered to try the all-American route to the Yukon.

The Yukon today is more similar to that early period than it is to any later period. Within two decades it was to become crowded with steamers, thriving communities, roadhouses, police stations, mail service, courts of law, and customs stations. A traveler on the river could never be more than a few miles from a trading post, a roadhouse, a Mountie station, a wood camp, an Indian village, or a miner's cabin. Today the river is even less populated than it was in 1886. Then, besides the few miners who had already penetrated the country, there were Indian villages and fishing camps from Lake Bennett to the Tanana River. Today there are no steamers, no miners, no trappers, no Indians. Except for Whitehorse, the towns are deserted or nearly so, and except for Eagle, the Indian villages are abandoned. Fort Reliance is gone. Not a timber remains standing, not a rotting log is left to indicate the site. There are only some depressions filled with shoulder-high weeds marking the underground living quarters of the Indians who gathered around the station. Forty Mile, the first town, is a forsaken national monument, as is Fort Selkirk.

3

Skagway,
Home of the Cruel Wind

T THE HEAD OF THE LYNN CANAL, the terminus of Alaska's inland passage, are twin fjord-like valleys lying between rugged mountains. One is Dyea, the other, Cqague, home of the cruel wind.[1] Stampeders wrote the name as Skagway, and to them it was not the home of the cruel wind but the beginning of the White Pass route to the headwaters of the Yukon, less direct than the more notorious Chilkoot Pass route only a few miles away, but preferred by many stampeders because of the reported horrors of the Chilkoot Pass.

When news of the Klondike strike reached Seattle and San Francisco, the only people living in the valley of the Skagway River were Ben Moore and his daughter, working a homestead of 160 acres.[2] Within a few months the valley was invaded by men more cruel than the cruel wind. Without regard for laws or property rights, gold seekers, speculators, and ruffians invaded the Moore homestead, took what land they wanted, set up tents, built docks, laid out streets, sold lots, and established businesses. Within a year Skagway was reputed to be the largest town in Alaska. It was far and away the busiest. Thousands of cheechakos trudged through the streets under full packs, heading for the Yukon. Thousands of sourdoughs came swinging down out of the mountains to wait in Skagway for the next ship south. Everything to help a cheechako on his way was in Skagway, everything to make the stay more pleasant for a sourdough awaiting a steamer

—banks, stores, outfitters, packers, information agencies, restaurants, hotels, saloons, and dance halls.

To the miner on his way out of the Yukon, this was civilization. After months on a remote creek, with perhaps a visit to Dawson, Skagway was a hectic metropolis. To the newcomer a few days out of San Francisco or Seattle, this was the end of the world, primitive chaos and confusion, the threshold of wilderness. To Londoners, New Yorkers, even Midwesterners, Seattle had seemed the rude end of urbanization; but Skagway, scooped out of the mountains, with its brawling glacial stream, its dark spruce forests, its raw, unformed conglomerate of stampeders, made Seattle seem in retrospect the very hub of the world.

Ships discharged passengers and cargo with little consideration for order or convenience. Ship captains were intent only on returning south as quickly as possible for more passengers and cargo. Docks were piled high with freight, and when no room remained, luggage, equipment, and stores were stacked on the mudflats in a welter of confusion. Days could be spent in searching out a scattered outfit. Carefully selected food items, camping equipment, prospecting tools, and medical supplies were lost or stolen, and these had to be replaced. In addition, wagons, boats, special items of clothing, mosquito repellent, and lightweight foods that had not been considered when outfitting below were now sold to credulous buyers.

Such a melee of disorder and confusion was made for unscrupulous speculators, confidence men, and scoundrels, and they arrived on the scene early. The leader of the most notorious gang was Jefferson Randolph "Soapy" Smith, who had earned his nickname by selling cakes of soap wrapped in five dollar bills for a dollar. Although much has been written about "Soapy" Smith, so vivid was his imprint on Skagway and the Yukon stampede as a whole that it is essential at least to summarize the myths and truths of his brief period of ascendancy.

"Soapy" Smith was one of the most colorful and some say the most adroit of confidence men, outlaws, and crooks in American history. He was not a desperado or a quick gunman, but he did combine a flair for the gyppo game carried to its ultimate with an ability to gain the confidence of suckers. In addition, he was a literate man with highly developed social instincts, which unfortunately he never allowed to inhibit him. "Soapy's" philosophy was not simply don't give a sucker a break, but in the more sophisticated reasoning of his warped moral values, he conceived of his activities as being beneficial both to the United States and to the individuals robbed. By relieving a stampeder of his money in Skagway, "Soapy" stated that he was stemming the flow of capital to Canada, where it would be spent in Dawson City. He considered his efforts to part a stampeder from his money as his contribution to America's economy. Furthermore, "Soapy" reasoned, if a man was so gullible, so lacking in instincts of self-preservation as to allow himself to be taken in Skagway, he had little chance of survival on the trail or in the Klondike. He was far better off to learn of his weaknesses and inadequacies while he was still in a place from which he could return to the States easily.

To assure his philanthropy of being as inclusive as possible, "Soapy" carefully screened all arrivals. A reporter on his payroll interviewed passengers on every ship and advised "Soapy" of any person who appeared well-heeled. "Soapy" would then assign one of his men to assist the newcomer. There were the Reliable Packing Company and the Skagway Information Agency, both places to be visited. For a dollar, the Skagway Information Agency would provide a map of the trails, advise as to the best route, recommend a boarding house in Skagway, or an outfitting store for equipment overlooked—any information or advice sought was available for one dollar. The one dollar was not important to "Soapy." The important thing was to get the prospect to produce his wallet, to show his roll. When that happened, the excitement would start. A person would bump into the customer, or someone from outside would dash in and grab the roll. In the ensuing scramble to seize the culprit, the victim would be knocked down, the doorway jammed with bodies, and the robber invariably would escape. The money would find its way to "Soapy," who would see to it that the injured party had enough to buy a ticket back to Seattle. By this kindness he earned a reputation for philanthropy and kept Skagway free of aggrieved men.

During the Spanish-American War, "Soapy" not only raised a company with himself in command but set up a recruiting office. Patriotic young men rushing to enlist were given what passed for a complete medical examination; and while the recruit stood naked before the doctor, the doctor's assistant made a more thorough examination of the recruit's clothing, removing all money and valuables.

If all else failed, if a person was about to escape Skagway unscathed, there was, as a final inducement to leave some money for "Soapy," the telegraph office, where a person could send a message anywhere in the United States for five dollars. Here was a last chance to communicate with loved ones, "Tomorrow we push off." The remarkable thing was that there was nearly always a reply from the loved one, and the more remote an address, the faster the reply. A wire to New York was almost certain to produce a reply within twenty-four hours, collect. And most amazing, all this was done several years before the first telegraph service was inaugurated in Alaska.

"Soapy" was a complex person who seemingly wished for respectability but could not resist taking sucker money. His men would rob a preacher, and "Soapy" would help to get the minister's church built and give a large donation. If one of his thugs killed a man, "Soapy" would provide for the widow and children if any. Up to a point, he enjoyed playing Robin Hood and liked to think of himself in the hero role. It is reported he paid William DeVere, "The Tramp Poet," $1,000 for a poem entitled "Jeff and Joe, A True Incident of Creede Camp, Colorado." The hundred fifty-two lines of narrative rhyme include the following, suggestive of Mr. Smith's philosophy of what constitutes moral rectitude:

> And as for Jeff, well, I may say
> No better man exists today.
> I don't mean good the way you do—
> No, not religious—only true.
> True to himself, true to his friend;
> Don't quit or weaken to the end.
> And I can swear, if any can,
> That Jeff will help his fellow man.[3]

The following letter from a friend adds to the portrait of a man having social graces not associated with a ruffian or a cheap con man:

San Francisco, Nov. 29, 1897

JEFF R. SMITH, Esq.:

Dear Sir—"A friend in need is a friend indeed." I'm busted—up a stump, and about as desperate as you were when we first met.

That Spokane trip cost me about $4,000, in all, including $3,500 I advanced you. When I got back and paid some debts, helped along some poor people, I soon found myself down to cases, or within a few hundred of being so. It was a case of "dig up," again, so I started for the Klondike. A party here agreed to pay my wife and children $50 a month for a year, in consideration of a half-interest in what I located. Well, I didn't get there. Our river boat broke down and we were frozen in at the mouth of the Yukon. I had to borrow money to get back to Frisco.

I don't know which way to turn. As I had about $7,000 only a few months ago, those who knew me naturally think I ought to have money now. I don't know anybody I can borrow of, and I must raise at least $200, but actually need $300. Hell is to pay all around. If I had $200 to $300 I would get on my feet and pull out. I have a chance to book 100 people for Dawson at $300 each, including 1,000 lbs. of provisions, beside transportation. That would give me $30,000. I can get a 150 ton boat, to carry 100 passengers, delivered at St. Michaels, for $20,000. Such a boat would give 100 tons freight capacity, aside from the 50 tons allotment to passengers, and at 5¢ per lb. I can take in $10,000 from freight. Thus I would take in about $40,000, while $30,000 would pay for boat, grub, etc. That would clear the boat and give about $10,000 in cash, and to that could be added what the boat would earn next year on the river. I would let her freeze up somewhere near Dawson and use her for a hotel for 8 or 9 months. I have two or three capitalists on the string for this plan, but that is for the future. I'm dead broke now, and I want you to be my friend if it breaks a leg—or breaks somebody else.

My wife often speaks of "Dr." Smith and always says: "Jeff will pay you when he prospers." I feel sure you will too, but a little now is an absolute need.

In Seattle recently I heard you had been in town and was flush. I met Mr. Thompson, who told me you had gone to Nashvill. I wired you there, to the track. I am sending this letter to Mr. Thompson to forward, as he probably knows your address. For the gods' sake do not disappoint me. My wife sends best wishes for your happiness.

Yours truly,
H. B. MULGREW.[4]

Whether or not "Soapy" Smith answered the plea for help is unknown. He probably did if he was in the money, but he was addicted to faro and could lose money as fast as he made it.

"Soapy" Smith was at the apogee of his life at this time. He had raised a company of men and volunteered his services to his country in the war with Spain. He had received a letter from the Secretary of War declining the tender of his volunteer company, "on account of the cost of transportation," but the Secretary accompanied his declination with warm expressions of the government's appreciation of Mr. Smith's patriotism. His brother was an editor of the *Evening Star* in Washington, D.C. He had a large correspondence with leading politicians. Although having friends and admirers who recalled his many benefactions, he lacked the ability to temper greed with discretion. He could not sense the changing temper of the times. So thoroughly and easily had he browbeaten Skagway that he thought he could not be checked.

Skagway was a new town and the businessmen were fighting with Dyea, Valdez, St. Michael, Edmonton, and the Stikine route for preeminence as the gateway to the Klondike and the profits that could be made from the traffic flowing in and out of Dawson. Reputable people had invested in stores, hotels, banks, transportation companies, breweries—businesses that depended upon Skagway being the preferred route for the Yukoners. A reputation for lawlessness threatened to destroy Skagway's advantage as the shortest route to the interior. These businessmen were becoming restive, knowing "Soapy" Smith was giving Skagway and the White Pass route a bad name. But Jeff did not see the signs or, sensing them, was unwilling to trim his sails to weather the rising storm. If he had, he might have gone on to be a figure of civic importance. Alaska in 1898 could take a lot but not as much as he demanded. At 9:30 at night on July 7, 1898, his domination of Skagway was ended.

On the morning of July 7 a young stampeder by the name of J. D. Stewart was robbed of his poke of gold. He had just returned from the Klondike and was desirous of selling his gold before shipping out for the States. Bowers, a known member of Smith's gang, represented to Stewart that he was in Skagway for the purpose of buying gold for a big assaying company. Unfamiliar with Skagway and Smith's gang, Stewart accompanied Bowers to the rear of Smith's place on Holly Avenue near the Mondamin Hotel, ostensibly to make an assay of the gold, which varies in value according to its quality. Two more of Smith's gang were waiting there. The three overpowered Stewart, wrested the sack of gold, worth an estimated $2,670, from his hands, and disappeared from sight around adjoining buildings, leaving Stewart with nothing to show for his year of mucking in the gold fields.

News of the blatant daylight robbery circulated the city instantaneously, igniting the already smouldering indignation. People were shocked by the flagrant outrage of the act. It was bad enough to take advantage of the credulous cheechakos going in, but to rob a sourdough who had made the long trip in and out, who had endured the hardships of the Yukon for a year to make his stake, and to do it in broad daylight—this was too much. It threatened the legitimate economy of Skagway.

The honest businessmen of the town assembled. There was no question in anyone's mind. This was the work of "Soapy" Smith's men. They discussed the deed and its implications. Their normal anger only supported their rational appreciation of the threat to Skagway's business of such unchecked lawlessness. A committee of the most influential citizens of the town called on Smith and flatly informed him that the gold must be returned. They did not ask Smith if he were responsible. They just told him to return the gold. Furthermore, Smith was advised that he and his gang must leave Skagway.

Smith made a vague promise that if the incident was kept out of the papers the gold would be returned by four o'clock in the afternoon, and that he would use his influence to prevent his men from interfering with returning Klondikers in the future. If Smith had kept his promise, if he had been able to appreciate the seriousness of the protest and the mood of the citizens, history might have written a different ending to his life. But he did not keep his promise. He did not understand the mood of the town. Instead, he started drinking heavily. The more he drank, the more intemperate he became, talking in a rash and defiant manner.

As the deadline for the return of the gold came and passed, public indignation mounted. There was talk of vigilantes, of lynching, but the Smith gang was tough and known to be well-armed. Calmer voices did not consider a direct confrontation wise. At nine o'clock a spontaneous meeting started in Sylvester's hall, which proved too small for the crowd that gathered. The meeting was then adjourned to the Juneau dock, where a meeting was called to order "to devise ways and means for ridding the city of the lawless element, which for some time has infested it." The meeting was opened by the foreman of the Skagway *News,* who suggested the election of Thomas Whitten of the Golden North Hotel as chairman. The chairman appointed a committee of four, including Frank H. Reid, city surveyor, to guard the approach to the dock in order that no objectionable characters might be admitted to disturb the deliberations of the meeting. The four stationed themselves at the end of the dock, when "Soapy" Smith appeared carrying a Winchester rifle. Truculent with drink and months of unchecked power, he walked up to Reid and demanded to know what he thought he was doing there. At the same time, he struck at Reid with the barrel of his rifle. Reid grabbed the gun in his left hand, pushing the muzzle toward the ground, drawing a revolver with his right hand as he did so. The two men fired almost simultaneously. Smith was killed, shot through the heart. Reid was mortally wounded.[5]

With the passing of Smith, Skagway became a respectable, if still boisterous, law-abiding town. The Smith gang was methodically rounded up in the ensuing days and sent south. A citizen's committee was formed for this purpose, excluding Deputy Marshal Taylor, who had been affiliated with the Smith gang. Members of the gang who could be found immediately were thrown in jail. Every wharf and dock was posted. A detachment of deputies was sent to Dyea and another to Lake Bennett. There was no escape except into the wilderness, which was sure death. Eventually the entire gang was sent out with warnings not to return.

The original prognosis for Reid was favorable. The shot had entered two inches above the groin, passing an inch to the right of the pelvic bone. It was felt that a man who could ask for and stoically smoke a cigar while bone fragments were being removed from his back could survive anything. But he died.

If Skagway was the most lawless town in America in 1897–98 and "Soapy" Smith the epitome of that lawlessness, it was not a condition imposed upon the community solely by "Soapy" Smith or by his men. It was a result of the times and the people. The bunco artists, the confidence men, and the robberies, even the murders, were a reflection of the uncontrolled individualism. The Smith gang merely took advantage of a condition that existed. The law of established society was not administered here.

A special code dictated law, a specific morality associated with the trail and the sense of urgency to clear the port and be off to the Klondike as soon as possible.

Take the shooting of McGinnis, for example. McGinnis was a loudmouthed blowhard, given to talking when he should be listening. When someone in a bar asked about a sloop that had arrived off Skagway, McGinnis was the one who knew all about it. The sloop was loaded with whiskey, belonging to a bootlegger. He knew. He nodded wisely, suggesting specific intelligence, secret knowledge that gave him special understanding of events. Now, bootlegging and liquor were important matters in which the law of the States spilled over into Alaska and found acceptance among the stampeders, who feared the possible danger from Indians under the influence of alcohol. Liquor and Indians didn't mix. So to suggest someone was bootlegging a sloopload of whiskey was pretty stiff talk. The sloop actually belonged to Jack Dalton, who had blazed the trail bearing his name from Haines Mission to the Yukon, and Dalton did not relish such loose talk about his ship. He searched out McGinnis and demanded an explanation. McGinnis, not knowing the sloop belonged to Dalton or anything about the cargo, talking just to puff his own importance, was only too willing to repeat his story.

Dalton called him a dirty, lying sonofabitch and demanded a retraction or it would be the last time McGinnis would ever shoot his mouth off about someone else's business. McGinnis tried to bluster his way out of the position in which he found himself. Dalton's response was to pull a gun and shoot McGinnis six times. He then went to the deputy marshal and surrendered himself. A trial was convened the same day, and Dalton was acquitted. He was an honest trader, as everyone knew, and McGinnis was a loudmouth who got what was coming to him.[6]

But Skagway was not all violence. It was a town with opportunities for anyone, man or woman, with the toughness of spirit and perseverance to seize the advantage. "Ma" Pullen was such a woman.[7] A penniless widow with four children and a knowledge of horses and five Indian dialects, she arrived on the beach of Skagway in September 1897. A man canvassing new arrivals for a cook hired her immediately for $3 a day. In her spare time, she made pies. So successful was this sideline that she went into business for herself and soon accumulated enough capital to send for her three sons and seven horses. Baking was all right for getting a start but packing, "Ma" Pullen felt, was a better business for her. Anybody could set up a grub tent who had food and a stove. No special skill was required; the customers were not choosy and the clientele was transient. Accordingly, competition kept profits low. Packing was different; it took special knowledge and both animals and equipment were in critical supply. And a report was being circulated around Skagway that the Mounties were going to insist that each man have a minimum of one thousand pounds of food in addition to his other equipment. The packers could not have asked for a more favorable regulation.

With all her money tied up in the new venture, "Ma" Pullen suffered her first reverse; all her packing equipment was stolen from the beach while she was getting her horses to shore from a scow. Broke, with three hungry boys and seven idle horses to feed, she went back to the pie business. Every extra dollar went to the purchase of pack saddles and harness, and it wasn't long before "Pie" Pullen was "Packer" Pullen, the only woman packer on the trail. When the Brackett toll road was opened over the White Pass, she added a wagon to her resources and rented the outfit to another, so she could devote her energies to a restaurant. It was at this stage in her life that she allowed herself for the first and only time to be caught by the chimera of gold. Infected by the excitement of the Atlin stampede, she sold out and hit the trail. Always a businesswoman with an eye for profit no matter how small, for $10 she hauled another miner's outfit over the Pass with her own. Then reaching Lake Bennett, she purchased a large boat for $100, giving the owner a $10 deposit. With the option on the boat, she sold passage to ten miners for $10 each, raising the purchase price and recovering her $10 deposit.

This enterprising woman never had a chance to prove herself as a miner, for no sooner had she arrived at Atlin than she fell and broke her arm. So, drastically cured of the gold fever, she returned to Skagway. Exhausted from this adventure and realizing that the days of packing were numbered with work beginning on the White Pass Railway, she turned to the hotel business. She rented a large house Bon Moore had recently completed and contracted to rent furniture from a speculator who had brought it to Skagway for a dance hall only to find the influence of "Soapy" Smith too tough to buck. Not wishing to pay the protection money required for running a dance hall, he agreed to rent the furniture to "Ma" Pullen. However, before she could open her hotel, the speculator changed his mind, recovered his furniture, and went into the hotel business himself. But "Ma" Pullen was early Skagway. She didn't complain or sue for breach of contract or give up. She just worked harder. She found other furniture, placed orders in Seattle, and went ahead with her usual drive and determination. Within a year the Pullen House had proved so popular and her management had been so successful that she owned the house outright.

Although today the Pullen House is a derelict shell surrounded by weeds, in its heyday it was a palatial two-story building with formal gardens and lakes and ornamental bridges, a civilized delight on the raw road to the North. It was the gathering place for the weary mucker and the rich miner, and "Ma" Pullen knew most of them. She knew "Packer" Jack Newman and Mike Bartlett, Ben Moore and "Soapy" Smith. She knew the good, the bad, the indifferent from daily contact. Her job was to serve people, not to judge them. Even the notorious "Soapy" did not draw her censure, and she was among the few sorry to hear of his demise. She knew him as a kind, gentle man. No mother, and "Ma" Pullen was no exception, could consider a man bad who always had a cheerful word for her sons and would give them a small nugget or coin from time to time, a man who befriended stray dogs and men down on their luck.

"Ma" Pullen was probably the most successful of Skagway businesswomen, but she was not the only woman to seek a livelihood on the stampede trail. There were surprisingly many who came alone or with husbands, drawn by the excitement of the stampede, fired by stories of easy money. None aroused as much attention or caused as much trouble in so few years as Mollie Walsh.[8]

Alone without help
This courageous girl
Ran a grub tent
Near Log Cabin

During the gold rush
Of 1897, 1898
She fed and lodged
The wildest
Gold crazed men
Generations
Shall surely know.
This inspiring spirit
Murdered Oct. 27,
1902.

So reads the inscription on a marble shaft supporting the bronze bust of Mollie Walsh in a vacant lot overgrown with wild grass and weeds in Skagway. This monument to a woman of the stampede stands there because one man was in love with Mollie Walsh and continued to carry his haloed vision of her in his heart the remainder of his life, though she spurned his love. This man was "Packer" Jack Newman.

Before a railway was built, he ran a mule train, packing goods for the stampeders across the White Pass to Lake Bennett. It was on this trail that one night, his left hand badly frostbitten, his eyes almost blinded from the snow, numbed, nearly frozen, "Packer" Jack stumbled into Mollie Walsh's tent, where she served hot food and provided rough shelter.

Mollie was no rawboned frontier woman. She was a petite, black-eyed, dark-haired Irish colleen with a face and figure that made both sourdough and cheechako alike sore in heart that they must pass on and not linger in the presence of such beauty. She had come north like the others to seek her fortune, leaving behind a widowed mother and younger sisters depending upon what she earned for their support. In this tent, "Packer" Jack found hot coffee and solicitude. From that moment on, he worshipped Mollie Walsh.

Jack Newman made a habit of stopping at Mollie's tent at every opportunity, and as a packer he had many. But Mollie was not lacking for male admirers. One who perhaps considered himself in more serious contention for her affection than he should have was a faro dealer in Skagway. He wrote a warning to Newman advising "Packer" Jack to stay way from Mollie Walsh's tent. "Packer" Jack was not the type to take kindly such a warning. Before coming to Skagway, he had fought Indians, he had sailed before the mast, he had driven pack trains in Arizona and Colorado. He was a tough cookie who knew his way around in a man's world. He oiled his holster, strapped his gun to his side, and called the faro dealer out. Apparently, it was a fair call because according to report, although "Packer" Jack shot and killed the faro dealer, there was no trial, let alone a conviction.

Having thus laid his life on the line, so to speak, having challenged in fair duel another man for the hand of Mollie Walsh, Jack Newman now felt he had proprietary interests which Mollie had never granted. About this time, Mike Bartlett, a rival packer on the trail, also found the charms of Mollie Walsh irresistible. As he passed back and forth across the White Pass frequently, he became a too regular visitor at the grub tent for Jack Newman's peace of mind. "Packer" Jack had no concern for the propriety of Mollie Walsh's position. It was axiomatic during the stampede days that any woman was completely safe among the horde of single men. It was an integral part of the code of the North. After serving food to the men who stopped at her grub tent, after washing up the dishes and pots, Mollie would hang a blanket across the back end of her canvas shelter, making a flimsy wall between herself and the dozen stampeders stretched on hemlock boughs laid on the floor. With only this token protection to her bedroom, "Packer" Jack later wrote that although "she fed and lodged the wildest and most persistent men Alaska ever saw, she remained as clean morally as the snow that fell on her tent." But he was jealous of any man who paid Mollie attention and particularly a rival packer. Even as the faro dealer had overplayed his hand, so did "Packer" Jack. He told Mollie Walsh not to let Mike Bartlett into the grub tent.

Any girl might resent such proprietary orders, and Mollie was no exception. Self-willed, independent, high-spirited, a successful businesswoman taking care of herself, her mother, and her younger sisters, she took orders from no man. The one thing she did want, yearned for more than most women because of the hardships she had already endured in her short life, was a home of her own with a husband to provide for her. The vine-covered cottage to her was a psychological necessity. Security was her goal. Jack Newman promised these things, but she was not sure of him. His background made his promises suspect. He was given to profanity and drinking, characteristics a young girl does not attribute to a man of a stable, homemaking disposition. Whatever the reasons, or whether it was pure spite for Jack Newman giving her orders, she married Mike Bartlett.

She moved into Skagway, where the Bartletts lived until, with the coming of rail transportation, packers were no longer needed. "Packer" Jack and Mike Bartlett both became anachronisms to the Skagway scene. But they had both done well. They had both made money, far more than most of the stampeders who had sought their fortunes on the tributaries of the Klondike. The Bartletts are reported to have gone outside with $100,000. "Packer" Jack, the dean of the White Pass packers, probably had as much or more.

Mollie had her security. Whether she had her vine-covered cottage is not recorded, but something went wrong. The reality of marriage was perhaps too restricting after the freedom of Alaska, too mundane for Mollie Walsh, the entrepreneur, the young businesswoman. Or perhaps the dependable, home-loving Mike Bartlett was not what he had seemed. Mollie Walsh ran away to Mexico with a John F. Lynch, taking with her as much of her husband's money as she could lay hands on. When the money was gone, Mollie returned repentant, and Mike Bartlett took her back.

They returned to Seattle, where Mollie lived with the Klein family in an alley between Seventh and Eighth near Pike Street. Here, on October 27, 1902, Patrolman Claude G. Bannick, the first policeman in Seattle to cover his beat on horseback, heard a shot in an alley. He wheeled his horse as he saw what looked like a small girl dressed in a white nightgown, running through a gate screaming. He kicked his horse into a gallop as a man with a pistol emerged in pursuit. Before Officer Bannick could reach her, the man raised his pistol and fired again, and the girl collapsed in a white heap on the pavement. As patrolman Bannick threw himself from his horse, the man turned the gun on himself and fired a third shot, but this time with less success, only wounding himself slightly.

Bannick wrested the gun from the man—Mike Bartlett—who yielded without a struggle, muttering about Shorty being the cause of it all. Whoever Shorty was, or might have been, is not known, for no Shorty was found or came forward at the subsequent trial of the murderer of Mollie Walsh, the little girl in the white nightgown, still petite, still a lovely young girl in her twenties, who died before Officer Bannick could get medical help.

Bartlett was indicted for murder and a year later stood trial in a packed courtroom, where the romantic background of Mollie Walsh Bartlett was developed in all its detail by the prosecution. The prosecution might have used the very words later used by Jack Newman: "If there are still men on earth who ate Mollie's frugal meals, and were sheltered by her tent, let them thank their God for having had that lucky chance, for as sure and as long as snow falls on Alaska, Mollie Walsh will be remembered as the girl on whose headstone could be most fittingly inscribed: Here Lies Drama! Murdered by her husband, Oct. 27, 1902." The attorney for the defense brought out Mollie's escapade with Jack Lynch, but his main defense was temporary insanity. It was proved that Mike Bartlett had visited a Seattle doctor, claiming that he had a ball of alcohol in the back of his head and wanted it drained off. The evidence of witness after witness proved that Bartlett had gone to pieces after the shooting. Mike Bartlett was acquitted on grounds of temporary insanity and sent to an insane asylum as a victim of dementia. After two years he was released as cured, but he was no sooner out than he committed suicide.

Whatever the evidence, whatever the facts, hazed as they are by prejudice and legal verbiage, through all that happened, Jack Newman's love for Mollie Walsh remained intact, as he said, "A guiding light to his life. Each time he thought of the angel Mollie in heaven, it played on the strings of his heart as an angel might play on a harp."

Twenty-eight years after the death of Mollie Walsh—and she was never referred to as Mollie Walsh Bartlett by "Packer" Jack —he commissioned the bust that now stands in an empty lot in Skagway. The commissioning itself almost caused marital troubles. Even in death, Mollie Walsh was trouble. Jack Newman had in the meantime married another Irish lass. After twenty-four years together, she did not take kindly to her husband's spending his money and romantic attentions on a youthful dream. It is reported that she took her husband to task because not only had he commissioned the bust of Mollie Walsh, he had also been the principal in erecting a bronze monument to pack mules who had given their lives to get the effects of stampeders across the White

39

Pass. "Look here, Jack," Mrs. Newman is quoted as saying, "If you are going to devote your life to putting mules and horses and Mollie Walsh in bronze, where do I come in? Now you listen. You get me, your wife, in bronze, and be real speedy about it, or else you are going to get into serious domestic trouble." Today, set in a building on the corner of Sixth and Union Streets in Seattle, there is a bronze medallion to Hannah Newman, while the bust of the "wonder girl" of the White Pass stands neglected among the weeds, having been moved three times by the disinterested citizenry of Skagway.

If Skagway was a tough, wild town, it at least bred a tough, independent breed of people for whom nothing was impossible, men who could build roads over passes where even foot trails were treacherous, men who could carry pianos over Chilkoot and haul steamboats over mountain trails to the interior.

In the deep gloom of the spruce forests lie giant boilers that once provided steam for heat and power to help the stampeders on their way. If the movement of such equipment with nothing but sleds, mules, manpower, and gut determination does not rank with the building of the pyramids, at least it is a rare tribute to the men who did not know the meaning of impossible and could not wait for the day when power equipment would replace ingenuity.

With the death of "Soapy" Smith and the expulsion of his gang, Skagway went on to become the most important town in Alaska at the turn of the century. A railroad was built connecting Skagway with the steamer traffic on the Yukon at Whitehorse. Known as the White Pass Railway, it was completed in 1900. Later, it merged with a major steamship company plying between Dawson and Whitehorse, and the line became known as the White Pass and Yukon Route, by which name it is known today, though the Yukon portion has ceased to function.

Today Skagway is but a faint shadow of its glory days. Its beauty is unchanged. It is still the end of the steamship run. Tourists coming by sea still disembark at Skagway, still take the White Pass and Yukon Route with their automobiles on flatcars to Whitehorse, driving from there to Dawson. But the excitement, the bustle of Skagway in 1900 is gone. It is a quiet, peaceful town surrounded by mountains and glaciers. The old Pullen house is still there, drenched in a rank growth of summer weeds. The monument to Mollie Walsh can be found, but it is not con-

At its peak during the last stampede Skagway was probably the busiest port per capita in the world. The White Pass Trail to the Yukon began at Skagway. (E. A. HEGG)

At Trail Street, Dyea, began the famous trail to the Chilkoot Pass. Dyea rivaled Skagway as a port in 1898, but not a building remains today. (E. A. HEGG)

spicuous. Of the saloons of the last stampede, only the Packtrain saloon and the Soapy Smith saloon remain. The former is unchanged from the days when stampeders crowded the single room for warmth and Dutch courage to face the trail before them. Its primitive furnishings, its casual friendly service, even the clientele have altered little. The Soapy Smith saloon, an unpretentious headquarters for the most pretentious man in Skagway, is modified in use only. Now it is the most complete, jampacked museum in Alaska, thanks to the efforts of one man, George Rapuzzi, who has lived in Skagway since the reign of "Soapy" Smith. Crowding every inch of wall space, every square foot of the floor and even the bar are mementos of history so brief in years and so remote in terms of technological and political change in the life of America.

Skagway is still the most appropriate approach to the Yukon. It is the beginning of the White Pass and the Chilkoot trails. This is the way most of the stampeders to the Yukon came. It is symbolic of the best and the worst of the last stampede, of the "Ma" Pullens and the "Soapy" Smiths.

A new boom for Skagway is in the air. Large asbestos mines on Forty Mile are shipping their ore out through Skagway. Japanese industrialists are investing millions for the exploitation of mineral resources in the Yukon Territory. The White Pass and Yukon Route is to be modernized and strengthened. New docks for giant ore-carrying Japanese ships are to be built. But instead of being a boom by and for individuals as was the last stampede, it will be the boom of industry and corporate capital. The excitement of the former cannot be recaptured. The new boom may bring economic benefits to those associated with the development, but it will not capture the imagination of the world as did the last stampede, of which Skagway was an important part.

4

The Chilkoot Pass

HREE MILES NORTHWEST OF SKAGWAY was Dyea, the beginning
of the Dyea Trail to the headwaters of the Yukon River via
the Chilkoot Pass, the traditional trading route of the Chilkoot Indians. In 1880, the year that the Northwest Trading
Company established a post in the Dyea valley, twenty-three prospectors, backed by the guns of the U. S. cutter *Jamestown*, established the right of white men to use this trail to the Yukon. Two
years later Arthur Krause went over the Chilkoot Pass and made a
sketch of the area for the Bremen Geographical Society.[1] The next
year, 1883, the United States Army sent a small surveying party
under the command of Lieutenant Frederick Schwatka to gather
information on the Yukon River. Anticipating the stampeders by
more than a decade, Schwatka followed the Dyea Trail to the
headwaters of the Yukon, where he built a raft to float thirteen
hundred miles downriver.

The trading post in the Dyea valley had an Indian school and
a post office before Skagway was started. With the beginning of
the Klondike stampede, the town of Dyea quickly developed and
by 1898 rivaled Skagway for preeminence. Dyea had the largest
brewery in Alaska and a baseball team that challenged the Skagway
team on the Fourth of July. Both towns had saloons, hotels, restaurants, mail service, telephone companies, churches, hospitals,
smithies, transportation outfits, drayage, lightering, and all the

businesses related to moving men from sea to shore and over the mountains to the Yukon. Each town had certain advantages and disadvantages. Skagway had piers stretching out into deep water, but it had "Soapy" Smith and his gang. Dyea had no docks or deep water adjacent to its waterfront. The shallow, silty coast forced ships to anchor well offshore and lighter freight and passengers by barges which, in turn, had to unload into wagons driven into the water up to the horses' bellies. But Dyea was safer, more law-abiding. Skagway was the approach to the White Pass, and Dyea to the Chilkoot. The former provided a more gradual ascent over the rugged Coast Mountains, but it was longer. The Dyea Trail was more demanding, but it was shorter.

Although the early prospectors, Krause, and Schwatka had crossed the Chilkoot in the summer, the Klondike stampeders crossed mostly in the winter when the frozen rivers and snow made possible the use of sleds. With no blizzards or avalanches to threaten the traveler, the summer crossing was less dangerous, and with adequate funds to hire Indian packers, the trek across the pass was not long. Lieutenant Schwatka, with enough Indians to transport everything in a single portage, made the crossing to Lake Lindeman in four days. For the stampeder relying upon himself alone to move his outfit, summer meant no frozen rivers for sledding. It meant scrambling up hills with a heavy pack, working through dense forests and undergrowth, climbing over huge roots, across bogs, ravines, and innumerable ridges of boulders and uprooted trees. Torrential rivers had to be crossed and recrossed twenty to thirty times. Viciously stinging devil's club was everywhere. The shortest route up the final slope to the summit was a barren talus slide impossible to climb in the summer. A longer route to the right was still blanketed with treacherously melting snow, the thin crust concealing crevices and boulders among which the stampeder might fall if he did not proceed with the greatest caution, probing each step as he advanced. The descent from the pass on the Canadian side of the border was across a glassy snow field dropping hundreds of feet into Crater Lake. In the winter the devil's club was dead. The frozen rivers provided an uneven but passable roadbed, so that with sleds a man was able to move greater loads in a single trip. It was not necessary to take to the ridges and dense forests to avoid streams. The impassable talus slope was blanketed with ten feet of snow, so that steps cut into the icy surface provided the shortest route to the crest. An equally important factor in favor of the winter crossing was time. It took between one and two months to move an average outfit from Dyea to Lake Lindeman, about twenty-five miles. Crossing in the summer would put a man on the Klondike too late to be ready for mining the coming winter. By packing over the pass and building a boat in the winter months, a stampeder would be ready to start downriver as soon as the ice went out. He would reach Dawson and still have a couple of months to prospect, find a claim, and build a cabin before winter, when all important mining was done.

Summer or winter, however, it was a long and arduous trip from Dyea to Lake Lindeman for the stampeders who could not afford packers to help with their two-thousand-pound outfits, the average load of a miner. To prevent avoidable personal hardships in the interior, the Canadian government insisted that each man have a year's supply of food with him. It was estimated that a thousand pounds of food would satisfy this requirement. In addition, each man had to carry his prospecting and mining equipment, cooking utensils, stove, boat-building tools and materials, tent, and clothing, all of which amounted to another thousand pounds. Since most men could figure on packing only fifty pounds at a time, moving an outfit from sea level to 3,739 feet[2] and down to Lake Lindeman was a time-consuming process. A base camp would be established with a relay point about three miles up the trail. Shuttling between the two points, a man might move one hundred fifty pounds a day, or more if he had a sled. When his entire outfit was moved forward to the cache, that would then become his new camp, and another relay point would be established further along the trail. Such piecemeal movement was possible only because the theft of an unguarded outfit was rare. A man's cache was considered inviolate. What horse thieving had been to an earlier generation in the West, cache robbing was to the men of the last stampede. A man caught pilfering another's cache was tried on the spot by a stampeders' court. He might be stripped of his belongings and banished if he was lucky, but he was more apt to be flogged or shot.

Alden R. Smith's trip over the Dyea Trail is probably typical of how it seemed to most of the young men crossing that first winter after the report of the strike on the Klondike reached the outside world. He was a farm boy from New York. In this too, he was probably average. There were clerks and professional men from the cities less accustomed than he to outdoor labor in all kinds of weather. There were also lumberjacks, muleskinners, and prospectors from the western states more familiar with the wilderness and life on the trail. He was also average in that he was not a loner. He was in a party of ten from Batavia, New York. In Seattle two of the men found their funds inadequate to continue the trip. Two more panicked when confronted with the reality of embarking for the wilderness to the north and abandoned the party; so there were only six men in the Batavia party when it landed at Dyea with its ten thousand pounds of provisions. They were two weeks out of New York—two weeks to cross a continent, to outfit themselves in Seattle, and to travel by steamer to the end of civilization. They were to be two months completing the next thirty miles.

Exhausted from unloading and assembling their outfit, Alden Smith blew fifty cents to spend a night in a hotel in Dyea and another fifty cents for dinner. After dinner, he drifted into the bar for the excitement and to see what the wild west was like. Facetiously, he noted in a letter home: "We could sit in the bar room in our hotel in Dyea for two hours with a room full of men and not see one of them drink anything but water. The saloons have to rob someone to get a little."[3]

He did see some excitement, however, though he made little of it: "There was a man shot in Dyea the first night we were there. There was four of them in the racket. It was a lot of gamblers. It would have been a good thing if each half had killed the other half of them."[4] Although the murderer was later caught and sent to Sitka for trial, Alden didn't think there was as much excitement over the shooting as there would have been over a fist fight back home.

Like most of the stampeders, Alden had no use for professional gamblers. He worked too hard for what he had to risk it on a game of chance. However, among so many men there must have been others who felt differently, for even along the sled trails there were gamblers with their canvas tables trying to catch suckers.

It seems strange that there would be gambling along the open trail, that men could be diverted from the immediate task of moving outfits toward the Yukon. But there was gambling, and the shell game was a favorite along both the White Pass and the Chil-

Stampeders on the Dyea Trail. The country has now reverted to wilderness. (E. A. HEGG)

Sheep Camp, twelve miles from Dyea. Arriving there after a month on the trail, stampeders found restaurants, hotels, a hospital, a postoffice, and telephone service. Nothing remains of the tent city today; even the site is lost. (E. A. HEGG)

koot trails. The con men apparently reasoned that anyone who would risk so much on the remote possibility of gold would ante up for a chance to win at the shell game. The attraction of the shell game to the con men was the small investment required and the ease of moving the equipment. The stock in trade was three English walnut shells, a small rubber pea, and a canvas table. A pea was placed under one shell, the three shells then shuffled about quickly, and an onlooker invited to bet on which shell concealed the pea. The adroit manipulator guaranteed his winnings by removing the pea before a bet was placed. Despite Alden Smith's conclusion that most men were not taken in by these games, still there were enough unwary ones to make it profitable.

When the Batavia party reached Canyon City after spending six days sledding their outfits the eight miles from Dyea, there were shell games in progress. At one, two shills were making easy money by correctly guessing the shell hiding the pea. Men, not able to make another pack trip that day and with nothing else to do, gathered around to watch the excitement. They cheered on the shills for beating the gambler at his own game, not knowing it was a put-up job. A young man and his wife joined the crowd. The gambler, experienced in spotting the gullible, persuaded the young man to lift one of the shells. "No obligation," he said. "Don't put any money down. Just lift the shell. If you guess right, you get twenty dollars."

The young man, embarrassed at being singled out, tried to draw back only to find himself pressed in by the crowd.

"Don't worry," the gambler wheedled. "It doesn't cost you a cent. Just lift the shell. If you guess right, you win twenty dollars for nothing. Buy the little lady a new parka."

Feeling that it would be churlish to refuse so generous an offer, the young man awkwardly picked up a shell, and there was the pea.

"There you are," the shell man chanted. "You win twenty dollars. Now just to help you and the little lady out and to show these gentlemen that there is nothing wrong with the game, you put down twenty more and with what you already have you will win forty dollars; so you will get eighty dollars and risk only twenty."

The reasoning was too fast for the young man. All he grasped was put up twenty and win eighty; and since he had already won twenty, it didn't seem that he could lose. If he had stopped to realize that he was being asked to bet forty, the twenty he had won and twenty more, he might have refused. The gambler knew this, and so did not give him time to think. Another twenty was put up. This time, the young man lost. Within a few minutes, the shell man had all of the young man's money. The wife tried to recoup and the shell man took all that she had. In this, the shell man made a mistake. A man could make a sucker of himself if he wished. That was his lookout. He might be ill-advised, a damn fool, but he had a right to be stupid in his own way. Let a woman be involved, and the repressed protective instinct of the men would be fiercely aroused. If a man tried to take advantage of a woman, and especially if a gambler tried it, there would be as many avengers as there were men available.

A large crowd had gathered during the fleecing of the young couple. It closed around the shell man. He was advised with words that left no doubt as to the sincerity of the speakers that it would be good for his health to give the money back to the lady. He understood and complied before leaving the scene. However, he was still the eventual winner. The two shills mingling in the crowd managed to recover the money for their partner before the unfortunate couple could escape from the press. The stampeders, frustrated in their act of gallantry, did not hesitate to take up a collection on the spot, raising a nice purse for the young couple.[5]

From Dyea to Canyon City was eight miles, and it took the Batavia party, working as a team, six days to move their ten thousand pounds that far. It was only five miles more to Sheep Camp, but it took seven days to complete that move.

There were no sheep at Sheep Camp, and never had been. There were, however, mountain goats on the cliffs and peaks surrounding the valley, and hunters used this site for dressing out game after a successful hunt. These were the sheep of Sheep Camp. By 1898 it was a forward depot for the stampeders. Thirteen of the seventeen miles to the summit of the pass were behind the stampeders when they reached Sheep Camp, but the next four miles was the worst; so they stopped here to catch their second wind before moving on to Stone House and then the Scales at the base of the Chilkoot Pass.

Sheep Camp was a fair-sized community at times, as many as a thousand and more transients camping there in tents and lean-tos. There were the usual restaurants and hotels as well as a hospital, postal service, telephone communications with Dyea, and packing outfits. Men got mail and bought two-week-old newspapers in Sheep Camp. Eggs shipped from Seattle and packed up the trail from Dyea were only 35¢ a dozen.[6] Alden Smith spent three days in the hospital here, for which he was billed nineteen dollars, and glad to get out alive apparently, as two of the nine patients who shared the hospital with him died during that time.

While recuperating, Alden again moved into a hotel; but in this rustic camp of tents and a few shanties built from rough lumber, the best hotel, or any building for that matter, would have been considered inadequate for a cow or horse stable back in New York. Still, with snow four feet deep, Alden Smith felt any solid shelter was better than a tent while getting his strength back.

Some of the boys, impatient at the enforced delay, hiked up to the summit to get a look at the dread Chilkoot Pass. They reported back that the climb was not as steep nor as high as expected, which was good news. However, with Alden still weak from his illness and considering the difficulty of moving their provisions and equipment this far, they decided on some help, at least to the Scales. Alden, being from a farm, was for getting horses, but they cost $200 apiece and feed was scarce. Dogs seemed to be the thing for this country and were comparatively cheap, the price being only about half what it would be for a good dog in New York. But for people unfamiliar with dog teams, all reports were that it was harder to make the dogs work than it was to do it oneself. And again food was a problem with dogs as well as for horses. In the end they decided on professional packers. From Dyea over the pass, the charge was 6¢ a pound, which would have come to $100 apiece. This was prohibitive. However, from Sheep Camp to the Scales was only 1¢ a pound. This much they could afford. From the Scales, they would have only the short climb to the summit, and then it was all downhill to the lakes.

Although the Scales are three miles beyond Sheep Camp, the Batavia party, like most others, remained in Sheep Camp while moving their loads to the summit. This made for a good hike every morning before starting with the packing, but it also made for economical and more comfortable camping. On the summit, wood was 5¢ a pound and water the same price per glass. They could haul their own wood and water, but it was easier to hike the three miles up and back each day. They could have had their goods packed on over the summit. From the Scales, horses, mules, oxen, Indians, and—after April 19—a tram service were all available for those who could afford 1½¢ a pound to move their outfits over the summit. However, the Batavia party had taxed its budget to the limit hiring packers to the Scales. They were young and healthy. Toting fifty pounds each, making four trips a day, they managed to move all their food and equipment over the summit in eleven days—not eleven successive days, but a total of eleven days packing. There were interruptions.

On April 1 a storm came up just as the boys were ready to leave for the Scales. They knew from experience and from reports that when it was storming at Sheep Camp, there would be a blizzard at the summit. Only fools and the most impatient tried to pack in such weather. It was not only difficult and dangerous, but a cache left on the summit could be burried twenty feet under snow before the storm passed. It was still snowing on April 3, a heavy wet snow. The impatient, taking advantage of the light traffic on the trail, tried to pack over the summit. The wind had died down, so they thought it might be safe. They should have known better when they saw all the Indian packers leaving the Scales and heading for Sheep Camp, but they ignored this warning. When small slides started on the Summit, it was too late. They tried to get down to safety. Some were killed on the slope or at the Scales. Others made it to Squaw Hill only to be caught by an avalanche that swept thousands of tons of wet snow into the valley. About one hundred people in all were buried. For four days all traffic stopped as every available man turned out to dig for survivors.

Men responded as always in the face of tragedy. Confronted with a common crisis, they temporarily put aside personal considerations. They rescued those who could be rescued. Twenty-seven were dug out still alive. The bodies of some sixty who lost their lives were recovered. Men helped each other search for outfits buried in the snow. In the rush to reach the gold fields, men could still take time to perform their ritualistic functions. Bodies of the dead were wrapped in blankets and sent back to Dyea for burial. The Freemasons, of whom Alden Smith was one, convened a meeting and raised money to ship home the bodies of fellow members.

Then the stampede went on. Men were back on the trail.

Packs were shouldered and the assault on the summit continued. The North-West Mounted Police continued their checks to make certain that each miner had his thousand pounds of food. Canadian customs officers again collected duty on all goods brought into Canada.

Having negotiated the climb to the summit, having cleared through customs and received the approval of the Mounties, the stampeders were ready to descend to the Yukon. Behind them and far below was American territory. In the summer it was a lush landscape of green meadows, dense forests, and cascading streams. Even in the winter, the spruce forests laid a soft blanket of green over the rugged mountains. Ahead was the interior, Canadian territory, a barren prospect of snow, ice, and rocks. Treeless ridges formed a jumbled mass to the horizon. Directly below the summit, a vast snow field concealed the frozen surface of Crater Lake, the beginning of the Yukon, whose waters were to carry them to the Klondike. It was a bleak introduction to a country where men hoped to find their fortunes. Some took one look and turned back, selling their outfits to speculators or abandoning them, rather than pack them back down the trail they had just climbed. But most went on. They had overcome too much already not to push on and try for the gold which had lured them to the North. They reshouldered their packs and joined the steady line of men beating a treacherous path down the frozen slope leading to the Yukon that lay somewhere under the snow below.

Down they went with a fresh sense of anticipation. The dreaded Chilkoot Pass was behind them. Ahead, eight miles or so, was Lake Lindeman and beyond Lake Bennett. Many would join the sprawling camp on the western shore of Lake Lindeman. Others would attach sails to their sleds and move their outfits across the frozen surface of Lake Lindeman to Lake Bennett to join the stampeders there who had come across White Pass. Here, at Lindeman or Bennett, the exhaustion of backpacking behind them, the stampeders pitched camp. They set up tents or built cabins and waited for the ice to break up so they could start down the Yukon.

Alden Smith and his group were among those who continued on to Lake Bennett. By the end of April they had all of their goods assembled at the head of Lake Lindeman. They loaded their sleds with about one thousand pounds each, rigged a mast and sail and ran the sleds to the foot of the lake, where they set up a cache. From here, they pulled their sleds over the frozen stream connecting Lindeman and Bennett.

Like all young men away from home for the first time, Alden Smith longed for news, letters or newspapers, and preferably both. At Bennett, he found both. The Seattle papers came in regularly and sold for 25¢ a copy. Letters cost the same. Men acting as self-appointed mail carriers charged 25¢ for a letter brought in and 10¢ for taking one out, going on the principle that news-hungry young men would pay almost anything for a letter but wouldn't send letters if the tariff proved too high.

May 28 was an expensive day for Alden Smith. He received five letters that day, the most recent being dated only May 12, taking sixteen days to make the trip that took him two and a half months. Apparently, his mother expressed concern, as mothers will, as to whether he was getting enough to eat, because the next day he wrote home to put his mother's mind at ease. "Ma wants to know what we eat. Well, this morning we had pancakes and bacon and oatmeal. This noon we had vegetable soup and bread and pork and beans. Sometimes we have pies or fried cakes or anchor pudding which is made of bread dough and fruit and boiled in a pan of water until it is done. It is so heavy that the boys say it will make a good anchor for the boat, so it is called anchor pudding. Now we get enough to eat and it is good enough, what there is of it." Then he added: "I must tell you about the ladies up here for there are a good many of them on the trail. They wear man's pants and coats and rubber boots and it is hard to tell them from a man if their long hair does not give them away. And of course they have no whiskers on their faces. Most of the men have not shaved since they landed and their faces are the same color except two niggers who are a little darker than the rest of us and not so red, but I see they wear sun glasses the same as the rest of us."

Alden Smith may have played down the difficulties of the trail and the rigors of camp life to quiet his mother's fears. If he did, there were many others who exaggerated the dangers to titilate home readers. Then, as now, tales of tragedy were more commonly accepted by the press than reports of the ordinary and kept the home public in a constant state of alarm for the safety of their relatives on the trail to the Yukon. In another letter, Alden told his mother not to worry about him. She had heard that twenty-one people were drowned along the trail. "I did not hear of it," he wrote, "unless it was up on the trail above Lindeman. We heard such a story there, but as there was not enough water there to drink, I do not think it probable. Some fellow told it, I reckon, to get people to go over the other trail past his restaurant." He went on to explain that a pilot at one of the rapids saw a man in a boat without a pilot drown about every trip through the white water, but no one else saw them and the men were never missed.

To the men on the trail, there was beauty as well as hostility in the wilderness. The excitement of the prospects and the exhilaration of the rugged life were more significant than the small problems of daily life. However, the Dyea Trail was rugged. It demanded long hours of hard, cursing work to negotiate its length. The struggle over the Chilkoot Pass was a challenge to endurance and patience. But the very hardships which confronted the men tended to draw partnerships together into a closer relationship. In contrast, the easier life of camp at Lake Lindeman and Lake Bennett had the opposite effect. The enforced waiting for the ice to go corroded patience and strained friendships.

When men were confined to close quarters, living together in the most intimate relationship, frequently sharing beds and blankets for warmth, the trivial became magnified and petty irritations became major problems. It might be snoring, or it might be that one partner did not appear sufficiently fastidious to the other. Perhaps one seemed to eat more than his share, or he made too much noise masticating his food, or one seemed to use more than his share of hot water for washing. These little things were the rocks on which partnerships foundered. The more trivial the cause, the more heat it engendered.

The one problem which caused the greatest animosity among friends was the whipsawing of lumber. To make boats, the stampeders had first to fell logs which they then dragged into camp. There a saw pit was constructed, so that two men, one working below a log and one working on top of the log, with a long two-handled saw could rip the trees into planks. This was a time-consuming ordeal and one which tried the patience of men. The man working below would get sawdust down his neck and in his eyes. He felt that he had the worst of the situation. The man on top, who had to pull the saw against gravity, too often felt that the man in the pit was not contributing his share of effort, that he was perhaps hanging onto the saw or not pulling hard enough or not helping with the return. For two men, even the closest of partners, to survive the ordeal of whipsawing trees into planks required much patience, a sense of humor, and forbearance. Without these attributes, many a partnership foundered in a saw pit as tempers would flare over some imagined error on the part of the other.

With the breakup of the ice on the lakes, a great fever of excitement would invade the camps. Along the shores of Lindeman and Bennett every man wanted to be the first out. Every day, every hour, every minute was important. Each felt involved in a race against time and against his fellow men to reach the Klondike. Boats were hastily launched, masts stepped, gear stowed. Some started too soon before the ice was completely gone and ran into trouble. Others risked launching when the wind made the lake too rough for travel. Inexperience with boats resulted in too frequent mishaps or personal tragedies.

Harry Grow, a thirty-four-year-old Midwesterner, farmer, railroad man, roustabout, and cook crossed the Chilkoot Pass at the same time as the Batavia party. However, he chose to stay at the Lake Lindeman camp rather than proceed to Bennett. Having purchased a knocked-down boat in Seattle, he did not have to make one. With the instructions supplied with the boat kit, he managed to assemble it, but then he was confronted with a problem. He knew nothing about boats. He had never handled one in his life and had no idea how to go about rigging sails or how to manage them when rigged. Inquiring around camp, he met a man named Jack Darrow, who had neither a partner nor a boat of his own. Darrow claimed to know all about boats. In return for the contribution of his experience, Grow agreed to take him along.

By June 3 the lake was sufficiently clear of ice for them to start. Darrow rigged a boom and jib sail, and with Darrow at the tiller, they set off. A stiff breeze filled the sails, and they were soon passing rafts and slower craft as they headed down the lake. It was cold on the water, but they were moving toward the Klondike and moving fast. Grow was thinking how smart he had been to buy the boat in Seattle and how fortunate he had been to meet up with Darrow, when they approached the end of the lake. Darrow pointed to a cabin on the shore near where the lake emptied into rapids leading to Lake Bennett and told Grow they would land there so they

Stampeders gathered at the Scales for the climb over the Chilkoot Pass. The solid line of men marks the short route; beside it are slides used by returning men. To the right is a longer but more gradual route. It took ten days for a stampeder, making four roundtrips a day, to move his outfit to the summit.　　(E. A. HEGG)

U.S. mail arrives at Lake Bennett, 1898. Mail was brought from Circle to Bennett, nearly 800 miles, by sled in winter and by boat in summer. (E. A. HEGG)

At Lake Lindeman the stampeder built a boat and waited for the ice to go out. A cemetery, a plank cabin, and overgrown refuse heaps of tins and bottles are all that remain of the transient town. (E. A. HEGG)

could line the boat down the rapids. Following instructions from Darrow, Grow tried to lower the jib sail so they could come about at the cabin. In his excitement and inexperience, he fouled the lines and the jib stuck. Darrow, with less experience than he claimed, let the situation get out of control. The boat swept past the cabin and into the rapids. With the double force of wind and current, it was impossible to control the boat. They piled up on a rock half way through the passage, damaging the boat and ruining much of their outfits.[7] At that, they were luckier than many who lost everything they had on the Yukon.

Haste coupled with inexperience was the usual combination that led to trouble. But for one young couple it was not being able to swim. They had married only days prior to departure for the Yukon. The steamer trip to Dyea was their honeymoon. A tent was their first home. Together they had worked their outfit up the Dyea trail and over the Chilkoot Pass. Unlike Grow, they did not stop at Lindeman; they pushed on to Bennett. Like others, they had to construct a boat. As did the others, they had to wait for the ice to go out. The bride was not a great help in whipsawing lumber. The groom was not as fastidious in his personal habits as he had been. The strain of waiting developed little cracks in their marital relationship. The weather was unusually warm and by May 12 the first mosquitos made their appearance. Sleep became an ordeal. Little differences that might have been made up in bed were only aggravated by the threatening drone of mosquitos. Patented mosquito repellents were of little use. They were both bitten and irritable. But the universal excitement of the break-up of the ice in the lake revived their spirits. The waiting was finally over. They stowed their supplies in the boat, stepped the mast and took off, only to be confronted with a final difficulty. Unaccustomed to small boats, the wife, attempting to move forward to create a better balance, fell overboard. Unable to swim, she screamed for help. The unfortunate spouse was equally unfamiliar with water and hesitated in despair. Should he go overboard, knowing he could not swim and they both might drown, or should he stay in the boat and hope his young bride might somehow get close enough so that he could pull her in? While he struggled with this quandary, a stampeder from a neighboring boat jumped into the lake and rescued the young woman. He helped her into his own boat and put to shore, where a fire was built so that both could dry out. When the husband managed to get his boat to shore and joined his wife, she turned on him in disgust. "You are no longer my husband. This man," and she pointed to her rescuer, "was willing to risk his life for me. He was willing to plunge into the icy lake and bring me to safety. If he wants me, I am his."[8]

The startled rescuer accepted the proposal and declared he would take this woman to be his wife. The discarded husband protested to no avail. A gathering of stampeders who had either witnessed the near tragedy or heard accounts of the event agreed unanimously that the young woman was within her rights. The previous marriage was declared nullified by the cowardice of the husband and his lack of responsiveness to marital obligations in the face of danger. By consensus of those present, the new partnership based on proffer and acceptance constituted a legal marriage in the eyes of God and man.

The throng is gone today. The excitement of the stampede is absent. The shell games, the snow slides, the restaurants, the hotels, the companionship—all that is historical memory. The Dyea Trail could be given back to the Indians, except they too are gone. Hardly a trace remains of the populous city of Dyea. In this day of urban sprawl, when orchards and truck gardens are being replaced by tract houses, it is interesting to know that occasionally the reverse can happen with equal rapidity, for this is the history of Dyea.

In 1899 Emile Klatt was a farmer in Wisconsin. Times were hard. Dawn to dark toil produced barely enough income for himself. As to thousands of others, the stories of the riches of the Klondike promised a possible release from the seemingly hopeless treadmill. He sold his farm and headed for Dyea, the Chilkoot, the Yukon, and so to the Klondike. But he knew nothing of mining. The streams were all claimed long before he arrived. The stories of easy wealth which he had wished to believe, of gold to be picked up from the stream beds, he found to be myths. He tried working for others; and although the pay was good, it was not his kind of work. He was a farmer. He was accustomed to working for himself. Discouraged, he started the long trek back. When he arrived in Dyea, he found it deserted. Not a hotel, not a restaurant, not a store was occupied. With the railroad operating out of Skagway, every businessman had moved to that town and all traffic was now funneled through that port. He wandered over the narrow valley

floor he recalled teeming with activity. He noted the shallow Dyea
River and the flat lands from which all timber had been cleared by
the early stampeders, and as a farmer, he liked what he saw. Not
particularly wishing to return to Wisconsin penniless, his farm
gone, he homesteaded 160 acres, including the entire city of Dyea,
and started farming.

The first year he put in five acres of potatoes and turnips, and
at the end of the first season he knew he had struck it rich. He had
a stake better than any placer claim on some miserable creek. He
had struck paydirt that would never play out as long as there were
bellies to be fed. His potatoes and turnips brought him $600 an
acre, far better than mining, and to a farmer, more satisfying. He
put in more potatoes and turnips and some hay. He moved into
the best house in town. It was all his, part of his homestead. He
helped himself to dishes and pots and pans. He had his own smithy
fully furnished. When he extended his acreage, no trees had to
be cut or land cleared. He burned down some buildings, first removing the windows and fixtures that might prove of value later.
Nor did he have to work as hard as he had in Wisconsin, plowing,
disking, fighting weeds. The first year he had followed the old
customs, but he found that the long days of sunlight produced
vegetables too large to bring the best market price. The next year
he planted narrower rows and let the weeds grow. This not only
reduced work but resulted in a bigger crop of smaller-sized vegetables that brought premium prices.

In 1907 there were still great warehouses standing, the empty
Klondike Trading Company and the Sunset Telephone Company,
which advertised communications with Skagway and all points on
the Dyea Trail. The Information Center was still standing with
its weathered sign offering information about the trail for $1.00,
the trail that was no longer used. That year Emile Klatt burned a
hotel to make room for a cabbage patch. Thus Dyea died as the
farm of Klatt gradually consumed the city.[9] Today both the town
and the farm are gone. Only the river, the trail, and the pass remain.

Gone too are the civilized landmarks of the Dyea Trail—
Canyon City, Sheep Camp, Stone House, Squaw Hill, the Scales,
and the great camps at Lindeman and Bennett. The trail itself
is more primitive and wild than it was in 1880, when the first
prospectors crossed the pass, and the Chilkoot Indians maintained

a well-marked path from Taiya Inlet to the headwaters of the Yukon.

From Dyea to Canyon City the trail is maintained by the state of Alaska, but Canyon City is only a couple of disintegrating shacks and a rusting boiler. Beyond, the trail is vestigial, scrambling up steep hillsides, over innumerable tree roots and rocks, down gulleys and gulches, over piled up rivers of rocks and uprooted trees. In the winter it is again the silent wilderness unmarked, unmarred by the passing of thousands of stampeders. In the summer, it is a wild valley of primitive beauty with water cascading down the mountains, pouring from solid rock, hanging like wispy festoons from towering precipices. High above the valley, blue-tinged glaciers lie cradled in the arms of the mountains, while the valley itself is lush with growth. Giant forests give way to willows, ferns, devil's club, and a riot of fireweed all cottoned with dew and shredded clouds.

Sheep Camp, which Alden Smith described as a city of a thousand tents and where the Batavia party found a hospital, hotel, restaurants, stores, and postal service, is vanished. Only a state cabin for hikers perpetuates the name. Stone House and Squaw Hill are but a guess. A flattened pile of lumber marks where the tram service started in 1898. Nothing remains of the Scales, where stampeders bought coffee and doughnuts, while waiting their turn in line to mount the snow steps to the summit. The barren cirque is a silent void, where once there was a tumult of motion as the stampeders were finally confronted with the reality of the Chilkoot Pass, which is hidden until this moment.

Beyond the pass the wilderness is even more pronounced. Looking east and north from the summit, Canada is a frozen, desolate country of barren, snow-covered mountains and ice-filled lakes. Any trail the Indians may have established is overgrown. A jumble of ridges sliding into a maze of ravines follows Crater Lake, Long Lake, Deep Lake to Lake Lindeman. Where a vast tent city stretched along the shore, there is now a forlorn cemetery and moldering heaps of rusting tin cans and broken bottles. The sandflats denuded by stampeders in their search for boat lumber and firewood are again covered with a spindly spruce forest.

Bennett was even more of a community than Lindeman. Some ten thousand men converged there from the White Pass and the

Chilkoot Pass trails and waited for the ice to go out. Today it is but a tourist stop on the White Pass and Yukon Route where passengers pause briefly to gorge themselves from huge platters of moose meat, boiled potatoes, beans, stewed tomatoes, gravy, bread, pitchers of milk, and pie set out family style on trestle tables. The only reminder of the transient city is a wooden church, propped up by huge timbers. It was completed in 1899[10] by an Episcopal minister who recognized the need of men delivered from the ordeal of the trail for a place of formal worship. He called for volunteers to build a church, and they came. Under the open skies of the north country, confronted with the transitory lust for gold, the men felt a need for the habits of their homes and abandoned societies. Rallying to the call, they felled trees, ripped planks and built themselves a church with high walls, windows, a sharply pitched roof, and a great steeple rising high into the air. They never got around to putting a floor in the church, and their structural engineering would have had difficulty passing contemporary building codes. That did not matter; they built themselves a fine, great church where they might worship and sing the familiar hymns. It was abandoned the next year when the railroad went into service and the need for building boats and rafts at Bennett ceased.

Bennett died like Dyea, Canyon City, Sheep Camp, Stone House, and Lindeman. The transient tents disappeared and were not replaced. Cabins were torn down over the years for firewood. Business establishments moved on to other places. Trees reforested the land.

5

Stewart River

WITH THE BREAK-UP OF ICE in the spring, with the opening of the Yukon, it was all downhill to Dawson. By boat, barge, or raft, the stampeders floated from Lake Bennett to the Klondike. It was, as an Australian prospector put it, a piece of cake. There was the inconvenience of running or portaging around Miles Canyon and Whitehorse Rapids, but for men who packed over the Chilkoot Pass in the winter, this presented no great danger or serious chore. There was Five Finger Rapids, but the five volcanic extrusions reaching out of the water like truncated fingers were more of a geologic oddity than a threat to navigation. To the imaginative, they might have seemed to tremble in the running water like the clutching grasp of some unplacated river spirit, but the length of the passage between them was not over sixty feet. They were so lacking in danger that the diary addicts of the Batavia party did not even note them in their logs.

To the men of 1898, their attention and effort concentrated on reaching the Klondike, the Yukon was simply a convenient route to be traversed as quickly as possible on the way to Dawson. They noted little of the Yukon country through which they passed. They swept past Caribou Crossing, sailed, rowed, paddled, or poled through the treacherous shallows of Tagish and Marsh lakes. A few lost their boats and supplies in Miles Canyon or the Whitehorse Rapids, but most took these dangers in stride, shooting the rapids themselves, employing professionals who waited there for hire, or hauling their outfits around the rapids on wooden rails built to facilitate the portage. Without stopping, they passed the flats where the town of Whitehorse was to be built and crossed Lake Labarge, on the marge of which Robert Service was to lay the cremation of Sam McGee. They scarcely noticed the beauty of the Thirty Mile River in their race against each other. They passed the Teslin River, where men had prospected over a decade earlier, Hootalinqua, Big Salmon, Little Salmon. Only out of curiosity did some stop at Carmacks, where the discoverer of the Bonanza once had a trading post.[1] Then Five Finger Rapids and Rink Rapids. At Fort Selkirk the men had to stop to show their customs papers and perhaps to buy some fresh vegetables from the little farm behind the trading post. And off again, past Selwyn, Ballarat, Coffee, Kirkman creeks, Carlisle Creek, Thistle Creek, and White River before reaching Stewart River, fifty-five miles from Dawson. The Batavia party stopped, but nothing in their diaries indicates they had any realization that here too was gold, that this was where the first stampede to the Yukon occurred.

In 1883 four men worked the Stewart River during the summer months, making on the average ten dollars a day.[2] Lacking supplies and since winter mining in the frozen gravel beds had not at this time been developed, the men went down the Yukon to the Alaska Commercial Company's Tanana Station and wintered there. In the spring two of the men sought new streams in other parts of the country, while Dick Poplin and Jim McClusky returned to the Stewart. Again they found gold and again with the coming of winter they headed out. This time all the way out, over the Dyea Trail and on to Juneau. They had been inside for two years and needed to restock.

Before 1885 the trading posts at Tanana, Fort Yukon, and Fort Reliance, in fact, all the trading posts along the river, had stocked only Indian trade goods for the fur trade. There might be enough flour, sugar, and tea on hand for the occasional prospector who ran short, but the stations did not have equipment for miners. Clothing and boots suitable for men working in the cold streams were not ordered. Beans, rice, bacon, coffee—food items of interest to the white men from outside were not available, nor were picks, shovels, hammers, saws, pans, and the like. But when he prepared his inventory in 1884, McQuesten ordered fifty tons of supplies specifically for the needs of prospectors, so they could replenish their larders and replace worn-out boots and broken tools without going out of the country at the end of the summer. With the arrival of this shipment the next summer and from then on, miners could remain in the Yukon country as long as they wished. They would be able to work as late in the season as weather permitted without fear of running short of supplies. Their needs could be filled locally from the shelves of McQuesten's trading posts, which moved with the shifting mining population.

In 1885 McClusky decided against going back to the Stewart, but Poplin returned with three other men, Wilbering, Morphat, and Bertrand. He found two others, Fraser and Tom Boswell, already there. The six men joined forces and together they sluiced over $10,000 worth of gold in two months. This was too good to quit working early in the season, which they would have to do if they went back to Dyea or Juneau to winter and get more supplies. Fortunately for them, Boswell and Fraser had spent the previous winter at Fort Reliance and knew that McQuesten had gone out in the summer of 1884 to order miners' supplies. These should have arrived by now, and if so, this would make it possible for the camp to obtain a year's supply without going outside. Instead, they could sluice until the river froze and then winter on the Stewart. Tom Boswell was chosen to make the trip downriver to get the food and necessary equipment, but it was decided that he should tell no one of the strike. They would keep this to themselves. If anyone asked how they were doing, he was to say that there wasn't much color so the men had decided to spend the winter in the back country, trying their hand at trapping.

Boswell built a crude raft at Stewart Island on which he floated down the Yukon past the Sixty Mile River, Indian Creek, and the Klondike River to Fort Reliance, where he arrived on August 6. There were no supplies, only a little flour. However, Boswell was not seriously disturbed. He knew that the ice conditions in the Bering Sea made it impossible for supply ships to reach St Michael until late in June or early July. After goods arrived at the station there and were reloaded onto a river steamer, it would take another month to reach Fort Reliance. His reasoning was correct, for on August 10 McQuesten arrived with fifty tons of miners' supplies.

With McQuesten were Joseph Ladue, Homer Franklin, Thomas Williams, Harry Madison, and Mike Hess, who had been prospecting farther down the river. They were all interested to hear what Boswell had to say about the Stewart, but they were not surprised to learn that it was not so good. Boswell bought what he needed for six men for a year, and then, as McQuesten was going up to Selkirk to trade for furs, all the miners boarded the boat for a free ride upriver. At Stewart River, Boswell got off to wait for McQuesten's return to haul his order as far up the river as possible. Franklin and Madison got off at White River to prospect, and Ladue, Williams, and Hess went on to Selkirk to build a boat and continue on to try their luck on the Teslin. When McQuesten returned to the Stewart alone, Boswell finally told him why the party planned to winter on the Stewart and how much they had taken out already. McQuesten was shocked. All sourdoughs, as a matter of common practice, told others whenever they made a good strike. A discoverer of a good strike had the right to two claims, a principle respected by the other miners; but in return, it was expected that the discoverer would tell others so that they might also have a chance to work a promising area. By not telling them, Boswell had denied five men the chance to get gold from a proven stream. McQuesten said nothing at the time. There was little to be gained from recriminations, but he soon had an opportunity to correct Boswell for his breach of the miners' code.

Twelve miles up the Stewart, they encountered a camp of six prospectors who had come in from Juneau after Boswell had come downriver. There were Frank Dinsmore and John Hughes, Isaac Powers, Steven Custer, Hugh Day, and Albert Day.[3] They were all experienced prospectors and suspected Boswell must have something to be coming in with a boatload of supplies. Although Boswell still stuck to his earlier story that they had found nothing of consequence on the gravel bars and so were going to try to recoup some of their expenses by trapping for the winter, McQuesten would not let him get away with this again. He told the new men that Boswell and his group had been making $20 a day. Boswell was not discomfited. He said he had been away for several weeks and didn't really know how the boys were doing.

All but Dinsmore and Hughes joined McQuesten and Boswell on the boat, but they were able to go only fifteen miles before the river shallowed out. Here they unloaded and established a cache. Normally, McQuesten would have returned to Fort Reliance, having completed his contract, but there seemed to be the making of a good strike. He wanted to see it for himself. Besides he had been a miner before becoming a trader and still liked to prospect occasionally, though he no longer had the urge like his partner Harper, who could never keep away from prospecting for long.

Together, he and Boswell canoed the rest of the way to the camp on Steamboat Bar. He tried his hand at working the river bars for five days and made $250. Satisfied with what he found, he returned to Fort Reliance, telling everyone he met on the way about the strike. By the next summer there were over a hundred miners and a new McQuesten trading post on the Stewart.

This was the first of the stampedes to the Yukon. However, it was not long-lived since no other good strikes were made along the Stewart, and a year later most of the miners left in the stampede to the Forty Mile. With the succeeding stampedes to Circle City, Dawson, Nome, and Fairbanks, the early importance of Stewart River was forgotten. But there were always some miners on the river, and as traffic along the Yukon increased, a roadhouse was built on Stewart Island, a telegraph station established across the river. John Lawrence, who came to the Yukon as a boy when gold dust still shimmered in the air, knew them both. His unleavened story of life there is refreshing in its contrast to the yeasty accounts of boisterous rudeness untypical of the times, but perpetuated by the prose and verse of Jack London and Robert Service.

Jack London, who wintered on the Stewart River in 1898, caught the spirit of the cold northern country, but he was more interested in fiction than fact. The brutal side of life attracted him unduly. The riot of drunken lust and reckless gaming existed but, in well-policed Dawson, was not a prominent part of life. Robert Service, who arrived in the Yukon after the stampedes were over, pictured the people as they wanted nostalgically to think of themselves as being bigger, more riotous, more boisterous, more sentimental than life. John Lawrence simply recalls it as it was.

John Lawrence was a Midwesterner, a farm boy. His mother was dead, his father a struggling failure. When the insanity that was Klondike swept the world, his father, like many others, saw the Yukon as his last chance for success. He could continue on all his life scraping a bare subsistence from plowed fields or he could go to Dawson and make a fortune. Leaving John Lawrence with an aunt, the father disappeared into the North.

A year passed, stretched into two, then three, paced by a daily round of chores. The drudgery of life was buoyed by daydreams of the Klondike, Bonanza, Eldorado, Dawson, the Yukon. He could not remember his father as a person but rather conceived of him as a heroic figure, a gold miner, one of the stampeders, a part of the glittering panoply which was the life in Dawson as portrayed by the periodicals of the day. Then came the day when a letter arrived with money, instructing him to join his father in the Yukon. Not yet thirteen, with the beginning of summer, he closed his schoolbooks for the last time; and with visions of gold and high adventure, he took a train for Seattle. Each stage of the trip was more exciting than the last. To a boy from the flat farm land who had never traveled, the train was a thrilling experience, the endless miles of plains, range land, the first sight of mountains, desert, the somber gloom of pine forests. Then Seattle, a big city, a seaport, the embarkation point for the stampede trail, and the steamer to Skagway. Each experience a first, magnified by its relation to the goal, the Yukon. The magnificence of the inland passage with spruce-clad mountains rising into the clouds, every peak and precipice dripping water in cascading streams and plumed falls. The glaciers and blue-tinted icebergs drifting on the still waters of the sheltered passage. And finally the Lynn Canal and the Taiya Inlet like a microscope exposing in its narrow focus the grandeur of Skagway. The railroad starting up the main street of Skagway, over the White Pass to Lake Bennett to Carcross to Whitehorse and, finally, the Yukon and a gleaming white sternwheeler, almost as large as the ocean-going steamer he had taken from Seattle but drawing only three feet of water.

John Lawrence did not remember much of the trip down the river, but as they churned across Lake Labarge in the middle of the night, with the pale, washed-out skies crimped along the horizon in a golden glow, he surely experienced, if only subconsciously, the beginning of that feeling peculiar to the Yukon. This was inside —saucered by scalloped mountains rimming the timeless distance that slides into pale skies fading to infinity—all the world beyond is outside. He could not recall sleeping, although he must have. There was too much to see. Down the Thirty Mile River looking for moose, which he did not see. There was too much traffic then for these great beasts, which today wander carelessly along the banks. A shudder through the thin planking of the steamboat, as the Teslin joined the Thirty Mile to double the flow of the Yukon.

Brief stops at isolated camps to take aboard endless cords of skinny spruce to fire the boilers. Past Indian camps, Carmacks, Tantalus Bluff, Five Finger Rapids, which must have appeared a terrifyingly narrow passage for the bulk of the steamboat, Rink Rapids, a short rest period at Fort Selkirk to leave mail and supplies. Then off again, for Stewart Island, the end of his saga. His excitement mounted as he anticipated reunion with his father. But how would he recognize this great gold miner, this stranger who was his father? For the first time, as the moment of reunion approached, he realized he could not recall his father. Try as he would, he could evoke no picture, only an emotion.

As they swept around a final bend in the river, the pilot gave two blasts on the whistle. "There she is," a deckhand said. "That's Stewart Island."

John Lawrence looked, but he could see only a flat piece of land that looked like part of the shore. "Where?" he asked, already feeling the vague disappointment of reality. There was only desolate river wilderness. He did not know what he expected, but it wasn't this. It was something made up of gold and palatial saloons and gay throngs and men, bigger than life, striding solemnly about with pokes of dust and nuggets.

"See that clearing there? That's Ma Shand's. Your pa's cabin will be back in there somewhere."

Bitter tears burned his eyes, and a constriction in his throat made it impossible for the boy to speak.

"It's too shallow to land there now," the deckhand continued. "We will have to pull in on the other side of the river; but don't worry none, sonny, they heard that whistle and your pa will be there to get you."

But he wasn't. As the steamer dropped away with a final blast of its whistle, leaving John Lawrence on a sharp mudbank with a bundle of clothes under his arm, his only reception was from a swarm of mosquitos. There was no sign of activity on the opposite shore. No boat. Not one person. The rising crescendo of excitement that had been building up in the past two weeks had ended as a dull clink on a broken triangle instead of culminating in a crash of brass and timpani. Fortunately for his self-control, a long, narrow flatbottomed boat appeared from behind some sweepers down river. It was being poled, rather than rowed, by a young man. As the boat slid effortlessly against the current, he got his first intimation that the Yukon was not to be what he anticipated, for the young man was not the rudely dressed miner he thought everyone in this country would be. He wore knickers, a Norfolk jacket, and a broad-brimmed hat.

"I presume you are John Lawrence," the boatman said, as he thrust the boat into the bank and held it there with his pole.

The voice too was a surprise, for it was a cultured British accent. John nodded.

"I do think you better come aboard before you are utterly consumed by those wretched mosquitos. Easy though," he warned, "the boat is a bit tippy."

When they had pushed away from the shore and the fury of the mosquitos, the man introduced himself as the local telegraph operator. "You see, I live on this side of the river rather than on Stewart's Island, so your father asked me if I would meet you. He had to go to Dawson for a couple of weeks. Until he returns you can stay at Ma Shand's roadhouse. She's expecting you." Having delivered John Lawrence to Ma Shand and having extended an invitation to the boy to come across and visit, the young Englishman left.

"Hmph," Ma Shand sniffed, as he departed, "him and his airs. Just look at them dude clothes. Too good for common folk. He could of boarded here," she said, exposing her bias, "like the operator before him did. But no, he's got to live over there by himself with all his books and things. Well, as the feller says, it's no skin off my nose. Now," and she planted her mind solidly confronting a new subject, "what are we going to do with you until your pa comes back? The Devil finds use for idle hands. Up here everyone pitches in and helps, you know. Not like outside." Years later when *Little Mother of the North* was published extolling the life of Ma Shand, John Lawrence recalled that "if she was a mother to me, she sure made me work for it."

It was a lonesome, homesick boy who had to wait two weeks for the climax to his long trip, for the reunion with his father; and then when his father did arrive, he was far from the romantic figure the boy had evoked in his mind. In the Yukon, like so many men, Mr. Lawrence had found something other than fortune. He found religion, and forsaking the Klondike and the glitter of Dawson, he had settled on Stewart Island to earn a bare subsistence commensurate with the suffering which he felt was man's lot on

*Fort Selkirk was the headquarters of the Yukon field force.
Stampeders stopped here to have their customs papers
checked.* (E. A. HEGG)

*The first Yukon stampede began after gold was discovered on
the Stewart River in 1883. Fifteen years later stampeders
on their way to the Klondike still stopped at the mouth
of the Stewart River.* (E. A. HEGG)

this earth. Mr. Lawrence was a thin man who had become stooped both by the toil of making a living and from the weight of the problems on his mind. His drooping moustaches accentuated the lugubrious appearance of his melancholy face. He was the opposite of the great smiling man expected, who would greet his son with a shout of welcome and clasp him with exuberant abandon. Mr. Lawrence was a quiet, serious man, whose eyes burned with a fierce glow of moral rectitude rather than sparkling with the bubble of life. The father acknowledged his son with a simple nod and led him from the big roadhouse, redolent with warm life, off through the woods and down-timber to a mean little shack, which was to be their home. To a boy fired with the glowing expectations of romantic youth, this was almost more than he could bear.

Fortunately for John Lawrence the Englishman (no name is given) who had met him on the bank of the Yukon was an educated man and took an interest in the boy. For over a year John Lawrence went daily to the telegrapher's cabin, where he found friendship and a more pleasant way of living than he had in his father's miserable cabin. Nearly every morning he would have breakfast with the telegrapher, who would then take down one of the many books he had in his cabin and start the young boy on the reading which they would later discuss and analyze, thus developing John Lawrence's thinking and mental processes. The young boy learned how to operate the telegraph key, so that later he too became a telegraph operator. By chance, while looking through his host's library, he found novels written by the telegrapher, and so it was he learned that his mentor was an Oxford graduate who had published several books. However, after inheriting ten thousand pounds, the Englishman had abandoned writing in favor of gambling. He developed a system to beat the house, or so he thought, and went to Monte Carlo to put his theory to the test. The test cost him exactly ten thousand pounds. To reestablish his fortune, he had come to the Yukon, where failing to find gold, he had become a telegrapher. He hoped that the money he saved from his job, plus what he might make from a new book he was writing, would enable him to resume the life he had led before the Monte Carlo fiasco.

When an old trapper died, leaving John Lawrence a cabin with guns and traps, the boy moved out of his father's cabin before he was fifteen. With his own home, with guns and traps, he became independent. He hunted moose for the miners and cut wood for the steamers. During the long winter nights he passed his time at the Shand roadhouse, where the men gathered to play poker.

One night, when barely turned fifteen, he sat in a poker game. He had been watching the play for some time and, being a smart-aleck young kid, thought he could play as well as the men, and certainly better than those who had been drinking; so when a player dropped out and some of the men, more as a joke than in seriousness, urged him to sit in, he did.

One of the players at the table was Blackie Morgan, a huge black-haired, black-bearded miner with a violent temper who hated to lose. Anything to beat Blackie was popular, because he took it so hard.

The boy did not have much money, but he had sold a moose that afternoon and had about one hundred dollars in his pockets. By playing carefully and perhaps with the connivance of some of the men at the table, he ran his pile up considerably. It was nearing midnight when, in a game of draw poker with nothing wild, four kings and a three were dealt to him. He felt his heart pound with excitement. From watching poker many nights, he knew he had a winning hand. The possibility of anyone beating four of a kind was slim, and to beat four kings was virtually impossible, requiring four aces or a straight flush. There were six men in the game at the time, including himself. The opening bet was a dollar, which was raised to ten and then fifty before it got around to John Lawrence. He called and raised fifty, his hands sweaty with the excitement of such a raise. Although he knew it was virtually impossible for anyone to beat him, still the risking of so much money on the turn of a card was frightening to a young boy.

Three players called the fifty, including Blackie, who called and raised a hundred. To Blackie, poker was a game to be won. If a kid wanted to play, that was his tough luck. He would have to take his knocks along with the men. If he wanted to bet with the men, he would have to meet the stakes, and he scowled at the boy as he shoved in the raise. John Lawrence hesitated. A hundred dollars was a lot of money. It was an impossible amount to risk on cards. He might lose. Blackie was the kind who just might draw out on him. But he had no choice as everyone turned to watch him, to see what he would do. He had to call the hundred. He knew he should raise, but he could not do that. His throat was dry and his voice broke as he squeaked, "I call," and pushed in one hundred dollars.

Only one other player stayed, who felt that perhaps Blackie was trying to crowd the boy out of the game and might have nothing, and so hoped to back into a win if the boy dropped under pressure.

The dealer called for cards. John Lawrence was under the gun. It was up to him first to declare. He hesitated, thinking that perhaps the best way to play the hand was to draw one, hoping to convince the other two that he was drawing to a straight or trying to fill two pairs to get a full house. But one of the old-timers standing behind the boy, accidentally kicked his chair; and as the kid looked around, the old-timer imperceptibly shook his head. John Lawrence knew this meant to do nothing, stand pat and make them think, as they must already think, he had a pat straight or possibly a flush. The next man threw in two cards and drew two. Blackie studied his cards, scowling at the table. Finally, he said, "Okay, there's got to be one honest bastard in the crowd, give me one." He dropped his discard and picked up the single. Without looking, he began sifting his cards.

The opening was up to Blackie, who had been called. Slowly, he raised his cards to eye level, fanning them one at a time. Then with a deep sigh, he shoved in five hundred dollars, just matching the pot. The kid watched him, terrified. He had still five hundred in front of him from the evening's winnings. This was more money than he had ever possessed. He could keep the five hundred and drop out of the game. But he knew this was impossible. He had the winning hand. He had watched too many nights to believe otherwise, but the gut-aching reality of play was a far cry from watching.

With an abrupt, jerky movement, he pushed in all of his money. "Call," he croaked.

The third man threw in his cards. He was not about to back into a pot. Blackie slammed his cards to the table, spreading them out. Full house, jacks up. "There you are, kid," he said gruffly. "You got to learn some time. That'll make a man out of you."

Feeling weak and exhausted, John Lawrence spread his hand. "Four kings," he whispered.

Blackie stared at the winning hand. "By God," he roared at last, "Four of a kind and you stand pat? You miserable little son of a bitch," and he rose from the table and stalked out, followed by the hoots and the hollers of the other poker players. They slapped young John on the back and shouted his praise. One of the men gave him a cigar. "By Gawd, you're a man, boy. Light up and have a drink."

John Lawrence recalls that, when his father heard of the poker game, he was furious. He took the $1,500 from the boy and forbade him ever to go to the bar again. He put the money in a Dawson bank and said it would stay there until the boy was twenty-one. It didn't, because his father died before then, but John did not return to the bar or the poker games. For one thing, he had found out what it was to win big, and it had scared him. It did not get into his blood and excite him to try again. He did not wish to go through the ordeal a second time. Furthermore, a Mountie, hearing about the escapade, told old man Shand, who ran the bar, that he was contributing to the delinquency of minors, and if he let the boy in again, the bar would be closed.

Boys became men fast in the Yukon. The Mounties might deny a boy access to a bar, but there was no child-labor law to prevent his earning money by hard work, nor did society frown on manual labor for growing boys. He was earning his own living and did not need the $1,500. He cut wood for steamers at $7 a cord. He hauled freight up the Stewart River for 5¢ a pound. The moose he killed he sold for 17¢ a pound, and the animals usually dressed out at around 600 pounds. He recalls walking to Barker's and taking a dog team from there to Thistle Creek. It was St. Patrick's Day. At Thistle Creek they had a dance that evening, but there were only two girls—Anne Schoolman and Maggie Shaver. By the time he got up courage to ask Maggie Shaver for a dance, both girls were too tired to dance any more. Besides, as he remembers, he had not started to get his growth yet, and the girls thought he was too small.[4]

Later John Lawrence had his own telegraph station on the upper Yukon until the decline of Dawson and the coming of the telephone made the telegraph line obsolete. He went outside. Although he lived the rest of his life in southern California, his early years at Stewart Island and along the Yukon remained his most vivid memories.

Today Thistle Creek Lodge still stands, its vine-covered verandah overlooking a lovely sweep of the Yukon, but there is no dancing in its empty halls. The telegraph line lies forgotten among the down-timber along the Yukon. The miners have left Stewart River. Ma Shand's roadhouse is gone. Of the settlement that once existed, there remains only the home of the Burian family, who trap, do a little prospecting, and keep open the last trading post on the upper Yukon. An anachronism in a world of conformity, they maintain the independence of individualism that here made the first sizable strike of the last stampede.

6

The Klondike,
Bonanza, Dawson

ROM THE STEWART RIVER, the Yukon flows north some seventy
miles before making a question-mark sweep to the west.
Here a sparkling, clear river enters the silt-umber Yukon. On
July 17, 1883, Lieutenant Schwatka's exploration party
beached their raft at the juncture of the two rivers, believing they
were in the proximity of the Canadian-American boundary.
Schwatka says in his journal that this stream was called Deer Creek
by the traders, because of the large numbers of caribou or woodland
reindeer seen in this valley at certain times of their migrations.
Actually McQuesten, the only trader in the immediate area, knew
the stream by its Indian name, Trundeck,[1] a name popularly
mispronounced by stampeders, Klondike.

Sixteen years later George Washington Carmack, a Califor-
nian, was fishing there with his Indian friends when a passing
Canadian prospector, Robert Henderson, told him of finding gold
on a Klondike tributary; and it was this information which led
Carmack to his own discovery of gold on another tributary. At
least, this is the popularly accepted story.[2]

Who actually discovered gold first in the Klondike region?
Who was responsible for the Klondike stampede? The official
Canadian version credits Robert Henderson, perhaps because he
was a Canadian and the only Canadian even remotely connected
with gold discovery in the Klondike region. Others say Arthur

Harper or George Pilz or Joseph Ladue first discovered gold there. Whoever the discoverer was, the immediate catalyst for the stampede was Carmack, but for prejudicial reasons, even those who credit him with filing the discovery claim tend to denigrate his character and question the propriety of acknowledging him as the man responsible for the greatest stampede on the Yukon. The truth is clouded by contention.

The first white gold-seekers on the Yukon were Harper, Mayo, McQuesten, and their associates, who came down the Porcupine in 1873. It was in that year Harper worked the White River area, eighty miles above the Klondike. From 1875 to 1878, Harper and Mayo were at Fort Reliance, but Harper was never one whose mind was far from prospecting. Although it is not reported, it is safe to assume that Harper prospected all the creeks in the area of Fort Reliance. This would certainly include the Klondike, which is only about five miles upriver from the station. In 1883 George Pilz, the German engineer credited by many, himself included, with the discovery of gold in the Juneau area, came into the Yukon and claimed to have prospected the Klondike without finding anything of great interest.[3]

In May of 1886 Peter Nelson, Dan Sprague, Joe Ladue, and John Nelson prospected various creeks emptying into the Klondike but did not consider the area of particular significance, "as we could make all the way from $50 to $100 a day on the Stewart River bars, if we caught low water."[4]

Frank Buteau gives Henry Willet and Joe Wilson credit for the initial discovery: "In 1892 they went up the Indian River and located gold near King Dome. Four years later, in 1896, Bob Anderson and Andrew Hunker went over the hill to find the gold Willet and Wilson had located. They found it on Gold Bottom and Hunker Creek, which flow into the Klondike, and up at the head of Dominion Creek, a tributary of Indian River."[5]

Joe Ladue was then running a trading post at Ogilvie, near the mouth of Sixty Mile River. He made it his business to know of gold strikes in the area, so that he could encourage miners to work the streams within a reasonable radius of his post. As the Indian River was only about ten miles downriver from his store, when Robert Henderson arrived at the Ogilvie trading post in 1894, Joe Ladue painted a glowing picture of the prospects there. Henderson, accepting Ladue's account, started up the Indian, prospecting along the way. He went as far as Quartz Creek, and up Quartz to the divide of the Klondike watershed. Finding no good prospects, he returned to Ogilvie for provisions.

The next year Henderson followed the Indian to its headwaters and crossed the divide to Gold Bottom, a tributary of the Klondike. Here he found fair prospects. He wintered on the creek that year; and the following summer, convinced now that he had a good strike, he made the long trip back to Ogilvie for more supplies. This time he was able to settle up his account with gold, and he told Ladue where he had made his strike and how promising it looked. Together, they figured out on a homemade map just where Henderson's find was located and determined it would be easier for him to return via the Klondike, instead of portaging over the divide from the Indian. When Henderson reached the mouth of the Klondike, he met George Carmack, fishing for salmon with a couple of Indians, and he told Carmack of the strike on Gold Bottom.

To this point, most versions of the discovery of gold in the area are in agreement. According to the official Canadian account, which credits Henderson with starting the Klondike stampede, he told Carmack of his gold find and continued on to Gold Bottom. Later, Carmack and the two Indians, while hunting moose, did visit Gold Bottom and tried a few pans on the stream. They did not like what they found and left, after promising to inform Henderson if they found good prospects on Rabbit Creek, where Henderson had suggested they try their luck.

Carmack's account differs in important details.[6] He and his Indian friend, Skookum Jim, had explored the country the day before Henderson's arrival and had selected Rabbit Creek as a likely stream to prospect. He agrees that Henderson told him of Gold Bottom, but he was not particularly interested. Later, with Skookum Jim and Tagish Charlie, he did go up the Rabbit and found good prospects. The three men then crossed over to Henderson's claim and tried Gold Bottom, which they did not find as good as Rabbit Creek. Carmack says he told Henderson this and advised Henderson to come over to Rabbit Creek.

Carmack and the two Indians then returned to Rabbit Creek, where they found richer prospects than before. Those who try to discredit Carmack say that Skookum Jim and Tagish Charlie found the gold while Carmack was sleeping. Others say that Kate Carmack, his Indian wife, found the gold while she was washing up after lunch.

Whatever the version accepted, Carmack did go to Forty Mile and was the first to record the discovery of gold on a tributary of the Klondike. He says he reported his find to half a dozen prospectors he met along the way, men looking for Henderson's strike, about which they had heard from Joe Ladue. Certainly the Rabbit was heavily staked within a few days. Even before Carmack could return to his claim from Forty Mile, there were some fifty miners in the area. A miners' meeting was held opposite Number 17 Below Discovery on August 22, at which twenty-five miners were present. David McKay was elected local recorder, and Rabbit Creek was officially renamed the Bonanza.

Piecing together the reports of men who were in the Yukon at the time and the writing of Carmack himself, the following would seem to be a reasonably accurate synoptic biography of the discredited discoverer of the rich placer deposits on the Bonanza, which precipitated the Klondike stampede.

George Washington Carmack was born September 24, 1860, on a cattle ranch in California. When twenty-four, he shipped out of San Francisco, arriving in Juneau in March of 1885. With several other men, he went to Dyea and crossed the Chilkoot Pass to prospect the upper Yukon. With the coming of winter, he returned to Juneau. The following year he joined the Ogilvie survey party, guiding them to Lake Bennett. There he left the party and returned to Juneau to buy trade goods for trading with the Indians along the Yukon. But he didn't trade that year. Returning to Dyea, he threw in his lot with the Indians, whose philosophy of life he preferred to the establishment-inclined traders or the monomania of the gold seekers. He hired out as a packer over the Chilkoot, carrying hundred-pound packs along with the Indians. Here he met Skookum Jim, a Tagish Indian, whom Carmack described as having high cheekbones, a hawk-like nose, large, piercing black eyes; he was six feet tall, straight as a gun barrel and powerfully built, with strong sloping shoulders, tapering down to a narrow waist, giving him the appearance of a keystone. He was known as the best hunter and trapper on the Yukon. Here also Carmack met Tagish Charlie, a good complement to Skookum Jim, lean and lithe as a panther. The three men formed a tacit partnership, Carmack later marrying Tagish Charlie's sister, Kate.

Together, the three men hunted, fished, and prospected the tributaries of the Yukon. Carmack loved the country and liked to climb to high places and look at what God had made and write poetry. A loner, as far as white companionship was concerned, he preferred his Indian friends. Such a man, having rejected his own society, could not expect popularity. He had gone siwash, or native, for which he was considered queer and ridiculed by the white prospectors. In 1889 he and his Indian companions went to Forty Mile and on down the river to Fort Yukon and returned. In the following year he is reported to have found gold on Birch Creek, three years before the strike by Cherosky and Pitka, which is officially credited as the discovery leading to the Circle City stampede. For four years he maintained a trading post near the Five Fingers Rapids, probably at the present site of the little town of Carmacks. While there, he built a church at Fort Selkirk for Bishop Bompas. In 1896 he decided to open a coal mine, having discovered a good coal deposit in the vicinity of his trading post. But before carrying out this plan, he returned to Forty Mile, and then with Skookum Jim and Tagish Charlie, he visited the mouth of the Klondike to fish for salmon.

Whatever the truth concerning the disparate statements of Henderson and Carmack—whether Henderson suggested Rabbit Creek to Carmack or Carmack tried Rabbit Creek on his own hunch; whether the discovery resulted from an experienced prospector's appraisal of rock formations or was the lucky chance of hungry hunters dressing out a moose, as some claim; whether Carmack found gold or Skookum Jim or Tagish Charlie or Kate, as claimed by those who considered Carmack shiftless—there is no gainsaying the fact that George Carmack filed the first claim in the Klondike area.

Carmack does not himself take credit for finding gold on the Klondike. He admits that in 1895 Pete Nelson reported at Forty Mile that he, John Nelson, Dan Sprague, and Joe Ladue prospected the Klondike in 1886 and found gold. But Carmack was the first to file claims officially, not only for himself but for Skookum Jim and Tagish Charlie, thereby assuring his Indian partners of becoming wealthy men. According to a photograph of the original application for claim, it was sworn to and dated September

24, 1896, and signed on that date by Carmack and Constantine, commanding officer of the Mountie station at Fort Cudahy, Forty Mile.[7]

Why this date appears on the original application is not known, as there is no question that the discovery was made in August and Carmack first recorded his claim on August 21. A Mountie who was stationed at Fort Cudahy at the time wrote of the event, confirming August 21, 1896, as the date Carmack filed his claim. According to his ambiguous account of Carmack's actions, Carmack "took a few favored friends into his confidence in Forty Mile and came across to us next day" (the twenty-first). "When I crossed over to the town on the morning of the 21st, I was surprised to find it empty."[8]

In two sentences the Mountie confirms the date, suggests that Carmack was secretive about his discovery, that everyone in Forty Mile apparently knew of it, and that he was skeptical of Carmack's report, since he was surprised to find Forty Mile empty. However, he wasted little time in joining the stampede. He got leave on August 28 and reached Bonanaza Creek on September 1, by which date, he reported, all the claims below and for a long way above Discovery were staked out.[9]

How well Carmack did was never known. However, he did write his sister, Rose Curtis, not long after his discovery, saying he had taken out a considerable amount and could sell his claim any time for $25,000. "Then," he wrote, "I could sit around and smoke my pipe."

Those who would denigrate Carmack say he abandoned his family and went to New York, where he died penniless. This is incorrect. He left Dawson in 1898, taking with him his wife and daughter, Graphie Grace. The editor of The Klondike News, published April 1, 1898, reported of Carmack: "His love for new scenes has inspired in him the idea of building his own boat to visit the Paris Exposition in 1900, and he has selected for his tour an extended voyage through the South Sea Islands, Japan, China, through the Straits' Settlements and Suez Canal, taking in the Holy Land and the country bordering on the Mediterranean Sea, returning by way of the Atlantic." This was a typical romanticization of the use of wealth indulged in by writers more from a wistful desire to add glamor to the drab living in search of gold than from any real belief in the authenticity of what they were writing.

What Carmack actually did was go to California to visit his sister. When he returned to the Klondike the next year, he left his wife and daughter with his sister. But money changes people. The man who had sat on high places and written poetry, who had preferred the Indian way of life, who liked to fish and hunt but was not above the hard work of prospecting or cutting timber for steamboats or running a trading post, now found romance. In Dawson he met Marguerite Laimee, who had a tobacco shop there.

Marguerite Laimee was herself a free spirit. From Spokane in 1890 she had moved to Chicago and then to the gold fields of South Africa, before arriving in the gold fields of Australia. When the world was responding to the excitement of the Klondike, she too pulled up stakes and went to Dawson. According to her own estimates, she was worth $55,000 when she left Dawson with George Carmack in 1900. They were married the same year, on October 30.

Earlier, realizing his attachment for Marguerite Laimee, George Carmack had written his sister, telling her that it was all over between himself and Kate and asking his sister to send Kate home to the Yukon. He never saw Kate again, but his daughter, Graphie Grace, joined him and his new wife in Seattle, where Carmack built a hotel and an apartment house, opened the Blue Lodge Placer Mine on the American River, and was connected with other mining companies.

His daughter married the brother of her stepmother, though the brother's name is given as Jacob George Suftig, suggesting that Marguerite Laimee had changed her name to satisfy her own romantic inclinations. When Carmack died in Vancouver, the daughter sued Marguerite for her father's fortune. There is no record of the outcome of this suit, but the fact that after the suit George Carmack's widow went to the Blue Lodge Placer Mine and stayed there until she died would suggest that her brother and her stepdaughter cum sister-in-law had stripped her of the money her husband had left.[10]

Henderson was never allowed even a discovery claim, because he was lax in filing his strike on Gold Bottom. Hunker, who subsequently found gold on the same stream lower down but filed earlier, was given credit for the discovery, which meant that he could have two claims, the customary bonus for a discoverer of gold on a new creek. Henderson, who suffered a severe leg injury shortly after Carmack's visit, went out to Circle City for medical attention and so, according to some accounts, did not hear of the strike on the Bonanza until he returned the next spring. This is questionable, since news of the Bonanza strike was received in Circle City during the winter of 1896–97, and miners were already leaving for the Klondike during that winter. However, the accounts have it that when Henderson discovered what had happened and that he was too late for the rich strike, he sold his claim for $3,000 and left the country "an embittered old man." (He was probably not over thirty-four at the time.) But patience as much as luck is required in gold mining. The claim, which Henderson so disgustedly disposed of for $3,000, ultimately yielded over half a million dollars and then was sold for $200,000.[11]

While there may be a genuine difference of opinion as to who was responsible for the Klondike stampede, there is none as to who started Dawson. It was Joe Ladue. According to his own account, he was led to move from the Sixty Mile to the mouth of the Klondike because of Henderson's report of success on Gold Bottom. Familiar with the way of miners, Ladue knew that when word of Henderson's strike reached other creeks there would be a stampede to the new field. The Stewart River diggings had petered out. The miners on the headwaters of the Sixty Mile traded mostly at Forty Mile, and McQuesten and Healy had control of the business there. So Ladue pinned his hopes on a new stampede. Accordingly, in August of 1896 Ladue closed his trading station at Ogilvie and moved to the mouth of the Klondike to be ready for the stampede to Gold Bottom when it should develop.[12] At the time of his move, he knew nothing of Carmack's strike on Rabbit Creek. In fact, he arrived at the Klondike about the same time Carmack made his discovery. By a happy chance he was at the right place at the right time to capitalize on the biggest stampede on the Yukon.

With Harper as a partner, Ladue staked out most of what is now Dawson. He secured from the Canadian government a land grant consisting of the best part of the flat land lying between

Moosehide Mountain and the Klondike River. A year later he went to Ottawa and arranged for confirmation of the grant. The Canadian government gave him a patent, so that there would be no question as to the title of town lots in Dawson. Almost immediately, the enterprising Joseph Ladue was in the midst of everything. He located or purchased valuable mining properties, secured a timber grant, and set up his sawmill. By June of 1897, even before the great gold strike was heralded by the arrival of two ships in Seattle and San Francisco bearing tons of gold, Joseph Ladue was organizing in New York the Joseph Ladue Gold Mining and Development Company of the Yukon. This energetic opportunist and promoter was the man about whom Schwatka wrote in 1883 in rather contemptuous tones. He had met Ladue at an Indian camp between what was to become Eagle and Circle City and referred to him as a Canadian voyageur. Although Ladue accompanied Schwatka much of the way to Fort Yukon, which he would have missed completely but for the help of Ladue, Schwatka wrote on July 25, "I had suspicions that 'Jo' did not like the pace we kept up, or rather that he did not relish being awakened whenever his scow sought the quiet of an island shore." Schwatka was not alone in his inability to appreciate the man beneath the carefree exterior; Ladue had been unable to marry the girl of his choice in Pennsylvania because her father considered him a ne'er-do-well.

To this point, several truths seem apparent. The discoverer of gold in the Klondike region cannot be pinpointed. Henderson did make the immediate strike which precipitated a limited stampede, and prompted Ladue to move his trading post from Sixty Mile to the Klondike. Carmack's discovery on Rabbit Creek diverted the stampede from Gold Bottom to the Bonanza, which in turn triggered a major stampede from Forty Mile and Circle. The fortuitous juxtaposition of events made it possible for Ladue to established Dawson where the Klondike enters the Yukon. And the fabled Klondike, which attracted thousands, was not the source of gold. Gold was there, but its recovery from the broad, swift Klondike would have to await the introduction of dredges. Gold came from the tributaries of the Klondike—the Bonanza, the Eldorado, Gold Bottom, Hunker, and others. Ogilvie could justifiably attribute the gold rush to Henderson, but he could as well have tapped Ladue, Sprague, and Nelson for that honor.

Carmack, however, was the immediate agent responsible for the stampede.

When did the outside world learn of the rich placer finds in the Klondike region? The popularly accepted date is July 16, 1897. But Carmack had written his sister in California about his strike in 1896. Joe Ladue was in New York in 1897, trying to raise money for gold mining in the Klondike. In November of 1896 Black Sullivan, Dirty Joe, and Missouri Bill (these are the only names by which they were known) arrived in Seattle from the Yukon. They told of the great strike on the Bonanza.[13] But no one listened. Stories of gold were old hat. For the press and the general public the Klondike was not a reality until the summer of 1897, when the *Excelsior* steamed into San Francisco with an estimated $400,000 of Klondike gold. Two days later, on July 18, the steamer *Portland* docked at Seattle with $700,000 in gold. The Seattle *Post Intelligencer* bannered the news, "A Ton of Gold from the Fabulous Klondike." Actually it was closer to two tons. Miners returning aboard the ships were surrounded by reporters. Some, caught in the hysteria of the occasion, threw nuggets to the crowds in the streets. There could be no questioning of gold in this form. The country and the world were soon delirious with the news of the Klondike. Men hastily threw gear together and before the winter of 1897 some two thousand stampeders had managed to fight their way to Dawson. Several thousand more were stranded en route—in Juneau, Skagway, Dyea, Sheep Camp, Lake Lindeman, Lake Bennett. The rush was on.

And what were the times really like? Too often, to titillate the readers, writers about Dawson and the Klondike resort to brilliant reds, frostbitten whites, and grim blacks. The travail of mining is painted in its most tedious aspect. The world is usually blanketed in snow, the wind howling at fifty below; and in Dawson the reader finds only saloons, dance halls, and girls of the demimonde. Actually Dawson and the Klondike were made up of the usual cross-section of people. There was plenty of interest and excitement in the heady years of the early stampede, even when presented photographically. There is little need to color or exaggerate.

There were summers as well as winters. In summer there was no snow, the sun seemed never to set, there were berries of many types, the trees were in luxuriant foliage, and the streams ran full in their banks. Even in the winter the dry cold of the Yukon did not have the cutting quality of a wet gale off the Great Lakes. There were the gamblers, the cardsharks, the men who were paid to see that the house made a profit; but there were as many dealers who loaned money or pushed a stack of chips across to a miner who had just gone through his pile. There were women who sold their favors, who auctioned off their bodies for a night or a winter. There were also women who nursed the sick, who helped the needy. There were girls who sang and had nuggets and pokes of gold thrown at their feet. There were also women who set up restaurants and grub tents, who operated laundries, who ran missions, taught schools, and kept house.

The normal dress of the women was far from the décolletage depicted by artists who were never there or by movie producers ignorant of the laws of Dawson. The Mounties did not permit dress of questionable taste and this meant clothing which revealed too much. The usual costume on the dance floor was a starched white shirtwaist with long sleeves and high choker collar and a long dark skirt over an armor plate of corsets and three or four silk petticoats.[14] Queen Victoria was alive and this was British country. Besides, as Klondike Kate said, what men liked was not indecent exposure but the rustle of silk.

This is not to deny that there were women like the one who had an affair with the manager of the Dawson branch of the Bank of Montreal. When the man terminated the attachment rather abruptly, she sought revenge in a piquant manner. As a parting gift, she asked the manager for a large portrait of the bank's president which was hanging in the manager's office. Anxious to end the relationship, he acceded to the request. On the flip side of the portrait she had a local artist paint a florid picture of herself in the nude. When it was finished, she gave the painting to the most popular saloon in town where any who wished could gaze on the reproduction of her charms. She had a formal presentation with the usual draping of the portrait and the pulling of a string to expose it. When all greeted the appearance of the portrait with shouts and perhaps some remarks of questionable taste, and it was firmly established that the painting was there to stay, she rather offhandedly remarked about the difficulty of obtaining suitable canvas in Dawson for a portrait, so that she had to use the back of an old portrait a friend had given her; and with that she turned over the painting and revealed the portrait of the president of the

Stampeders at the boat landing at Dawson. (E. A. HEGG)

Lousetown was built across the Klondike River from Dawson. (E. A. HEGG)

The wedding banquet at Dawson of one of the men who struck it rich on the Eldorado. (E. A. HEGG)

The Monte Carlo was the finest pleasure palace in Dawson. (E. A. HEGG)

bank. Needless to say, all knew her friend, and the local manager was soon apprised of the situation; but the joke was too good for anyone to permit him either to have the painting removed from the saloon or to purchase it. The painting still hangs in Dawson; and if one is not familiar with the story he may see the painting and think it just another glorification of feminine pulchritude, little knowing of the subtle revenge incorporated in that voluptuous canvas.[15]

Along with women of this type, there were shrewd business-women like Belinda Mulrooney. She opened a restaurant in Dawson and then a hotel at a place she called Grand Forks, where the Eldorado and Bonanza meet. By 1898 she owned 22 Below on Henderson Creek, 27 Below on Dominion. She had an interest in 57 Above on the Bonanza and owned a sixth interest in the Bonanza Eldorado Quartz and Placer Mining Company. She had a half of 34 on Moose Horn, ten percent stock in the Yukon Telephone Syndicate, and a valuable claim on Hunker.

There was Nellie Cashman, who joined every stampede in the North and panned gold with the most rugged man. It is said that at one time she single-handedly saved Dawson from destruction by fire. A blaze had started and was threatening to engulf the principal establishments when Nellie Cashman rushed to the church, seized a bowl of holy water, returned to the scene of the fire, and threw the water on the conflagration. Whether this stemmed the blaze or the fact that at this precise moment the wind changed and blew the fire back upon itself may be debated, but Dawson was saved.

With the governor's wife presiding over society, with Salvation Army girls and nuns, Dawson had a moral tone, an air of propriety not found in any of the other stampede towns. And with law strictly enforced by the Mounties, Dawson had none of the wildness associated with Skagway, Circle, and Nome. Guns were not allowed; if a spell on the woodpile would not straighten a wrongdoer out, a rope around the neck would. The hanging judge, as he was called, enjoyed nothing more than to have a man presented to the court before breakfast, give him a good talking to as if that might be the worst the man could expect, and conclude with, "Now you are to be hung by the neck until dead." Then, with a feeling of contentment from a job well done, he would proceed to a big breakfast.[16]

The most vivid recollections of Frank Miller, a young man who worked in Dawson from 1897 to 1899, are not of gay night life, of wild debauched drinking, of dances, of girls, but of the strictness of the Mounties. At ninety-two, he is still active, running a hunting lodge and store at Miller House, Alaska. He doesn't recall the gayety of Dawson. He remembers the dullness of the long winters when men got cabin fever from being cooped up together with no entertainment or social life. He remembers the Mounties and the strictness with which they enforced law. One day in the winter of 1898 he dumped garbage on the frozen river. Along the Yukon it was routine practice to deposit the daily refuse on the ice, where it would freeze immediately. There were no flies; there was no odor; there was no decomposition. It just stayed there until the spring thaw, when it was washed away. And so, according to custom, he took his garbage to the Yukon and dumped it, only to be arrested. Unknown to him, the Mounties had set flags on the ice marking off an area within which garbage should not be dumped. Upon being advised of his mistake by a zealous young Mountie, he offered to remove it in compliance with the law. The Mountie would not permit this but demanded that the young man appear in court that afternoon. Fortunately, the judge was a man of more understanding. He dropped the case with the admonition that the garbage be removed and not again deposited within the staked area.

H. H. Scott, who arrived in Dawson in 1898, was not impressed with the town. He gave only a few lines in his diary to what should have been the climax of his trip from New York: "June 16 arrived at Dawson. Pleasant. Looked around town all day; not much excitement here. Slept in open lot. June 18. Saw Jonking [*sic*] Miller and Swift Water Bill. Started for Sulphur Creek at 10 p.m. by loas town. 50¢ to cross ferry."[17]

Alden R. Smith, who did not go to Dawson but went directly to Sulphur Creek, wrote in his diary for June 22: "Scott and Gillett got back from Dawson. Said Dawson dull and great crowd of people sore as though they had lost a presidential election." Later that year he did go to Dawson and found so little excitement or so little worthy of comment that in a letter home all he had to say about the biggest city of the North was: "I have been to Dawson since I wrote last. Bought two loads of grub there. Beef was 25¢ a pound by the quarter."

On the other hand, an American army officer who passed through Dawson in the summer of 1900 saw it differently. He described it as the warmest mining camp or anything else in the world: "Town full of gold dust, gold nuggets, gold bricks, and high prices, good fellows, girls, gamblers, saloons, dances, concert halls, etc. People go all night and sleep in the morning. I was anxious to go on at once the first day in Dawson, the second I was glad to stay one or two days, by the third I was in no hurry at all, but still I was glad to go and get away from my many friends who are too swift for me."[18]

Like all cities, Dawson City was different things to different people. To Father William H. Judge, it was not Mounties, or boredom, or excitement, not high prices or low prices, not girls or gold. He joined the first stampede from Forty Mile to Dawson to help his fellow men. He realized that, with the influx of miners, there would be disease and sickness and accidents. To him, Dawson was a place to build a hospital, which he did and staffed it with nurses. When it burned, he rebuilt it, driving himself to an early death.

To Bernard H. "Casey" Moran, a reporter, Dawson was a place where a man could use his imagination when hard news was lacking. When his editor ordered him to get a story that would build circulation, one that people would talk about from the aurora borealis to the Southern Cross, Casey delivered. Somehow, as only Dawson reporters were able to do when faced with an emergency like this, Casey stumbled across some Indians from far to the north, back up toward the Mackenzie and high up in the Ogilvie Range, which is unmapped even today. They told him of going far in search of food the past winter. They had circled east of the Mackenzie, deep into haunted country, where no Indians or Eskimos would dare go except under severe provocation when the caribou deserted their normal migratory trails, the moose were missing from the lowlands, and the run of salmon had been poor. Only when confronted with starvation would a reasonable person venture into this area. They told of reaching a high mountain and on top of the mountain they found a vast building, like a hundred villages built on a great canoe. From the appearance it was obvious that once this great canoe had been constructed of wood, but the cold hand of winter or the great spirit had turned the wood to stone. Casey found an illustrated Bible and showed the Indians a picture of Noah's ark, and all the Indians agreed the great canoe on the mountain resembled the ark in the Bible. Casey, a thorough reporter, got affidavits from the Indians certifying to the truth of what they told. The story did increase the circulation of the paper and cause people to talk. Rival newsmen sought out the Indians and tried to shake their story about the canoe without success.

To Big Alex McDonald, King of the Klondike, Dawson was both a center of business operations and a place of frightening social demands. He was involved in so many business schemes that whenever he met someone on the streets of Dawson, his opening remark would be, "Do I have a deal with you?" He pyramided a single claim into a string of mines and had his finger in nearly every operation in and around Dawson. It was thus only natural that he was selected to present a gift to Lady Minto when Lord Minto, Governor-General of Canada, arrived in Dawson. Big Alex was briefed thoroughly on a presentation speech. The gift was to be a pint-sized replica of a miner's bucket with the sides embossed with figures of miners, a shaft and windlass, and a scene showing the Yukon flowing past Dawson. The golden bucket with its friezes was heaped with nuggets and sprinkled with gleaming dust—a bit ostentatious perhaps. Indeed, some members of the committee selected to choose an appropriate gift were so in doubt that they thought it wise to ask Lord Minto in advance if Lady Minto would find such a gift distasteful or inappropriate. Lord Minto, speaking either for himself or from intimate knowledge of his wife's taste, is quoted as saying, "By jove, a splendid idea, my dear fellows. She will be no end delighted."

Whether she was delighted or not, certainly Alex McDonald was not happy with his part in the affair. The committee in charge of the presentation, appreciating Big Alex's inadequacies in the social graces, coached him thoroughly in a single brief phrase from Walter Scott. Alex was to hand over the gift while saying, "Not for its intrinsic value but as a token of esteem." Alex got the idea all right and remembered more or less what he was supposed to say, but not the exact words. When the time came he said, "Here take it, it's trash." The Dawson newspapers very kindly reported Alex McDonald's high social achievement with, "The presentation was made by Mr. Alex McDonald in simple but eloquent language."[19]

As Dawson at the turn of the century was different to each of these men, it is impossible to portray it in simple terms. It was a dull, unhappy place. It was a warm, friendly town. It was a place for rewarding, Christian work. It was where the Mounties watched for the slightest infraction of rules, where business deals were negotiated in the street and formal receptions were held for the Governor-General. Dawson was a composite of all these things.

In the same way, Charles John Anderson was a composite of the Klondike miner. There is hardly a book on the Yukon, Dawson, the Klondike, or the era that does not include something about this man, familiarly known as the Lucky Swede. The fact that nearly all versions are untrue only makes the man and the story more typical. A fraction of truth is woven into a morality play incorporating the prejudices and the hopes of the miners. In this case, the prejudice was against Swedes and the hope, as always, for a lucky strike. In each generation, in each society, some national or ethnic group is considered comic. In Alaska and the Yukon during the last stampede, the Swedes filled this position. They were the big, bumbling, stupid men, who could always be counted on to fall for a practical joke, who would work a hopeless claim, who would spend years on a creek that was known to be colorless; and it was proverbial that, despite their dumbness, they would be successful. A colorless creek would unexpectedly show gold, the hopeless claim would produce a rich vein.

Charles John Anderson was born in Sweden, June 2, 1859. After coming to the United States as a teen-ager and knocking about the country for six years, he went north in 1893, over the Chilkoot Pass, and down the Yukon to Forty Mile, the homing point for the stampeders in that year. Typical of the universal magnetism of gold is a list of the partners with whom Charley Anderson then worked a claim on Glacier Creek. Besides Anderson, there was an Englishman by the name of Hutchinson; a Norwegian, Lars Langlow; a Greek, Constantine Komentaros; and most unlikely of all, an Arab with the un-Arab name of Kotar Petros Boyhepapa. These men worked together until 1896, the year that George Carmack came to Forty Mile and filed a claim on Rabbit Creek, changing the life of the Yukon. Up to this point we have facts about him, as well as facts about the Yukon, which can be established. Here fiction replaces fact in telling the story of the Lucky Swede.

Three miners came to Forty Mile to file their claim on the Eldorado. The Eldorado, at this time, was considered a worthless little creek. It was too narrow, the water had the wrong taste, and the trees leaned in the wrong direction. But the Bonanza was staked up- and downstream from Discovery. Those who wished something could only stake the Eldorado, and they did. These men, having staked on the Eldorado and having filed their claim, now wished to make some profit from their enterprise. They had no expectation of finding gold. They had no hope that anyone would find color on the Eldorado. Accordingly, they had no intention of working the claim for unlikely profit. Rather, they wanted to sell, to dump it on some poor, unsuspecting sucker. But whom could they find stupid enough to buy a claim sight unseen on an unproven tributary even of the Bonanza? True, the Eldorado was a great sounding name, but so what? Had any gold been taken from the Eldorado as yet? No.

While trying to resolve their problem, the owners of the Eldorado claim happened to spy old Charley Anderson in a saloon. He had already had a few drinks, and when he was drunk he would buy anything or fall for any crackpot scheme. The men approached Charley, bought him a drink and started talking about the Eldorado, the richness of the creek, the great prospects, and of their own unfortunate poverty which precluded their working a claim already filed. Another drink or two and Charley Anderson found himself agreeing to buy the claim on the Eldorado for $800, all the money he had.

The story goes on to tell how the next day, sober and disturbed at the stupidity of what he had done, Charley Anderson tried to revoke the deed of sale. He approached the saloon-keeper who had witnessed the contract and got little sympathy. He went to the Mountie station, but the contract was valid. The Mounties were not interested in trying to protect fools from the consequences of their own avarice and their own drunken ineptitudes. So he was stuck with a claim on Eldorado. Having nothing better to do, he visited the claim and, being a Swede, started to work. He soon found that with a little work, there appeared a little color. As he dug deeper and approached bedrock, the color improved. In fact, the claim turned out to be one of the richest claims on Eldorado. The Lucky Swede. Some stories stop here. But this leaves the morality play incomplete, so most falsify further.

With all his money, Charley Anderson became the big spender of Dawson. He put men to work on his claim, while he spent his nights and days in riotous living. Gambling, drinking, and girls became his sole concerns. The gold came out of the ground, passed through his pockets and into the hands of the Dawson people. When one of the girls to whom he showed particular favor decided that she would trap this dumb Swede into marriage and get all his gold, there was a protest among the others. To resolve the dispute, it was decided that the girls should play a game of poker with the Lucky Swede as the stakes, winner take all. He agreed and refereed the game to see that no cheating took place. He married the winner and went to San Francisco. Here she soon managed to divest him of his money, leaving poor Charley Anderson penniless. He died deserted and without a cent in his pockets, with no one to claim the body that lay unrecognized in the San Francisco morgue.

It is perhaps improper to question such an appropriately moral conclusion or to strike out the words of a folktale with the editorial pencil of truth. What has so often been written as fact about Charley Anderson was the refined essence of the Yukon. It summed up both the wealth all hoped to find and the lucky way of finding it, which most realized was their only hope for success. It expressed the hope of all the hopeless that anyone might strike it rich, no matter how lacking in education or how far at the end of the line he might have been when brains were being passed out. And then the great finale—the women, the drinking, the gambling, and San Francisco, which was as high as those in the Yukon could aspire. Here was all that anyone who went to the Yukon coud desire. And so the story of the Lucky Swede, to its final homily, is a morality play. The truth is equally interesting. Indeed, the very difference between fact and fiction is an integral part of making the Lucky Swede a true composite of the Klondike miner.

When Anderson and his partners heard of the Carmack discovery and that it had become authenticated, they decided to leave Glacier Creek and try the new area for themselves. Since they were old miners not quickly taken in by every rumored stampede and had been more thoughtful than excited, by the time they reached Rabbit Creek, they found it had been renamed Bonanza and everything on the creek reasonably near Discovery was staked. Even the tributary, Eldorado, had been staked to its source.

Anderson and his party, disappointed but not discouraged, started over the hills toward some of the other creeks flowing from Queen Dome and King Dome which, together, formed the principal watershed for the Klondike. They headed first for Too Much Gold Creek, which someone had told them was not staked and was a good prospect. However, winter was coming. The first storm of the season hit them on the trail and decided for them that the best they could do was to return to Forty Mile. They always had their claim on Glacier, which paid a living wage. The return trip was difficult. The Yukon had not frozen solid yet, and the slush was running. It was dangerous and it was cold, but they made Forty Mile.

At the same time, Winfred Olar, Al Parks, and Al Thor arrived in Forty Mile. These men had staked Number 29 on Eldorado. More important, they wanted to sell. Charley Anderson heard about this, and since he had gone to the trouble to make the stampede to the Bonanza, he felt himself committed, though he couldn't have explained how. Rather than return to Glacier Creek, a tingling feeling, some feral instinct, drove him to the conclusion he should buy this claim if the men did not want too much. They wanted $1,200. Anderson had this money and could have paid it, but it was an asking price and he would be taken for a dumb Swede if he agreed to the first figure, so he counteroffered $800 cash for a quitclaim deed. The men, who were tired of the Yukon and had not driven a pick into their claim, gladly agreed to $800 cash, hoping to be able to get out of the country before the final freeze. Anderson actually had several thousand dollars in gold cached at the claim on Glacier. He borrowed the $800 at McQuesten's store, closed the deal, and then took off for Glacier Creek to get his gold.

Now that he had a claim on the Eldorado, the old excitement welled up—the possibility of great heaps of gold lying along rock bottom, of wealth for the taking. He could not wait, but immediately made up a pack and took off for the Eldorado. Besides, he knew as an experienced miner that winter is the time to mine. He did not need to prospect, he had a claim. All he had to do was sink a shaft to bedrock, if he could find bedrock, and hope for color.

Perhaps it is allegorical to say that he arrived at the Eldorado and camped for the first time on his new claim on Christmas Eve, 1896. But that is the truth. With a month of hard work, with pick and shovel, with wood fires to thaw out the frozen earth, he proved to his satisfaction that he had a rich claim. With spring and the influx of stampeders who could not find properties to stake, he was able to hire men to work for him. He paid the highest wages in the Yukon. He managed the workings himself. He was a miner and too busy mining to go to Dawson. The gaming tables, the drinking, the dancing, the girls were not for Charley Anderson. He never drank and never danced and had never played a game of cards for money in his life.

This was the Lucky Swede. But with any luck, and this is the part which folktales abjure because it is unpopular, there must also be some hard work and some perseverance. Charley Anderson worked hard to get to Alaska and the Yukon and the Forty Mile; he worked hard to get the money to buy the claim, and he continued to work hard after he bought it.

When he made his fortune, he did go to San Francisco, the never-never land, the great hereafter in the sky where the streets are paved with oysters Rockefeller and caviar, the pie in the sky for all wealthy stampeders. They might talk of Paris, they might talk of London, they might talk of ocean voyages around the world, to Japan, the Straits Settlements, the South Seas, and the Holy Land. They might talk of these, but they went to San Francisco.

But he wasn't a dumb Swede. At forty, he knew the meaning of money and investments. As many a hardheaded businessman before him, and since, had done, he invested in real estate. Now, no one can knock investing in California realty, especially San Francisco realty, and this is what Charley Anderson did. But this time his luck went bad. One day in 1906 earthquake and fire destroyed in hours the wealth he had accumulated on the Eldorado. This is the one point in which there is some truth in the story of the Lucky Swede; he lost his money in San Francisco. But he did not die there. Charley Anderson was a worker, an optimist, in good health. He went to Vancouver and worked in a sawmill and in other jobs in the lumbering business for many years. In his seventies, when last observed by those who would report the truth, he was still optimistic, still hoping in his spare time again to find a rich claim, still hoping once more to strike it rich, hoping that fortune having knocked once would knock again.[20]

The Lucky Swede is the composite, but Alden Smith is the average stampeder. He arrived from outside in 1898, after all the good creeks had been staked. He came well outfitted so that he did not suffer for food or clothing. He visited around the creeks before settling on a claim. He built a snug cabin with his partners, sank a shaft, mined, got some gold but not much. He ate well, did not find the weather disagreeable, and at the end of a year he returned outside with little more than he had when he arrived.

His letters home to his mother do not reflect hardship but the normalcy of life to a farm boy accustomed to hard work and winter chores. With the beginning of winter, he wrote: "It has snowed three or four times, but not much. We have our cabins built and the floors and bunks in them. It is comfortable and cozy inside. We are going to start two more holes tomorrow but it is not cold enough to mine yet. We stand it very well. I do not notice the cold any more here than we would at home at zero, but it is forty to sixty below here."[21] And again: "The week beginning December 8 was very warm some days 35 above. One day it rained a little. We all hoped for zero weather or colder. I have not worked in a coat any this winter. The sun does not shine at our house only forty-five to sixty minutes a day. There is about six hours of daylight though and we are all up and eat breakfast waiting for it so we can go to work."[22]

He warns his mother not to expect him to return rich: "I suppose the opinion on the outside is that everyone in here is going to be rich in a short time. Now the estimate of last year's output of gold dust for the Yukon River was $7 million. There is now estimated to be in Dawson and Klondike and the Indian River districts from 15 to 18 thousand miners and how many are down the river is hard to guess. If you just divide $7 million by 15 thousand you will have just $466.66 apiece, not enough to buy grub to go around."[23]

Nor does Alden Smith conform to the picture of the grub-hungry miner with only a little flour and such meat as he can kill. There was starvation and scurvy from improper diet; Jack London at twenty-one got scurvy the one winter he spent on the Stewart River. But the diaries of the Batavia party have these entries: "Aug 19. Shot five chickens. Aug 21. Picked 5 qts. cranberries. Aug 26. Had pot pies—duck and squirrels. Nov 24. Supper: moose, cranberry sauce, brown gravy, bread, cocoa, mince pie—a whole pie apiece."[24]

This was the reality of the Klondike, the Dawson of 1896–1900. But Dawson today is a putrefying body, still holding life but rotting slowly to death. It lives in the past; there is no pride in the present. The surrounding Indian population has moved into Dawson for the government dole and lives in a dingy row of uniform log cabins. The old-timers are kept alive in the hospital; the almost old-timers live in Sunset Home like specimen bottles on a shelf. No one talks of the present or the future, though there is more potential economic greatness in the Yukon Territory today than was ever dreamed of by prospectors. The people speak of the old Dawson, the Dawson of Klondike and Bonanza and Eldorado, of Louse Town and steamboats. They talk in muted voices of the old-timers who are gone, of the gold that was found, of the great stampedes as people talk about a great man on his deathbed.

The people are charming—Taffy Williams, who works for the city water works and has one of the greatest personal collections of records in all of Canada; Don Donnell, who collects stories as Taffy collects records; Syd in the bar; "Black Mike" Winage, who has forgotten the meaning of truth; Bombay Peg, the last of the madames of Dawson; Gumboot and Sox.

The city museum is a collection of junk intermixed with items of real value. Old record books, with no entries or with one or two pages containing undated entries of figures related to nothing, are stacked among original diaries. There is a private free museum out-of-doors of far more coherence and significance.

In the old cities of Europe, a visitor feels haunted by the history of greatness, but he also senses the pulse of a dynamic society. Not in Dawson. The banks are more museums than places of business. The hotels and restaurants are for tourists and are closed in the winter, when the people go outside. Interest may still be found in gold, a show of color, a possible rich strike. No one cares about asbestos or oil, iron or zinc. These minerals are intruders in a country that thinks only in terms of gold. A lonely prospector walking in with a $150 poke will cause more excitement than a construction worker in for a monthly spree with $500 in his pockets. The bartender forgets his customers in his haste to obtain an appraisal from the bank. The bank manager gives a quick figure and drops all other business as he heads off somewhere to see if he can get more for it. All the talk in the town is suddenly focused on a small jar of gold dust. The past and gold are the only realities of Dawson.

There is gold still in the Klondike. Go up the Bonanza past the derelict dredges settling in their sterile gravel pools, where once was a willow-clad stream. Go past 86 Below Discovery, 85, 84, past

76, Sourdough Claim, Gulch Claim, 48 Below. Cross over Boulder Hill to 37 Below, where the first white child was born, to King Solomon Hill, 43 Below, the Monte Cristo, the Bench Claims, where the hydraulics tore away the hillsides, gutting the land to lay bare the placers. Past Fox Gulch, Auro Fino Hill, 20 Below, American Hill, 10 Below, Adams Hill, Cheechako Hill. Then, Discovery, with a simple stone marker recalling that Carmack and Skookum Jim and Tagish Charley here found gold that stirred the world. On to 5 Above Discovery, Gold Hill, and finally, where the Eldorado enters the Bonanza, the town of Grand Forks with its sign, Pop. 9,000. Today there stands but one house and that house vacant. Here was the epitome of the last stampede—the Bonanza -and the Eldorado. Take a shovel and a pan. Scoop a pan of dirt from the bank where the streams meet. The easy stuff, the pockets of nuggets, the rich placers are gone. But gold is there. Watch the warm yellow glow of small flakes show through the black sand as the overburden is washed away. Feel your pulse quicken and the electric tingling along the surface of your skin and know what it was all about.

7

Forty Mile,
the First Stampede Town

THE KLONDIKE WAS NOT THE LAST STAMPEDE. It was not even the beginning or the end or the focal point for the majority of the adventurers heading north. During the Klondike's peak years, there were as many miners in Nome as in Dawson. Within a few years of its founding, Dawson's citizenry would be stampeding to Fairbanks. The Klondike was only the climax of the Yukon phase of the last stampede, an emotion-triggering name, a headline in the typographers' font of the day. The genesis of the upper Yukon placer mining was forty-five miles downriver from Dawson at a now-forgotten stream, Forty Mile, and the town of the same name at its mouth.

The Stewart River strike generated the first stampede on the Yukon, but it was a flash in the pan. After the Boswell party's find on Steamboat Bar, no other good strikes were made. No community larger than Ma Shand's roadhouse was built with Stewart River gold. As important as Stewart River may be in the chronology of the last stampede, it had no direct or immediate relation to the extensive prospecting that culminated in the Klondike.

If one place must be elected as the place where the Yukon stampede started, it must surely be Forty Mile, where the first major strike was made. Most of the great names of the upper Yukon are associated with Forty Mile. Here the men who were to become famous in Dawson first earned the name *sourdough*. The ubiquitous McQuesten and Harper founded the town of Forty Mile. The enthusiastic Ladue was here. Big Alex McDonald, the Daddy Warbucks of the Klondike, first mined on the Forty Mile. Inspector Constantine of the North-West Mounted Police, Mr. Law and Order of the Yukon Territory, was stationed at Forty Mile before Dawson was imagined. Sir John Dawson, after whom the city was named, was in Forty Mile. The Canadian surveyor, William Ogilvie, who surveyed the Alaskan-Canadian boundary and later became Governor of the Yukon Territory, spent time in Forty Mile. Bishop Bompas, whose diocese extended from Lake Bennett to Circle City, was head of the mission at Forty Mile. Pat Galvin, an ex-sheriff from Montana, one of the dynamic figures of the Yukon, got his start with a tinsmith shop in Forty Mile, where he made the famous Yukon stove favored by all sourdoughs. Arriving early in Dawson, he shifted from stoves to speculation. He established transportation companies, steamship lines, and trading posts, and had as many failures as successes.

There was Jack Smith, owner of the Monte Carlo with Swiftwater Bill. He entered the Yukon in 1895 and located at Forty Mile. A failure there, he was one of the first on the Bonanza, staking Number 7 Above. From this beginning, he went on to invest in other mines, Dawson real estate, lumber mills, and entertainment. Swiftwater Bill started in Forty Mile before striking it rich in the Klondike—Swiftwater, who married three sisters in rapid succession, more for ostentation than affection.

Andy Hunker, for whom Hunker Creek was named, started from Forty Mile. Hunker Creek was to rival the Bonanza. Father William H. Judge, who had no interest in gold, was in Forty Mile when the Klondike was struck. Early in 1897, foreseeing the need of a hospital in Dawson to care for the horde of stampeders who would come, he started construction of a two-story log building there. By August 20 the hospital was ready for use, except for one major drawback. Father Judge had made arrangements for the Sisters of St. Anne to furnish nurses. The nurses had been dispatched via St. Michael. But as so frequently happens on the Yukon, the steamer did not reach its destination. The river was too shallow that year, the boat carrying the nurses was stuck far down river, and the sisters had to winter along the Yukon. They did not arrive until 1898.[1]

Big Bill McPhee was in Forty Mile. He had come with the early ones, in 1888, and stayed until 1897, when he too left for Dawson; but in 1896 he was running the Caribou Saloon in Forty Mile, when Clarence Berry approached him. "I've got no money, no grub, no dogs," Berry said, "but I've got a hunch about that strike of Carmack's. I've got to go. Can you grubstake me?"

"Sure, Clarence. Here is the key to my cache," was Big Bill's reply. "Help yourself." That night Clarence Berry was with the stampeders going upriver. He struck it rich and, unlike many, he kept it. Returning to his native California, he invested in oil.

Ten years later, Big Bill had a saloon in Fairbanks. Having failed to strike it rich in Dawson, he had gone to Nome, where he tried his hand at lightering and freighting. Lack of feed forced him to shoot his horses and mules to prevent them from starving. From Nome, he went to Valdez, where he built the Keystone wharf for the railroad to the rich Copper River country, but the railroad was never completed. Again he failed and was forced to sell at a loss before the pile-eating worms should eat him out of business. It was then he opened a saloon in Fairbanks in a final attempt to wrest some success from life. But some people seem born to failure, and this time he was wiped out by fire. As he surveyed the blackened ruins of his last venture, he received a telegram from Clarence Berry in San Francisco: "I read of your loss, rebuild, restock and draw on me for all the money you need."[2]

One of the big sensations of the summer of 1893 was the arrival of Pete McDonald with the first team of horses ever seen at Forty Mile. The entire Indian community gathered at the riverbank to witness the strange new visitors to Forty Mile; but when the horses were brought ashore from the raft on which they had been floated down the river, every Indian present fled in terror.

Pete McDonald had earned and lost three fortunes before his arrival at Forty Mile. He hoped to recoup his losses with freighting to the mining camps on Forty Mile and Sixty Mile. But after one trip to Miller Creek, he decided that the country was too rough until a better trail should be made. Pete McDonald was a man who had made money by hard work and by taking advantage of opportunities, and he was to be one of the Dawson millionaires not through luck, but hard work. Pete McDonald's saloons, his opera house, his restaurant, and his music hall were to be the most popular in Dawson. With the thousands coming across his bars, he was to invest in innumerable claims along Bonanza and Eldorado until his income and fortune were beyond casual computation.

These were men of Forty Mile and Dawson. So was the Lucky Swede, Charles Anderson. And, of course, it was here that Carmack came to file his claim on Rabbit Creek.

It was at Forty Mile that McQuesten grubstaked two prospectors, leading to strikes on the Mastodon and Birch Creek, which started the Circle City stampede, the end of the opening phase of the last stampede. The first step was the trickle of men to the Teslin, Pelly, White River, Sixty Mile, and Stewart River. Then the Forty Mile strike, and finally Circle City. Each strike was greater than the previous ones and attracted an increasing flow of men and supplies into the North, culminating in the great strikes along the Klondike, in the Nome Peninsula, and in the Tanana.

The town of Forty Mile is in Canada. The river rises in Alaska and empties into the Yukon in Canada, but before an official survey was made, this was unknown. Today a wide swath cut through the trees stretches from the Arctic Ocean south marking the boundary, a tribute to man's nationalistic ardor. Nature makes no such concessions to claims of sovereignty. Until a boundary commission, headed by Senator William McKinley for the Americans, should adjudicate the conflicting claims and desires of the United States and Canada, the unmarked wilderness was subject only to the law of the miners there. McQuesten thought his station at Fort Reliance, five miles west of the Klondike, marked the boundary. His old record books from Forty Mile are imprinted, L. N. McQuesten and Company, Forty Mile, Alaska.[3] As late as June 21, 1899, a resident of Dawson had a power of attorney drawn up appointing, "M. Polley, of Forty Mile, Alaska, my true and lawful attorney."[4] In 1901, Colonel C. S. Farnsworth, commanding officer of American forces in northern Alaska, refused a request to assist in the collection of customs at Forty Mile, addressing his reply to H. E. McCarty, Deputy Collector of Customs, Forty Mile, Alaska.[5] Under the circumstances it is not surprising that the early miners, lacking maps, towns, or constituted authority, neither knew nor cared whether they were in Canadian or American territory.

The discovery of gold on the Forty Mile River is usually given as 1886 or 1887; however, as with the Klondike, the presence of

gold in the area was known before the first important strike. In
1881, the peripatetic Harper with a companion, Mr. Bates, crossed
from the Yukon to the Tanana River country via the Forty Mile
River. While fording the north fork, Bates was swept off his feet
and thoroughly soaked. It is almost axiomatic that the discovery
of gold is accidental, and this was no exception. Stopping to build
a fire to dry out Bates' clothing, Harper looked around, as was his
custom, and took a few samples of ore and gravel. Bates saved
samples of the ore and took them to San Francisco, where they
assayed at $20,000 a ton. When Harper learned of this the next
year, he returned to the north fork and searched for the location
of his discovery. He never found it, as the landmark had been
altered, the outcrop carried away by the ice going out in the
spring.[6] If it was a rich ore body, it is still there, undiscovered.

In 1883 Joe Ladue had a try at finding gold on the Forty Mile.
He had come into the Yukon the previous summer with three
others via the Dyea Trail. Working their way down the Yukon
River, they prospected the Sixty Mile until the coming of winter
forced them to seek Fort Reliance, where they went into winter
quarters. Seven more men arrived that fall and built cabins at Fort
Reliance. Although it is not immediately pertinent to the history
of Forty Mile, McQuesten's recollections of that winter provide
an interesting sidelight on the life of those primitive years.

He recalls with pleasure that except for one year, this was the
first time that anyone lived near him with whom he could con-
verse. The men would meet at the station in the evenings, and
"we would play cards, tell stories, and the winter passed away
very pleasantly."[7] On Christmas Day, among other things, they
had a shoveling match. The person who lost had to stand on his
head. It was here for the first time that most of the miners were
introduced to the Indian blanket toss. It started with as many
Indians as possible holding the edge of a large mooseskin and
tossing a young Indian into the air. The miners thought this great
sport and joined in. As could be expected, they expanded the
rules to include women, and soon were tossing the women on
the mooseskin. The Indian women, not to be outdone, in their
turn caught the white men and tossed them on the mooseskin.
This was to become an annual event at Forty Mile and later at
Circle City, where it was customary to start the proceedings by
tossing Jack McQuesten.

Miners at the mouth of the Hunker.   (E. A. HEGG)

Miners in front of their cabin at Number 6 Below on Bonanza.   (E. A. HEGG)

Shortly after New Year's day Joe Ladue visited a nearby rival post run by Moses Mercier, who had been in charge of the Fort Yukon post when McQuesten, Harper, and Mayo arrived in the Yukon a decade earlier. Here Ladue was shown a piece of gold-bearing quartz brought in by an Indian from the Forty Mile country. Borrowing an interpreter, a sled and dog team, Ladue set out to find the Indian who had brought in the sample, but he was unsuccessful. In the spring, he returned to the Forty Mile country in a renewed effort to locate the Indian and again was unsuccessful. Abandoning his hope of finding the Indian, Ladue, with three others, set out to find the outcrop themselves. They went up the Forty Mile, crossed over to the headwaters of the Sixty Mile and came down the Sixty Mile to the Yukon.[8] Although they passed over ground where good mines were subsequently found, they found nothing. Ladue, like Harper, was not among those destined to strike it rich in gold. Although he was among the first in the country and he prospected extensively, the rich strikes eluded him. Like Harper and McQuesten, he was to make his fortune from the Yukon in other ways.

In 1886 two newcomers, Homer Franklin and Madison, made a good strike on a small side-stream about twenty miles from the mouth of the Forty Mile. About the same time Michael O'Brien found a rich placer on the Forty Mile. With these two finds and with the continuing influx of miners, Harper decided that he and McQuesten should open a trading post at the mouth of the Forty Mile. Anticipating a stampede to the Forty Mile country, Harper wanted to get word to McQuesten, who had gone to San Francisco to buy supplies for the post at Fort Reliance. He wanted to tell McQuesten of the two strikes and suggest he increase his purchases considerably. There were no mail deliveries at this time, no stagecoaches, no winter riders. Any message sent would have to be carried by someone willing to undertake the five-hundred-mile trip to the head of the Taiya Inlet—up the frozen Yukon to Crater Lake, over the Chilkoot Pass in the dark of winter, and down the Dyea Trail to Healy's post in Dyea. With hard slogging and luck, the trip could be made in fifteen days. With possible storms or accidents, it could take a month. A traveler might find shelter and food with wintering miners at the mouth of the Stewart or the Pelly, or with Indians at old Fort Selkirk or Big Salmon or Hootalinqua, but a person could not count on this. He would have to carry enough supplies for the entire trip and for any contingencies. George Williams and an Indian agreed to make a try. For Williams it was a fatal decision. Driving themselves to the limit of their endurance, Williams and his companion made it to Crater Lake in record time. They fought their way up the north face to the Chilkoot Pass. There they were temporarily stopped by a howling gale. Snow poured over the Chilkoot like giant combers crashing over a reef. Exhausted from their efforts, nearly blinded by the driving snow, they finally managed to stumble down the south slope. With his companion's help, Williams reached Sheep Camp, but he could go no further. The Indian went on alone to Dyea. Help was sent back for Williams, but it was too late. He was carried into Dyea, but critically debilitated by the tremendous physical exertions and exposure, he died. However, the letter was forwarded by a winter ship and reached McQuesten in San Francisco in time.[9]

This was the beginning of Forty Mile.[10] With the return of McQuesten in the early summer of 1887, he and Harper opened a post at the mouth of the Forty Mile River, a post that was to become the first town on the upper Yukon. With the Spaniards in California and the Russians in early Alaska, missionaries pioneered many of the communities following the initial conquest by soldiers or traders. With the English and Americans, commercialism opened the way. Missionaries followed, but they did not initiate. Traders, such as McQuesten, Harper, Mayo, and Ladue, founded the trading posts. Miners gravitated around the posts, wintering in the vicinity if they had no claims to work. Indians settled near the trade goods, moving in ever-increasing numbers to the center of activity. With the growth of Indian settlements, missionaries arrived to establish schools and churches. Saloons, restaurants, and hotels were built. Smithies were set up to repair picks and shovels, sawmills to provide lumber for boats, sluice boxes, and coffins. Official representatives of a distant government would begin to arrive: customs collectors, postmasters, mail carriers, surveyors, law enforcement agents, and judges, gradually eroding freedom and individualism. In this way Forty Mile grew.

Sixteen young men arrived from outside to winter at Forty Mile and, given to tall tales, formed the Liars' Club. Indians formed a settlement near the trading post. Bishop and Mrs. William Carpenter Bompas arrived and opened a school for native children on an island just above the mouth of Forty Mile.[11] Ladue

brought a forge from Stewart Island for a blacksmith shop. Bill
McPhee opened the Caribou Saloon. Pat Galvin started his tinsmith shop. As late as 1898, after Forty Mile had passed its zenith,
Ogilvie reported two hundred and fifty white people there, including sixteen women. The Indian village had eighty at that time,
fishing and trapping, getting from 35¢ to 70¢ for ermine and up to
$700 for black fox. Over a thousand miners were still working up
the Forty Mile River, passing in and out of Forty Mile. The town
had two stores, two doctors, a theater, a brewery, several saloons
and eating houses, a library and reading room, and a debating
society, which mooted such vital questions as whether war or
liquor caused the most misery, awarding pragmatically the distinction of the greater evil to liquor. Roadhouses charged $1 for a bed
in common rooms or $2 for a private room. Meals were furnished
at $1.50 each.

Ogilvie adds a grisly footnote to this description of Forty Mile
in 1898. As lumber was always at a premium, he writes, it was not
an unusual sight to see a coffin going by with arms and legs hanging
out because the shortage of lumber dictated building coffins too
small for the corpses. However, it would seem to be another example of sensational writing to which even a man of scientific training
was susceptible when describing life in the Yukon. Such sights
could not have been frequent. Death was a reminder to the miners
of their wilderness surroundings and their remoteness from the
comforts of kin and civilization. Accordingly, they were meticu-
lously careful to observe the forms and rituals of civilized burials.
Coroners would be elected, proper death certificates drawn up,
relatives notified, and the effects of the deceased forwarded if possible. A headboard might replace the more customary headstone,
but otherwise proper services were observed, even though the reading at graveside might be from Shakespeare or a scientific textbook
in the absence of a Bible.

McQuesten's daughter, Crystal, tells an interesting anecdote
illustrating the careful observance of the niceties of burial. A
young man at a mining camp along the Forty Mile was killed in an
accidental shooting. After a proper burial, the deceased's effects
were searched and the name and address of his family discovered.
The man's few belongings were forwarded to the family along with
a letter advising them of the death of their son. As the family lived
in Boston, it was a year before a reply was received. With the reply

came a beautiful lead-lined coffin and a request to send the remains home for burial in the family plot. The miners who had participated in the burial had moved on to new creeks, but a deputation from Forty Mile attempted to comply with the wishes of the family. They searched the area around the old camp, but weeds and brush grow fast in the long summer days of the Yukon. They were unable to find the grave. They did, however, find a skeleton and decided this, if not the proper bones, would serve the purpose. So they put the skeleton in the coffin, sealed it, and shipped it off to Boston. The family, with the help of their doctor and an anthropologist friend, determined that the skeleton was not of their son but of an Indian. Appreciative of the miners' efforts to comply with their wishes but not wanting to inter the Indian bones in the family plot, they returned the coffin with the skeleton to Forty Mile with instructions that the coffin need not be returned. As no one had a right to the coffin and it was of considerable value, it was auctioned off for charity. An enterprising roadhouse owner bought it, removed the lid, and set it up in a lean-to as a bathtub. This, according to Crystal, was the first bathtub in Alaska.[12]

Law and order, as an official manifestation of government, came late to Forty Mile. It was the first town on the Yukon, and neither the government in Ottawa nor that in Washington was particularly interested in this remote wilderness. True, the United States Army had sent the Schwatka expedition to survey the Yukon in 1883, and Ottawa had dispatched the Ogilvie survey party into the Yukon territory in 1887, but these were isolated incidents rather than evidence of a persistent interest. To most of the early prospectors, this was the way they liked it. They had come north seeking the simplicity of the frontier as much as the gold. They came, for the most part, from the West—the Dakotas, Montana, Colorado, Wyoming, Idaho, Washington, Oregon, and California. Born to the free life or hearing about it from their fathers or Indian scouts, they were escaping the thousands moving west. They didn't need sheriffs or judges to tell them what was right or to prosecute what was wrong. They brought with them the traditions of the California mining camps and, more important, the American tradition that law was a personal affair predicated on the immediate needs of time and place. The rigidity of codified procedures or the less static common law handed down from remote seats of government were not for them.

Their principal interests were in protecting mines and assuring unmolested food supplies. If a miner had his claim jumped, it was to the interest of all that the fault be corrected. As for food, a miner built his cabin against the rigors of winter, and he established a cache where he kept his food. He might be gone for a year, but his food supply was maintained inviolate. It was the unwritten law of the Yukon that any person coming upon a cabin or a cache was welcome to live or stay in the cabin as long as he wished. He could help himself to such supplies as he needed without taking any with him; but he must replenish the cache, leaving something for what he took. Every cabin had its wood supply, and in the winter there was always kindling and dry wood beside the stove, so that a fire could be built immediately by a person stumbling half-frozen into a cabin, when minutes might mean the difference between a dangerous frostbite and health. When the chance visitor departed, he left behind him a clean cabin and kindling beside the stove just as he found it, so that when the owner returned or when another visitor reached the cabin, he too could easily start a fire. A person who robbed a cache, who stripped a cabin of its food, was as guilty of murder as if he had shot the owner of the cabin or cache. Before the advent of Canadian law, no miner was ever convicted of murder for killing a person found robbing a cabin of food or essential supplies.

The Canadians, bred in the British respect for order, preferred the established laws. When the size of a community warranted it, they requested the government in Ottawa to dispatch police forces to execute and maintain law and order. The Americans simply called a meeting, formed a mining district, elected a recorder, and proceeded to execute justice as required. There is no question that the Canadian practice did provide for a stricter and more successful legal procedure than the American laissez-faire method. It made Dawson a decorous city compared to the gustier life found in Circle City, Rampart, Nome, and Fairbanks. But the American system was more flexible and permitted the men to take their law and order with them, to execute it in the manner they felt appropriate to the occasion, and to maintain a psychology of independence and self-reliance. It also, however, permitted such characters as "Soapy" Smith to organize and establish themselves in Skagway and the Noyes gang to operate in Nome.

As might be expected, one of the early residents of Forty Mile most anxious for a formalized body of law enforcement officers was a London-reared Britisher, the Reverend Dr. Bompas, Bishop of Selkirk. In 1893 Mrs. Bompas wrote: "A terrible quarrel reported among the white men on Sunday night, resulting in one being shot through both legs, and another stabbed in the breast. Oh, for some police, or anyone to keep order." The Bishop wrote: "I hope for the arrival of some Government control, but the miners have themselves now checked the drinking among the Indians by deciding that the next person who gives a drink to an Indian shall receive notice to leave the country in twenty-four hours. As the alternative to obeying the miners' law is generally a revolver or a noose on the nearest tree, they are pretty well complied with, and they might possibly do the same with a policeman if he interfered with their own drinking."

And yet despite the complaints of the Bishop and his wife, these rough miners were not without sympathy and understanding and even respect for the clergyman. On Christmas, 1892, fifty-three miners from Forty Mile presented Mrs. Bompas with a highly personal and unique evidence of their Christian feelings. At one of the miners' meetings, which were the subject of the Bompas family complaints, it was moved and seconded, "to make a Christmas present to Mrs. Bompas, the wife of the Reverend Bishop Bompas (for which purpose a collection will be taken up amongst those who are willing to contribute), and that the present shall be in the form of a Forty Mile nugget, as most appropriate to the occasion, as a mark of respect and esteem from the miners of Forty Mile, irrespective of creeds or religions, and further, that it be distinctly understood to be a personal present to the first white lady who has wintered amongst us."[13]

Under the beards and shaggy hair, beneath the rude garments and customs dictated by the primitive conditions of the country, were frequently boys in their late teens or early twenties, sentimental youngsters who still thought in terms of mothers and sweethearts and tears. Frank Buteau, in describing his arrival at the headwaters of the Yukon, wrote: "In 1886 I and twenty-one others stood on the banks of Lake Linderman [*sic*]. We chose a

spokesman and pledged to each other: 'Here we are in the land
of ice and snow, we know not where we are going, we have seen
the tears rolling down from the eyes of our Fathers, Mothers,
Brothers, and Sisters and Sweethearts when we bade them goodbye, our hearts full of hope to see them once again—and now
as I see all tears falling here, I feel it is the duty of the last one
of us who remains alive to tell, not only what we have done,
but, also, what we have seen. So now forward into the land of
ice and snow and let this be, for all of us, not goodbye, but "Au
revoir " ' "14

Such sentimental young men composed the rough miners'
meetings. However, Mrs. Bompas and her husband, reared in
the polite society of Victorian England, might be excused for
failing to recognize the youthful simplicity behind the direct
justice of the miners' courts. Their reports on the arbitrary application of miners' law filtered to the outside and eventually to
Ottawa. But then as now, the wheels of government and bureauc-
racy moved slowly. It was not until 1895 that enough complaints
had accumulated and the belief had become established that
gold findings in the Yukon Territory were sufficient to justify
the expenditure of dispatching law enforcement agents into the
country. In that year the first detachment of Mounties was sent
into the territory to establish a post at Forty Mile.[15]

The North-West Mounted Police, popularly called Mounties,
who reported to Forty Mile in 1895 for duty, were not a mounted
force. With snow in the winter and muskeg and dense brush in
the summer, the Yukon is no place for horses. They depended
upon shanks' mare to get their man and relied on a rigid code
of moral rectitude to command respect for their enforcement
of law. As part of an elite force, they were sent to their frontier
outpost with a flexible set of orders to administer law and order
in the best way they could. Although there were specific laws
prohibiting liquor in the Yukon Territory, to avoid a critical
confrontation with the miners, the first detachment of Mounties
was instructed not to interfere in so far as the use of liquor was
concerned so long as men behaved themselves.

The first case requiring the attention of the Mounties did
not involve miners' law. It took place in the town of Forty Mile.
Shortly after the NWMP post was established, two men who had
been friends were reported to be carrying guns, determined to

shoot each other on sight. The reason for the falling out was the age-old cause, woman. The Mounties found one of the two men and arrested him on a pretext. It was then learned the second man was being married to the woman who had caused the trouble. A detachment of Mounties was sent to Bishop Bompas' residence, only to find that the energetic prelate, ignorant of the seamy side of life in his community, had already performed the marriage ceremony. He remonstrated with the officers for their intrusion on such a holy occasion. Upon hearing their charges, however, he let them into the room where the bride and groom had just been happily united. The Mounties seized a gun from the groom and arrested him for carrying it illegally. It was subsequently learned that the woman had already been married, though this was considered an allegation rather than a legal assurance, since there was no marriage certificate and how the marriage had been performed was unknown. At least it was ascertained she had been living with the other man concerned in the dispute. Both men were taken to the Mountie compound. However, the post had just been established and a jail was not yet built. Nor were there enough officers available to place a guard over the two men arrested, most of the men having been detailed to cut timber up river. The Mounties were confronted with several logistical and legal problems. Not only were there no jail and no men to act as guards, there was no charge against which a conviction could reasonably be expected. The only real complaint was bigamy, or more properly polyandry, and it was impossible to obtain evidence of a previous marriage, as the Mounties noted in their report, because of "The laxity of American laws regarding marriage and the remoteness of the place."

To resolve the problem, during the night one of the officers connived the escape of the prisoner who had that morning been married. The unrequited bridegroom was smuggled to a boat, given a piece of bacon, and put afloat on the Yukon. Since it was impossible to row against the current, the man could only go downriver. Although the boundary was not officially established, the Mounties, proceeding on the assumption that Forty Mile was Canadian, knew the man would soon be in Alaska and no longer their responsibility. Bishop Bompas, upon being advised of the outcome and upon hearing that there had probably been a previous marriage, declared with grave satisfaction, "In that case, the marriage I performed is null and void, and I have got the fees."[16]

The first conflict between the Mounties and the law of the miners' meetings was in the spring of 1896. A miner who had gone outside the winter before had let his claim to another for nine months. The lessee hired men to get as much as possible from the claim during the short period of his lease. As was customary, the muck from the mine was piled on the surface until the spring thaw. When water was once again flowing, the accumulated dirt from the mine was washed and the gold recovered. After the spring clean-up, the lessee disappeared with all the gold without paying the miners he had hired. The men held a meeting and resolved that the owner of the claim must be held responsible for the indebtedness. He was ordered to pay the miners. If he failed to comply, the claim would be sold to satisfy the debt. The owner naturally objected to the decision. He contended that the person who hired the miners was responsible for the debt. However, since that person could not be found and the miners felt they had a just demand for work performed, the claim was sold and the men paid off. The owner appealed to the Mounties. For the first time in the Yukon Territory an expedition of twelve armed Mounties was formed and sent up the Forty Mile River. Armed with Lee-Medford rifles, the men pulled their boats up the river, marched across country to Glacier Creek, and confronted a truculent mining community accustomed to being its own law. The Mounties took this action resolutely, though with some trepidation, as there were far more miners than Mounties. Fortunately, there was no trouble. The rifles backed by a small but disciplined force determined the outcome. The property was returned to the rightful owner and the miners were warned they had no right to take law into their own hands. They were given to understand that miners' meetings, which had been not only attending to miners' affairs and squabbles but addressing themselves with equal vigor to the private affairs of people generally, would no longer be tolerated. The law would henceforth be executed only by the Mounties.[17]

It is unquestionable that this prompt and decisive action on the part of the Mountie post at Forty Mile did bring into the area formalized law administered equally to each person wherever he might be. However, it could be questioned if the legal principle which had determined the Mounties in returning the claim to the owner was the most equitable. For the sake of one man and his right based upon remotely established precedents, many men were forced to have mucked in the frozen ground an entire winter for nothing. A man who had simply been fortunate enough to stumble on a good claim was given protection. Although legally proper, it is doubtful if the solution was as just as that provided by the miners' court.

The original Mountie post was not in Forty Mile, but on a small island across the mouth of the river from the town. Unsure of their welcome in a predominantly American society, they may have considered a more exposed site imprudent, or it may have been simple economics. Lots in Forty Mile were selling for $8,000, a bit expensive for a government budget. Or it may have been that Captain John Healy gave the land to the Mounties in the expectation that the proximity to his trading post of the only representatives of government would give him added prestige. A newcomer to the Yukon, in competition with McQuesten and Harper, he needed every gambit available.

From 1885 to 1892 Healy had a trading post at Dyea. After the Forty Mile strike, what he heard from miners passing along the trail convinced him that another commercial company could operate successfully on the Yukon. Armed with figures on the steadily increasing traffic into the Yukon and constantly rising gold production, he sold his idea to P. B. Weare and John Cudahy of Chicago. Together, they formed the Northern American Transportation and Trading Company, to be known on the Yukon as N. A. T. & T. The first post was to be established at Forty Mile, then the heart of the gold country and the mecca of all miners. As an intracompany political gesture, the initial post was to be known as Fort Cudahy.

For Forty Mile, 1893 was a frenetic year. Although there were only thirty permanent residents, there were many more on the creeks feeding into the Forty Mile River and on the creeks of the Sixty Mile, who relied on Forty Mile for supplies. Captain Healy arrived with the company steamer, the *Portus B. Weare,* named for the second partner. Since the steamer *Arctic* had already arrived with provisions for Harper and McQuesten, with the arrival of Healy's steamer, Forty Mile was for once well stocked. On the island across from Forty Mile, Healy immediately

set about erecting a two-storied building, the largest in Forty
Mile. With store and living quarters, he also planned a billiard
hall as an inducement for men to trade at his post. In Forty Mile
proper new cabins were being built, a restaurant was opened, a
dance hall erected. A new brewery had only recently been opened.
There were five saloons, with liquor being either brought over
the Chilkoot, up the Yukon, or made in the new brewery. If
these sources did not supply the demand, local saloonkeepers
made hootch.

A recipe for hootch left by a Forty Mile wag of those days
prescribes: Take an unlimited quantity of molasses sugar; add a
small percentage of dried fruit or berries; ferment with sourdough;
flavor to taste with anything handy, the higher flavored the better,
old boots, discarded and unwashed foot rags and other delicacies
of a similar nature; after fermentation, place in a rough still, for
preference an empty coal oil tin and serve hot according to
taste.[18]

Healy does not seem to have been too popular. He was not
as openhanded as good old Jack McQuesten, who was always
prepared to extend credit to a miner who had a bad season or
to give a deserving prospector a grubstake. The miners liked to
tell how the tightfisted Healy, claiming to have lost the combination to his safe, paid off O'Brien, who built his trading post, with
a $1,000 note. McQuesten gave O'Brien the $1,000, and then,
through the Alaska Commercial Company, presented the note
to Cudahy in Chicago, with interest. The miners themselves
would become involved when Mrs. Healy brought in a hired
girl with her to help with the housework. Unhappy with the
isolation of Fort Cudahy and dissatisfied with her employment,
the girl ran off to Forty Mile. Healy tried to get her back, but
a miners' meeting was convened and the case decided in favor of
the girl. Healy was ordered to pay her back salary and was told
the girl was free to do as she wished. In the absence of Mounties,
Healy had no choice but to comply.

In the days when Forty Mile was the center of life on the
Yukon, the prospectors who came in were mostly experienced
men, men who had peopled the camps of Colorado and Washington and British Columbia, who had been on the frontiers of
America in Montana, Wyoming, and the Northwest. They were
men who knew what it was to take care of themselves, who ar-

rived on the Yukon with adequate supplies for a year and when these supplies ran low, knew how to get food from the wilderness, how to hunt and fish, how to build log cabins that would turn the cold. They were men adjusted psychologically to the lonely winter nights, long periods of isolation, and the disappointment of barren holes and pans with no color. These were the men of the Liars' Club. They were the men of the miners' meetings who made their own laws, handled their own problems, decided their own justice. They were capable of providing their own simple entertainment and enjoyed the winter beauty when crystals of snow danced in the air like a spring hatch of mayflies, diffusing all the colors of the prism so the very night became alive with the glowing iridescence. Even their dances were uncomplicated.

The dance hall of Forty Mile was favored more by Indian than white women. On dance night, Indian women in heavily quilted skirts, soiled blouses, with blankets for shawls, would gather silently outside the door. Many would have babies strapped to their backs. When the door opened, one, then the others in single file, would slip into the dimly lit hall. Stacking the babies at one end, they would sit phlegmatically on a bench along the wall. When all were in, the miners arrived in ones, in pairs, or in joking groups, still wearing their gumboots or mud-caked work shoes. With the first squeal of the violin and thin notes of a tinny piano, the men would rush across the floor to seize whatever partners were available. In a silent frenzy, they would whirl the Indian women around the floor, stomping in time to the simple rhythm. There was no conversation, no singing, or shouting. Hour after hour, the gyrating couples would stomp about the floor, raising dust from the uneven planks, until the dancers could scarcely breathe or see from one end of the small hall to the other. Finally, as if a bell had tolled the hour, the dancing would stop. The Indian women would retrieve their babies and leave as silently as they had come. The dance was over.[19]

The American government geologist, Josiah Edward Spurr, included Forty Mile in his trip to the Yukon gold fields in 1896. Among other places he visited was Franklin Gulch, the site of the first big strike. The miners there were almost out of food, since the boat expected from Forty Mile had been unable to reach them due to low water. But this created no serious problem to these men. They shared what little they had.

Spurr asked one of the miners, "Doesn't it get lonesome here? Don't you find it a bit dull? What do you do?"

"Do?" puzzled the miner. "Do? Why God bless you, we have very genteel amusements. As for readin' and litrachure an' all that, why dammit, when the fust grub comes in the spring, we have a meetin' an' we call all the boys together an' we app'int a chairman an' then someone reads from the directions on a bakin' powder box."[20]

Spurr found the men along the creeks keenly interested in both domestic and foreign affairs. In the winter months with little to do but sleep and read, every man read voraciously whatever he could find. Nearly everywhere, Shakespeare was the favorite author, irrespective of the nationality or the degree of education. A clutch of houses or cabins that had a full set of Shakespeare considered itself in for a cozy winter. There were regular Shakespeare clubs where each miner took a certain character to read. Books of science and especially philosophy were widely sought.

Practical jokes were the basis for most humor, and a man who could not laugh at himself was unfortunate indeed, for resentment only increased the mirth. One who could take a joke and play it back on the practical joker received the respect of all.

Candles were an important item in the early years. They provided the only light in the windowless, or nearly windowless, cabins during the twenty-two-hour nights of winter. They were needed for underground mining in shafts sunk to bedrock. When candles were in short supply, and they were nearly always in short supply before a winter was over, a storeowner could ask almost any price for them. With nothing to do but think up mischief in December of 1895, Iowa John thought of a way to take advantage of a storekeeper's greed. With some old tin cans, he devised candle molds. With string for wicks, with a tin of evaporated milk and water, he froze up six dozen creamy-looking candles. For thirty cents worth of material, he had himself a lot of dollars worth of candles. With his trade goods, he went to the store and allowed as how he was heading downriver to Circle while the river was frozen and travel easy with a sled. He needed some bacon but didn't have any money, so he offered his candles in trade.

"How many you got, Iowa?" The storekeeper's cupidity was immediately aroused.

"I reckon around six dozen, give or take a few. But I weren't thinking of trading them all. I don't reckon I need that much bacon and you don't need that many candles."

The storekeeper figured fast, estimating what he could get for the candles come along about March. "Tell you what, Iowa, I'll give you a side of bacon and $5 a dozen for all your candles."

Iowa wasn't too sure, he was hesitant, he was unwilling, but gradually he allowed himself to be talked into the deal. It was that much less to transport and he could buy more candles with the money in Circle, where Jack McQuesten, who had moved to Circle, probably had plenty and selling them at half the price.

The storekeeper gave only a cursory inspection of the candles. They looked good enough. He left them in the box which he placed on a shelf.

Sure enough, in March candles were in real short supply. It was a candle famine, and the storekeeper offered to sell candles at $1 apiece. When a prospective purchaser remonstrated at the price, the storekeeper justified his price by saying that he had bought them from Iowa John and had to pay a long price because Iowa had gone to Circle and needed some money.

"That don't figure too well," the prospective buyer said, "I seen Iowa just last week up on the pup, where he's putting down a shaft."

"Well, then, he must of changed his mind and not gone to Circle, but he's sure been working in the dark because I bought his whole supply." The storekeeper reached for the water-stained box on the shelf only to find some congealed Swiss milk and six-dozen wicks.

When Iowa came to town after the spring wash-up, he said it was just a joke and offered to repay the storekeeper; but the storekeeper refused. It was a good joke and he could take it; and to show there was no hard feelings he had a twelve-gallon keg of whiskey he could let Iowa have at a good price. What with so many people going to Circle, he had more whiskey than he needed.

Under the circumstances, Iowa didn't like to appear ungrateful, but he didn't intend to be gullible either. He expressed doubts as to the amount and as to the precise contents. Upon invitation to see for himself, he hefted the keg and sloshed it. It was full all right. And when he removed the cork from the bung hole and poured himself a sample, it proved to be the real goods. It was right fine drinking whiskey. He bought it, paying with gold from the wash-up.

With a borrowed wheelbarrow and the help of some friends, he got the keg to his boat, where he and his friends proceeded to have an extemporaneous party before Iowa headed back up-river. But the party was short-lived. It took about ten drinks to drain the keg. Iowa shook his head in disbelief; but he had a sinking feeling that he had somehow been taken, his practical joke returned with interest. He rolled the keg. It still sloshed, but nothing came from the bung hole. In anger, he smashed in the end of the keg with the butt end of an axe. The barrel was full of water except for a whiskey bottle fitted into the bung hole.

Such practical jokes were the epitome of mining camp humor. They became part of the folklore of the country. From that day, Iowa was known as "Whiskey" John and the storekeeper as "Candles."

Spurr tells a whiskey story that was not a practical joke. To the miners working in icy streams or frozen underground shafts, whiskey, as the Russian priest at Nulato expressed it, was like mother's milk to a babe. The small settlement at Miller Creek had been without liquid rations for six months. The last of the community's potables had been consumed in a New Year's Day blowout. But late in June relief was in sight. In the excitement of anticipation, the men had given up all pretense of working. A hunting party had managed to bag a moose and preparations were under way for a barbecue. Some of the men and Mrs. Tremblay, the lone woman in the camp, were busy baking bread and cakes. A party of men, who had gone to Forty Mile for supplies earlier in June, had cached a keg of whiskey on the bank of the Forty Mile, unable to carry it with the other supplies in the portage to Miller Creek. Two men had been elected by lottery to go back for the booze, and the camp was now anxiously awaiting their return. It might seem a difficult assignment to make a sixty-mile round trip, with a twelve-gallon keg weighing nearly a hundred pounds to be carried on the return. But to miners who thought nothing of going hundreds of miles across country on a stampede carrying equipment and food on their backs, a sixty-mile hike was of no great consequence. With the prospect of whiskey, it was literally a stroll. It took the men only two days to reach the cache, but the return was a bit slower. Indeed, the men confessed that the keg had become a mite heavy and that it had become necessary to stop and lighten the load from time to time. No one at Miller Creek could really object to the logic of this reasoning and indeed felt that the men who carried the keg took only what was rightfully their due. Nor were they penalized when the moose was carved and everybody stepped up with a tin cup to draw his first drink of spirits since New Year's Day.

Although Mrs. Tremblay was the only woman in the Miller Creek camp, there were other women in the Forty Mile area; however, she did claim to be the first.[21] With her husband, Jack Tremblay, she crossed the Chilkoot Pass in the winter of 1893-94 on her honeymoon. Like those who preceded her and the thousands to follow, she stopped at Sheep Camp, where her husband left her, returning to Dyea for a final load of supplies. The connubial tent was lonely and dark that night, she recalls, but she apparently managed to sleep soundly, for she did not awaken until she heard men calling her name and asking if she was all right. She did not immediately appreciate their concern, but shortly afterwards she heard sounds of digging and then a man appeared at the opening in the tent to drag her out, sleeping bag and all. Only then did she learn that during the night a small avalanche had buried the tent so that only a corner protruded above the snow.

In later years Mrs. Tremblay was to remember her time at Miller Creek as among the most pleasant days of her life. If life was primitive, the excitement of gold and the genuine friendliness of the miners more than compensated for the hardships. Although she spoke only French upon arrival, she learned enough English to get along. There was always company in their cabin, and a body had no cause to be lonesome at Miller Creek.

Strangers were rare on Miller Creek, but those who did come would have concurred with Mrs. Tremblay. The greatest difficulty was choosing between the many hearty and sincere invitations to room and board. The miners, hungry for news from outside, were loath to be refused. Both intelligent and well-informed from extensive reading and endless discussions of philosophy, science, and literature, they were keenly interested in political and scientific developments. And contrary to popular misconception, the men were exceptionally courteous in these rough settlements where each had to travel and live on his own merits, each had to fight his own battles, and previous condition of labor or social standing counted for nothing.

The Tremblays were among the first to reach Dawson, and they saw it grow from a simple dream of Ladue to a thriving city. She was to become the leading couturiere there, specializing in the latest Parisian creations selling for over $1,000 each.

But Mrs. Tremblay was not the first woman in the country, as she thought. There was a Swede farther down Miller Creek whose wife had been there for three years without seeing another woman. There was Bishop Bompas' wife, who the miners said was "the first white woman to winter among us." There was Mrs. Healy and her servant girl and other white women in Forty Mile. There was Martha Carey, whose first child was born in Forty Mile in 1894. Her husband's biography is a vignette of the last stampede in both the romantic extent of his travels and the normalcy of his life.

Marion B. Carey came across the Chilkoot in the winter of 1886-87 with a small group of men. In the spring they floated down the Yukon to Forty Mile, where he spent the summer prospecting. Before the freeze-up, Marion Carey continued nearly six hundred miles down the Yukon to Nulato. Here he met and married Martha Duranduff. The next spring he and his bride worked their way up the Tanana River, more than fourteen years before the big strike that was to make Fairbanks. They crossed over from the headwaters of the Tanana to the headwaters of the Forty Mile, where they prospected. They wintered at Chicken, the principal camp on the Forty Mile in Alaskan territory and the site of a rich strike. (Some say it was called Chicken because the first gold found on the bars was the size of chicken feed. Others insist it was initially called Ptarmigan because of the great numbers of that tasty game bird found in the neighborhood; but when it came to putting the name on a map, no one could be found who would venture a spelling of ptarmigan, so Chicken was entered.)

In the spring of 1889 Carey, with his wife, was back in Forty Mile. In 1893 he joined the stampede to Birch Creek, which started Circle City, soon to outstrip Forty Mile as the chief city of the Yukon. The next year he was back in Forty Mile, where his first child was·born in 1894. In 1897 he was among the early arrivals in Dawson. Two years later he was part of the stampede to Nome. Then back to Circle City in 1900. He joined the final rush to the Tanana in 1905, where he and his wife settled in Fairbanks, which was to be his home until he died.[22] Although an early arrival in the Yukon and among the first in every major stampede, he never struck it rich. His is a typical saga of the stampede, and despite the paltry return on his efforts, he never begrudged a day of his life. For some, birds sing. For him, it was enough to have seen them and felt the shadow of their wings on his face in the summer sun.

No one struck it rich in the Forty Mile district. Franklin Gulch, where the first big strike was made, yielded no more than $30,000 worth of gold. The title of King of the Forty Mile was given to a miner who recovered only three thousand dollars in gold in a single season, hardly pin money for the kings of the Klondike or Nome. Yet to the elite of the sourdoughs, miners who had been on stampedes and come to learn that gold in the pan had more· value than the glitter of the horizon, the Forty Mile had a continuing appeal. Long after Circle City had drawn off the drifters and become synonymous with Yukon gold, long after the stampede to the Klondike, the Forty Mile district continued to draw prospectors and hold miners content with a reasonable return for hard work. Miller Creek had its permanent population. Glacier Creek continued to be worked until as late as 1964. The trading posts of Forty Mile supplied the camps with food and equipment, its saloons and theaters furnished a needed release for the isolated miners of the remote creeks. It was a town of consequence, not to be omitted from the itinerary of theatrical groups from the outside. Entertainment concentrated as much on sets as on music-hall girls from San Francisco. Experienced producers realized scenery was as important as the cast. A richly furnished and upholstered room with a heavily carved table, Chippendale chairs, rich curtains, and a finely carved buffet with crystal candelabra was amusement itself to men coming from the simplicity of log cabins with at most a slab-board bed, some boxes for chairs, and a rickety table.

Contrary to the complaints of Mrs. Bompas, the early Mounties found little objectionable activity to occupy their official attention.

In a few years, duty at Forty Mile became a monotony of routine. The weekly report submitted to headquarters at Dawson showed a daily schedule having scant relationship to police activity:

> Today, cleaned canoes. Rogers had town duty.
> Painted canoes. Rogers had town duty.
> Cleaned yard. Rogers had town duty.
> Finished papering barracks. If only had some dadoes, it would look real nice.
> Cleaned windows. Rogers had town duty.

In the absence of critical disorders, any event of even slight consequence merited a detailed report:

> Hotel managed by A. A. Gordon caught fire. Total destruction. The owner, Dud McKinney, was over on the Alaska side when the fire occurred. He is not expected back for a month. In his absence there is no one here who knows whether the property was insured or not. However, the talk around town is that the hotel was not insured. At the time the fire started, Mr. Gordon and the cook, Sam Hackney, were upstairs in bed. They just escaped with their lives, as the flames were in the room when they awoke. Sam Hackney was badly burned about the head, and both men had glass cuts about the face and on their arms from breaking out the window. Tom Smith had toes crushed on his right foot in helping to remove the billiard table from the burning building. However, he is getting around on crutches. The inmates of the hotel lost everything. Nothing was saved except a small stock of liquor and bar fixtures.

The reporting officer then neatly backs into the most interesting part of the report: "It is unlikely that Gordon will start up again as there is very little trade in Forty Mile for two hotels and Mrs. Gordon is about to leave him again and go outside with their bartender, Walter Jones. The couple expected to leave for Dawson today, but did not get away." With British understatement, the report continues, "Gordon, himself, feels very badly about what is happening but can do nothing to stop her."

The following week the report continues the story of the departing wife: "Mrs. A. A. Gordon left her husband on Saturday, departing for Dawson with the bartender, Walter Jones. If the couple remain in Dawson, watch them. According to reports, she is nothing but a common prostitute and will carry on her business outside, Jones acting as her macque [sic]."

A month later the Forty Mile Mountie Post reports: "Dud McKinney and Scotty Atkinson arrived. Dud had left valuables with the decamped Mrs. Gordon. Without making charges, Dud McKinney thinks, as do others, that the fire was not accidental."

This is the end of the report. What happened to Mrs. Gordon and her Mr. Jones is not known. Was the hotel insured? This is never stated. Did Dud McKinney ever recover his valuables? This also is not reported. And why was Dud McKinney unwilling to make charges? Was he also enamored of Mrs. Gordon? Or for that matter, why was Mr. Gordon sleeping with Sam Hackney, the cook, at the time of the fire?

Perhaps the matter was forgotten in an Indian scare which occurred at this time. Without giving credence to rumors, the Forty Mile post considered it necessary to report that Forty Mile Indians had become greatly excited over stories from Eagle that the Copper Indians, living in the White River district, were in rebellion and had already killed several men. Chief Copper Joseph was reported to have bought considerable ammunition and, after killing Indians in his area, was bringing his tribe downriver to attack the Forty Mile and Moosehide Indians. Lest he be considered an alarmist, the corporal, who was writing the reports, adds that the Indian marshal at Eagle, when questioned, said he considered the story a false alarm, and that if the Copper Indians had gone berserk, they would not come that way.[23]

Interspersed through these daily entries are monthly production figures on gold and discoveries of asbestos and rich coal seams. Despite the primitive conditions and very real hardships, life in the Yukon was not much different then from what it would be today, if the forsaken land were still populated. There were, of course, differences in customs dictated by the times. Honesty, for example. A miner entering a saloon in Forty Mile would drop his poke on the bar and call for a drink. The miner would then casually turn his back, while the price of the drink was weighed out. It was definitely bad manners to watch this transaction. Honesty was an accepted imperative. And there were superficial differences, such as the recording of temperature. The miners, knowing the dangers of venturing out when it was too cold because of the dangers of frostbite in freezing weather with inadequate medical facilities, would hang a bottle of mercury outside their cabins. When it froze, it meant the temperature was below minus forty, the freezing point of mercury. Hardier spirits, demanding a lower temperature to confine them to their cabins, would hang out a bottle of Davis Painkiller, a patent medicine containing a large percentage of pure alcohol. It was common knowledge in the Yukon that pure alcohol freezes at minus seventy-two, and when Davis Painkiller congealed, even the hardiest miner stayed indoors.

But comparisons cannot be made. Today Forty Mile is abandoned. It is one of the derelict towns of the upper Yukon, a memorial to the last stampede, which it fathered. Many of the buildings still stand in good repair, outlining the size of what was once a considerable townsite. The old customs office is still here; over its door hang two horseshoes. One is with the open end up in the conventional manner to prevent good luck from slipping out, the other is reversed to suggest the bad luck for those failing to obey the law of the country. To those who checked in at the customs post, the normal horseshoe symbolized good luck; for those who attempted to avoid customs duties and did not report in, the reverse horseshoe foretold the bad luck that could be expected to follow. Next to the customs office is the old general store, last owned by David Swanson. Artifacts of the community are hung from the walls or piled in the front yard—an old sled, a carriage, an ancient washing machine, traps, a pick, a gold pan—signs both of the store and of the requirements of the former residents. In front of the store is a lookout tower, a platform erected on timbers, from which the first steamer of the summer could be sighted. This was the big event of Forty Mile, when, after the long winter's isolation, communications were once again established with the outside world. Bets were made, pools formed with chances being sold as to the day, the hour, the minute when a line would be tossed ashore from the first steamer arriving upriver from St. Michael or downriver from Whitehorse. Frequently, the first arrival was a steamer which had been frozen in for the winter somewhere along the river. Then the newspapers and magazines would be already a year old, but even so they would make welcome reading. Supplies would come. People would arrive with news of the outside. During the winter, professional mail carriers brought letters by dog sled, but they could carry no bulky items like newspapers or magazines.

Farther upriver, hidden by trees, is a two-storied building

which once housed the North-West Mounted Police, its floor littered with newspapers from the turn of the century. The faded wallpaper is finished with a simple dado, indicating that head-quarters heeded the post's esthetic request. Next to the barracks is a rude church with a rickety steeple which once housed a bell. The prospect of the river curving west and north was once lovely. Today the view is largely screened by high grass, fireweed, and willows. Across a shallow slough is an island where the Liars' Club wintered in 1887 and Bishop Bompas built his mission. Helen Callahan, daughter of the man whose discovery led to the Circle stampede, recalls going to school here before the turn of the century. The teacher used to take her wide-eyed pupils for visits to see the marvels of the great town. She would show them the exciting stores of McQuesten and Healy, the firehouse, the smithy, the hospital, the Mountie post, and the huge steamers tied up along the bank. She remembers the Bishop as a tall, dour man in a Prince Albert coat and insists he kept rocks in the tails of his coat to facilitate flicking the legs of disobedient children.

Back from the riverfront are more houses. A faint trail winds away from the town, past the farms of Forty Mile, to a cemetery hidden in the gloom of spruce and willows. Faded headboards give truncated footnotes to the life of Forty Mile. "Joseph Nava-roo, died March 2, 1896"; "Barney Hill, died April 7, 1896"— two men who came to the Yukon to strike it rich only to die a few months before the stampede to the Bonanza. "Sacred to the Memory of Mrs. Mary Day, Died June 3, 1896." Was she the first woman to die in Forty Mile? And one marker for "Ralph and Homer Purdy, Children of Frank and Susie Purdy, Born Jan. 2, Died Jan. 3."

It is a quiet, forlorn cemetery on a knoll rising from the muskeg swamp. On the edge of the plot is a hexagonal house of unique architectural construction resembling a bizarre ark. The roof, walls, and base form the sides of the hexagon; the rear of the building slopes up slightly like a scow. This is the old charnel house. During the winter when the ground was frozen too hard to dig, the bodies were placed here to await the spring thaw.

Despite the cemetery, the chill charnel house, and the pulse-less buildings, Forty Mile does not appear a dead town. There is a sense of Rip Van Winkle, a town slumbering, awaiting an unknown cue to awaken and resume its interrupted life. Unfortunately, Forty Mile is being groomed for the waxen immortality of an enshrined corpse, rather than being permitted the vital respectability of a decent skeleton. The Canadian government has proclaimed it a national monument site and all the buildings are posted, "National Monument Site, Do Not Disturb." Swanson's store has a guest book for visitors. An airline has included it as part of a Fairbanks–Dawson package tour. The large asbestos mining camp of Clinton is nearby, and the workers come here for picnic lunches or barbecues in the evening. It is a posted wilderness inviting tourists, litter, and vandalism.

8

Eagle, the Loveliest Town
on the Yukon

ORTY MILE IS APPROXIMATELY HALFWAY BETWEEN DAWSON, the first capital of the Yukon Territory, and Eagle, the first administrative center of northern Alaska. Unlike Forty Mile or Dawson, Eagle was not just a stampede town, a sudden response to an overnight influx of miners. It was an Indian village, a trading post, a stopping place for river travelers, a small mining camp. As it grew, it became the military headquarters of the District of North Alaska. It was selected as the residence of the Judge for the Third Judicial District of Alaska, a district covering an area larger than Texas. It was a communications center with telegraph lines to Valdez on the coast and to Dawson in the interior. It was the port of entry and customs post for steamers and travelers coming downriver from Canada. However, even though not primarily a gold town, it was as much a part of the last stampede as any of the towns of the upper Yukon, its population rising and falling with the tide of the stampedes.

As an established town, Eagle is not as old as Forty Mile or Dawson, but its history antedates both. A trading post was established here in 1874 by Moses Mercier, who was then agent for the Alaska Commercial Company at Fort Yukon.[1] In 1883 Schwatka reported finding a deserted log cabin in good condition on the site, which he understood had been a trading post called Belle Island. McQuesten had a trading post here around 1886.[2]

Certainly, several factors suggest the presence of at least transient camps there for some years before the present town of Eagle was platted in 1898. There is an Indian village within three miles of Eagle. It was there long before gold was discovered in the Yukon and was described by Schwatka as "the first Indian village we had encountered on the river deserving the name of permanent."[3] This made it a logical place for a trading post. Mission and American creeks enter the Yukon here, providing clear water for travelers. Neither stream produced a rich strike but both yielded gold. It was accordingly a natural stopping place for trappers, traders, and, later, for miners passing up or down the river. The land, although flat, is well above the Yukon flood level and so a safe building site. Mining maps prepared in 1897 showed a community already established where Eagle is now located.[4]

By 1898 it had a newspaper and was sufficiently developed to have social factions, prompting Charles C. Carruthers to write in the Eagle *Tribune* on October 8, 1898: "While going to press we were informed that two dances were being prepared for this evening—the Upper Ten and Lower Five are to be represented. We hear the Upper Ten has the cake, the Lower Five the music —why this distinction? Who in our midst is separating the sheep from the goats? Who is it that has the temerity or ignorance to ventilate ideas of caste or of the shallow hypocritical pretensions to be better or think he is better than others in our midst? Who is it that is the first to cast the stone? In the great day of reckoning before the tribunal where no sham can exist, we are inclined to think that the harp and crown will be awarded in many instances where damnation was expected and vice versa."[5]

Eagle had a population of 1,300 at this time,[6] though like the other towns of the Yukon it was subject to the extreme fluctuations of stampede fever. Four months later, when Captain W. P. Richardson visited Eagle, he estimated the population at 600 with 250 cabins, but he was particularly struck by the peaceful and law-abiding nature of the community.[7]

From its inception, Eagle was a more orderly community than the other towns spawned in Alaska by the last stampede. The residents of the area showed an untypical respect for such laws as governed the territory. In January of 1898 the miners met, elected a recorder, and laid out the townsite of Eagle City with streets and blocks. The recorder then drew up an application for a patent to the ground included in the plat and forwarded it to Washington. With the end of winter they cleared the ground and began the erection of buildings. However, the application was disallowed as not being in accordance with the law. It was then redrafted and resubmitted. And ignored. Instead, the town-site as platted and built up by the local residents was included in a military reservation known as Fort Egbert.

The people of Eagle may have felt themselves badly used, but they preferred to follow legal procedures rather than take the law into their own hands. A chamber of commerce had been established, and through its offices the Secretary of War was petitioned for redress: "Now, we, the citizens of the City of Eagle, Alaska, through the Chamber of Commerce of Eagle, most respectfully petition your Honorable Department to use its best efforts toward getting a tract of land now included in the Military Reserve known as Ft. Egbert, Alaska, excepted therefrom, and placed in such condition that a patent for a townsite may be issued therefor. Said tract to be known as The City of Eagle, Alaska. . . ."

The petition pointed out that "This townsite contains the homes of from 500 to 700 people besides the plants of four large commercial companies, viz: The Alaska Commercial Company; The North American Transportation and Trading Company; The Alaska Exploration Company and the Seattle-Yukon Transportation Company, besides many smaller places of business usually found in a mining town, such as restaurants, bakeries, churches, stores, saloons, etc."[8]

The petition was eventually granted and Eagle became an incorporated city, but not without some misgivings and internal dissension. As part of a military reservation, it was under military control. While this was irksome, it assured domestic tranquility since the military was responsible for maintaining law and order. As an incorporated town, Eagle would become responsible for its own policing, sanitation, and other municipal activities. This in turn meant taxation to pay for the services. The commercial companies, figuring that the taxes would fall mostly on them, opposed separation from the military reservation. As the commanding officer of Fort Egbert wrote in his diary, "It is amusing to see how the zeal for freedom from military oppression is smothered by the discovery that the alternative is taxation."[9]

Despite the fluctuation in permanent population of the town, by the turn of the century Eagle was the most important American town on the Yukon River. It was the port of entry from Canada. It serviced more rich mining districts than any other American town along the Yukon. It was the logical entrepôt for the miners on the upper reaches of the Forty Mile River, which are in Alaska. It was conveniently located for the miners on the Seventy Mile, Nation, Charley, and Tatonduk rivers, all gold producers. Four trading companies had invested in permanent establishments there. As the closest of the Alaska gold camps to Valdez, the northernmost ice-free port in Alaska, it was the logical site for the terminus of a telegraph line from the coast. These reasons also dictated its selection as headquarters for the Third Judicial District of Alaska and the home of its first appointed judge, the Honorable James Wickersham, who arrived in Eagle City on July 15, 1900.

The Judge was given temporary quarters on the military post and offered all assistance consistent with military regulations. Judge Wickersham, who took the importance of his position seriously, was not one to consider this offer merely a courteous gesture. He immediately requested that the post sawmill prepare lumber for the construction of his own house, a courthouse, and a jail. The commanding officer of the post, Colonel Ray, having satisfied protocol in making his offer, proceeded now to fall back on regulations to prevent civilian encroachment on military autonomy. He did not have the authority locally to permit the use of military installations by nonmilitary personnel. However, if the Judge could obtain permission from the Department of the Army in Washington, D. C., he might then use the post sawmill. Despite his political influence in Washington, it took Wickersham nearly a year to obtain the necessary authority. By then, Colonel Ray had been replaced by C. S. Farnsworth, who made the facilities of the sawmill available only with the understanding that the Judge would have to hire his own help to run the mill and should buy his own logs on the open market. Military personnel could not assist in a civilian operation.

Judge Wickersham may have felt that Farnsworth was being unnecessarily rigid in binding himself to the letter of his regulations, but then the commanding officer of Fort Egbert was a professional soldier with many years of experience. He was acquainted with the difficulties Captain Richardson had with Washington over the funds for the building of Fort Egbert. Relying on the word of headquarters in Washington that funds would be available for the construction of the fort, Richardson had purchased lumber and hired labor for the work on barracks and quarters, only to find the money needed to meet his obligations tied up in Washington with red tape. Farnsworth's predecessor had complained bitterly to Washington "that the Quartermaster Department recognize the fact of our great isolation and deviate slightly from the rules where work can be done by telegraph. To call for estimates *from here* for work already commenced, when it takes months to make the exchange in correspondence necessary to make the funds estimated for available, may not seem to amount to much to a person in Washington, but becomes serious here on the banks of the Yukon facing a crowd of hungry men and no money to meet the issue."[10]

From his own service experience and with such an immediate example, Farnsworth was only too familiar with the accounting procedures and auditing practices of headquarters in Washington. The Judge, on the other hand, was serving his first government-appointed position. He had yet to learn that Washington, although remote, is godlike in its attention to even the smallest detail of government procedures. But he soon learned.

The steamer on which the Judge and his clerk were traveling, on an official trip to Circle, was stranded on a sandbar. How long the steamer might be stranded the Captain could not predict. The water might rise overnight, freeing the steamer quickly, or the water might drop, leaving the steamer stranded for months or years. The passengers had no choice but to proceed by lifeboats. Since it was late in the year with the nights growing cold, the Judge and his clerk, as did other prudent passengers, included in a basket of food one bottle of Cyrus Noble Kentucky whiskey. When the accounts were later prepared for Washington, the clerk, realizing that whiskey might be disallowed by persons unfamiliar with the rigors of the open river, entered the charge for the bottle in the accounts as "One bottle of subsistence, $5."[11] Three years and many letters later, the clerk, who had paid for the bottle out of his pocket, was still seeking reimbursement and Washington was still demanding an accounting form more acceptable to its practices.

Judge Wickersham may not have seen eye to eye with the military commander of Fort Egbert, but otherwise he enjoyed his few years in Eagle. He loved the Yukon country and the rough, independent nature of the people. He was a man who was exhilarated

by the vastness of Alaska, by the challenge of its winters, its towering peaks, its total wilderness. He enjoyed people and tall tales and
the camaraderie of the trail. His circuit included Circle, Fort
Yukon, and Rampart, making a round trip from Eagle of nearly
one thousand miles. In the summer he could travel with comfort
by river steamer, unless it became stranded on a sandbar and he
had to take to a rowboat. During the winter the circuit had to be
made on foot with a dog sled—either behind the sled or breaking
snow ahead of the dogs—for a distance equivalent to walking
through winter snows from New York to Chicago or San Francisco
to Seattle. If his planning was correct, he would reach a rude roadhouse before night where he might get a bed or more often a place
on the floor or, because of the prestige of his office, the top of the
dinner table after supper. He did not care. He reveled in the life—
the men, his job, the country. He was himself the stuff of the last
stampede, while being the carrier of the virus that would end it.

The rich tributaries of the Forty Mile, the gold fields downriver, and the proximity of the Canadian border made Eagle important commercially. With the building of Fort Egbert, it became
the military headquarters of North Alaska, and Judge Wickersham's arrival made it the judicial center as well. In 1903, when the
telegraph line was completed from Valdez to Eagle, it became the
communications center for the Yukon. Two years later, for this
last facet of its eminence, the Norwegian explorer, Captain Roald
Amundsen, sought out Eagle to announce to the world the de-
nouement of a four-hundred-year drama of history.

From the earliest history of the Western Hemisphere, men had
sought a northwest passage, a short route to the Orient. Within
five years of Columbus' discovery of America, John Cabot had
sailed as far north as Newfoundland in search of the short passage.
In the succeeding centuries Cartier, Frobisher, Hudson, Baffin,
Parry, and countless other adventurers braved the ice packs and
winter gales of the Arctic Ocean and turned back in defeat or were
lost. It was Roald Amundsen with his forty-seven-ton *Gjoa* who
succeeded in 1905, where all others had failed. Although this was
one of the great news stories of the time, only a few newspapers
carried it, and then only in a truncated form, noting briefly that
Captain Amundsen had reached Eagle by dog sled from Herschel
Island. "While the message is incomplete in details," one paper
reported, "it purports to be from a member of an exploring party

sent out by Nansen and states that the party is safe with the *Gjoa* wintering at Kay Point."

According to Amundsen, the *Gjoa* wintered at King Point, about thirty-five miles from Herschel Island, where five whalers were wintering. In October the captains of the whalers sent a mail sled to Fort Yukon for mail and messages that might be there containing instructions from their principals. Understanding that there was a telegraph station at the post, Amundsen decided to accompany the mail sled. This would give him the first chance in three years to communicate directly with Norway, and he was understandably anxious both to let relatives and friends know the *Gjoa* was safe and to advise his country that a Norwegian had discovered and successfully navigated the Northwest Passage. Barring. this opportunity, it would be another nine months before the Arctic sea-lanes would be open, and he could continue his voyage around Point Barrow and through the Bering Strait to Nome, the next closest place from which he could communicate with Oslo. Accordingly, on October 20 he left King Point with the mail sled bound for Fort Yukon.

For a month they were on the frozen trail, east along the coast to the Peel River, up the Peel to Rat Portage, and across the five-thousand-foot mountain range to the Porcupine. With a brief stop at Rampart House, they continued down the Porcupine to the Yukon. They reached Fort Yukon late in November, only to find that the nearest telegraph station was at Eagle City, over two hundred miles farther south. Disappointed but determined to complete what he had set out to do, he hired a local guide and proceeded to Circle City. There he joined up with a Mr. Harper, the mail carrier who was also heading for Eagle.

Following the well-established mail route along the Yukon, they reached Eagle in mid-December, where his first order of business was to send a telegram to the King of Norway announcing the successful navigation of the Northwest Passage. Amundsen was so beguiled with the hospitality and pleasures of Eagle that he remained for two months as the guest of Frank N. Smith, manager of the Northern Commercial Company's post there. Then, in the coldest season of the year, Amundsen made the return trip to the ice-imprisoned *Gjoa* with letters and newspapers for his men.[12]

That was 1906, a vintage year in Eagle. There was Herman

Coomer, who took wide-angle pictures of the town and photographed Amundsen. Horace Beiderman, a famous mailman of the Yukon, mushed between Eagle City, Circle, and Fort Yukon during the winter when the river was frozen and the only mail call was made by dog sled. Charley Ott had a store with Shield, a tinsmith, who made long bathtubs a person could sit in without hunching up his legs. Herman Coomer, besides being a photographer, was a miner associated with the Crooked Creek venture on the Seventy Mile. A. E. Robinson was already an Eagle old-timer by then. One of the most famous characters of Alaska, he typified the last stampede. He prospected and mined in a desultory fashion, but he was more interested in the free life of the Yukon than in gold.

Robinson was reputedly a famous marksman, who had won medals for sharpshooting in national competitions in the United States. For this reason, he was called Nimrod, the only name by which he was known in Eagle. In Alaska, a country of hunters, he was not interested in marksmanship. He hunted, but only for food, not for trophies. He was born one of that special breed who instinctively, it seems, can make anything with their hands. His dream was to make an airplane, but he never did.

He came to Eagle around 1900, soon after the town was established. He had a little jewelry shop where he made rings and trinkets for people. He could take a gold nugget and string out a thread of gold from it so thin it could scarcely be seen. But he had no feeling for money, and was almost ashamed to ask people to pay for what he enjoyed doing. It was said of Nimrod, he could make anything but a living.

A Dutchman by the name of Dick Bauer had a mine on Fourth of July Creek, up from Nation. He was running some hydraulic equipment and broke a gear in the machine. He went to Nimrod and asked him if he could make a gear. Nimrod studied the broken piece of equipment and said he could but it would be too expensive, Bauer would be better off ordering a new gear from outside. But to the Dutchman time was money. A man didn't make a living sitting on an idle mine; so he told Nimrod to go ahead and they would see when he finished if it were too expensive or not. Nimrod made the gear. It was not a complicated piece of machinery but one that had to be made precisely to fit the working parts and to withstand extreme pressure. When he finished, he showed it to Bauer and asked if $3.50 would be too much.

The first town on the Yukon, Forty Mile, is now deserted.
A few supplies are on the shelves of the general store for
the use of travelers, but there is no storekeeper and no charge.

A view of the river, looking north, from Eagle, the loveliest
town on the Yukon.   (PHILIP HYDE)

Like all people on the Yukon, Nimrod had his claims along the river or up the creeks, in which were wrapped his hopes for fortunes, with his jewelry store being a place of livelihood when he couldn't work his claims or couldn't be out prospecting. And like most men living this way, he never had an abundance of funds. His eating habits were irregular, and as might be expected he lost his teeth sooner than he should have through lack of proper diet. The story is told that one day, short of food, he killed a bear that had torn up his cache and in retaliation took the teeth out of the bear and made himself a set of teeth with which he could eat the bear.

The story is true in that he did make his own false teeth. The way in which it is reported is fanciful and has been passed on from journalist to journalist because of its color. Actually, the first set of teeth he made for himself were all aluminum. With balsa gum he made an impression and then molded a plate from aluminum and fit them with aluminum teeth. They were light and handy, but they proved too unattractive and had a strange, harsh feel in his mouth. This original set of teeth he left in his cabin up on Flume Creek, though it was not really his cabin but belonged to Barney Hansen. Barney found them there some years later, lying on a table with some diaries belonging to Nimrod. When Barney returned to the cabin after Nimrod's death, the teeth were gone, as were the diaries.

Nimrod made a second set of teeth. Again he used an aluminum plate, but this time he used bear and sheep teeth, which he ground down and fit into the aluminum plate. A dentist from Seattle, visiting Eagle in the late twenties, was intrigued by the home-made set and offered to make Nimrod a regular set of false teeth in exchange for the aluminum plate with the animal teeth. Nimrod agreed and the exchange was made. Nimrod always complained that the Seattle teeth just didn't fit as good as his own set.

Most old-timers never retired. Nimrod never admitted that life might come to an end. For him, life was lived day by day. He enjoyed each new day with expectations of a greater day to come. At eighty-seven he was working a claim on Seventy Mile. As usual, he was not eating as he should—just a little flour he baked into bread. It got cold early on the Seventy Mile and he started for Eagle. He never made that trip alive. Nimrod always said he did not want anyone to have to break his bones to get him into a pine box, as was frequently the case when frozen bodies couldn't be made to fit the ordinary rectangular space. Perhaps he had this in mind as he lay dying by his campfire, where he was found stretched out on a blanket with his hands crossed on his chest ready for his last resting place.[13]

Borghild Hansen, herself an integral part of Eagle, remembers Nimrod well. Although not a stampeder, her story is important to the understanding of Eagle and the last stampede. She is as much a part of the Yukon as John Lawrence, as much a piece of the history as Mollie Walsh and Ma Pullen.

She had not intended to go to Alaska. In the Midwest, she had done what many girls do who wish to have a profession; she went to normal school to become a teacher. If she had heard of Alaska, it was in terms of Jack London or Rex Beach, or old stories of the Klondike, stories which had little reality to a person in Chicago. Her ambition was only to be a teacher in Chicago or maybe downstate Illinois in some country school. But one of her classmates was a girl who had been in Alaska for a year. She was filled with the memories of that year. All she could talk about was Alaska, the vast horizons, the long winter nights, the never-ending days, the great sense of freedom in that last outpost of America. It struck a chord in the heart of the young midwestern girl.

In her last year of normal school, she applied to the Department of the Interior for a teaching position in Alaska. The Department probably did not receive too many applications for that far land and was pleased to select someone so well-trained. She was given an appointment to a school in the Indian village at Eagle.

One can imagine the thrill of a young girl receiving a letter from the Government of the United States with an official appointment as school teacher, giving her not only her first assignment, but an assignment to Alaska about which she had already heard so much. And not only to Alaska but to an Indian school.

These were momentous days for her. June and July in preparation for a new life, the final days with her family, farewell parties with her friends. In August, as the time drew close when she must assume the responsibilities of school-mistress of her own school, the departure from Chicago for Seattle, the first long train trip, the first break with the past, the first departure from what had been the realities of life. The arrival in Seattle, a coast city, facing the Pacific Ocean, for a young girl raised in the interior of America must have been rare excitement. The scent of the salt sea, the wharves, the docks, the fishing boats, and the great ocean liners. Then the steamer from Seattle to Skagway. The beautiful passage through the islands off the coast of British Columbia and the panhandle of Alaska. The towering mountains that come down to the coast waters, the glaciers, the vast spruce forests, the cascading falls that drop sheer from mountain bluffs into the ocean. At the end of the voyage, Skagway, the gateway to the Yukon. A frontier town that had maintained its life as the terminus of the Yukon and White Pass Railroad. And then the train trip, winding up over delicate trestles, under sheer rock cliffs, to the White Pass, which the stampeders had crossed on foot before the railroad was built. Each point on the trip must have seemed more remote, more forlorn, more isolated, more the end of the world. Seattle, from Chicago, was the Far West, the edge of the wilderness. Skagway was absolutely the end of the world; and then the train trip ending on the Yukon at Whitehorse, a town in the midst of a vast forgotten country. It too seemed a finality in itself, though it was only a moment to catch her breath before the next stage—the Yukon steamers, the great sternwheelers with their shallow-draft bottoms, the huge stacks belching smoke from the cords of burning wood. Down through the wilderness, and yet not a wilderness she had anticipated, at the same time being all she could have expected. The great pine forests of the coast did not exist here. The trees were small and spindly. The mountains instead of being sharp and precipitous, rolled off into the far horizons or skimmed saucerlike into the sky. Through Lake Labarge. And down the Thirty Mile River, to where the Teslin merges with the Yukon. Moldering cabins could be seen, hanging to the banks. An occasional cow moose with its calf would pause in its browsing along the shores to watch unalarmed the passing of the steamer. Past the Pelly and the ruins of old Fort Selkirk, where a little village was still alive at that time. Past the White River which poured its murky silt into the Yukon making its clear waters opaque, and Stewart Island and finally Dawson, the capital of gold, with shreds of glamor clinging like gauzy veils to an overaged actress playing the part of an ingénue. Here, finally, must be the real end of the world; there could be nothing further from civilization than this. And here she met her first disappointment. The Whitehorse steamer had been late, causing her to miss connection with the Dawson–St. Michael steamer. It had left the day before. It was late in the year, and whether there would be another steamer was unknown. However, Percy De Wolfe, the mailman, was going downriver with his long flatbottomed boat, and he offered to give the young girl a ride. She had no choice but to accept. From a steamer she came down to an oversized rowboat for the final leg of her journey.

Three days later the small mailboat swept around a bend and ahead lay Eagle Bluff. On the left bank was a miserable village. Ragged children waved and shouted; dogs barked. But from the distance she could not distinguish the appearance of the people.

De Wolfe turned to the young girl. "There's your home, ma'm. Shall we land there?"

She was suddenly frightened and a loneliness she had been too busy to feel engulfed her. The gap between reality and expectation was too great. "Is that Eagle?" she managed to ask.

"No ma'm. Them's your Indians. Eagle is a short piece down the river."

With a sense of reprieve, she suggested she had better go to Eagle first; and since De Wolfe had been only "spoofing the schoolmarm" and had no intention of arriving at Eagle without the new teacher, they continued on to Eagle City. It was a primitive cluster of buildings to go by the name of a city, but it did have an air of substance. There were docks and whitewashed buildings, stores, churches, a customs office. It was not what she had expected, but then she could not have expressed what she thought Eagle would be like. It was both ruder and lovelier than she had been prepared for; it was more remote, beyond the beyond. When she stepped ashore, the first man to step up asked her if she were the new schoolmarm, and upon receiving her answer said, "Well, we sure been expecting you. We've been holding a room for you at the hotel. If you will come along, I'll show you the way."

The nausea of fright and loneliness dissolved. They expected her. They knew who she was. Never, from that moment, was she allowed to feel herself a stranger in Eagle. This was her home. She belonged, she was part of the town. Immediately she felt closer to these people than she had ever felt to any people elsewhere.

The next day she started her final trip. She decided to walk to the Indian village to see her school. Although advised not to go alone, she could not wait for an escort. She had to see her school. The proprietor of the hotel advised her to carry a heavy stick because Indian dogs are a bit touchy about strangers, he said. But a good blow with a stick soon convinces them of your peaceful nature. So with a heavy stick and a fast-beating heart, she started out by herself, a young girl in a new country, moving toward her first job.

In August the days are long. The sun is warm in Eagle and the grass is lush, frequently standing high above a person's head. She had gone about a mile when, at a sharp turn in the trail, she was confronted by two young Indian men. Her pulse, which had slowed to normal under the blandishment of the friendly country-side, quickened again. She stopped and the two Indians stopped.

"I'm going to the village," she said. "Is this the way?"

The two Indians looked at her mutely. Then finally one said, "Why you carry club?"

She explained about the dogs.

The Indian reached for the stick. "You no need club. You our teacher. No one harm you in our village. Come." And the two men turned and started ahead of her down the trail. She followed. Thus she was escorted out of the high grass into the clearing around the straggling Indian village that is still perched along the banks of the Yukon two or three miles above Eagle.

She was immediately surrounded. The entire village came out and the chief, who was an old man, made a welcoming speech and sent a boy back to his hut. He returned with a key which the chief handed her. "This is the key to your school," he said. "It is yours. Take it." Then he led her to the school and as the entire village stood around, she stepped forward and inserted the key in the door and threw it open to see the one room with its benches and few rough tables. She walked in with the village crowding behind her and moved to the head of the classroom which was to be her position of responsibility, her forum for the years ahead from which she was to impart education and understanding to the young Indians of the village. She turned and summoning up a smile said, not being sure whether she meant it or not, "I am happy to be here." But even as she spoke in the shock at the frugality of her pedagogical diocese, she sensed the anticipatory pride in the people awaiting her reaction to the grandness of their school with its swept floor and real chairs and tables and glass windows found nowhere else in the village.

The chief came forward and proudly opened the door at the

back of the schoolroom, revealing the one room attached to the school which was to be her home. It was a meager room, but it had a wooden floor, a big stove, a bed, a chair and a table, a window, and a door in the back where the chief proudly showed her a vast stack of firewood.

"This is your home," he said. "We do not have much in this village, but we have fish and we will get you caribou and moose meat and bear. You will have plenty. We are happy you are here."

She did not stay there that night. The home was really not ready for her yet, nor she for it. She returned to Eagle City, and that primitive outpost on the banks of the Yukon now seemed a thriving, complex city filled with people, restaurants, stores, hotels, and offices. And looking back, there was Dawson, which in retrospect was a veritable Paris. But this was her home; this was what she had chosen. She was content. She still is.[14]

At the turn of the century Eagle, though small, was one of the most varied and complete communities of Alaska. On October 31, 1900, the dedication of a reading room was an important social occasion. Judge Wickersham was asked to make a few remarks as the representative of civilian authority. Father Monroe represented the clergy and Major Farnsworth the military. The remarks of the latter on this occasion have a nostalgic preachment of self-reliance missing in today's social philosophy. Speaking of the philanthropies represented by the reading room, he said: "People are asked to donate to this civic benefit for three reasons: one, to increase the size and equipment of the institution; two, to make the people realize they have a financial interest in the work; and three, and most important, to prevent the donation causing a feeling of dependency and implanting in the people that most degrading inclination to shirk their proper duties and shove the labor and expense of social duties onto the heads, hands, and pocketbooks of others. In other words, the third object is to prevent a debasing spirit of pauperism from arising among the people who derive the benefits of the institution."[15]

In 1900 Eagle was a town with a complete set of contemporary problems. Today it is free of these worries. The military is long since gone; the fort was deactivated in 1911. The office of the Third Judicial District was moved to Fairbanks. The telegraph service fell into disuse and was abandoned. The steamers have stopped plying the Yukon. The customs duties are performed perfunctorily by the postmistress. There is one store where bread can be purchased for 75¢ a loaf, a small restaurant and lodge, a post office, meeting hall, many vacant buildings and churches, and about twenty people. As an Alaskan wit jibed, it is now a town with more churches than houses, more houses than people, and more people than necessary. But one problem still exists.

Situated safely above flood level, overlooking a ninety-degree sweep in the river, given perspective by the towering Eagle Bluff under which it nestles, with hills to the south and to the north across the river, with lovely shade trees not found in the other towns of the Yukon, with wide streets and clear streams, Eagle presents the most attractive pastoral scene on the Yukon. Yet beneath this serene and bucolic exterior apparently still lie factious tendencies. At once friendly, hospitable, and charming, the community is seemingly riven by domestic problems.

In 1968 gregarious Master Sergeant Harvey D. Black, recruiting officer for the United States Army in Fairbanks, had a cozy log cabin in Eagle, which he kept as a retreat well supplied with beer and recordings. Like most sergeants, he had it all figured out. He was going into insurance when he retired. But upon retirement he went to Eagle and sold liquor, instead of insurance. The neighboring Indians could buy liquor, but it was customary in most stores, to restrict sales to them. They have the strange concept that money has no meaning in itself but only in relation to what it can buy. Having been raised without expectations of a Sears, Roebuck world, they bought what was available when they had the means, and bought until they divested themselves of their money. If permitted their natural inclination, they would spend what they had on liquor. This created an unfortunate situation both for the families of the Indians, who might need clothing or food or schoolbooks, and for the community in which they proceeded to get uproariously drunk. And so, as in other places, the custom in Eagle was to restrict sales of liquor to Indians.

Sergeant Black wanted to change this custom. He felt it was an insult to the Indians, a restriction of their freedom to do as they wished with their money. He considered it also a restriction of his right to make as much profit as he could. He brought in beer and instituted unrestricted sales. The community objected to no avail. Failing moral suasion, the town voted itself dry. Sergeant Black, a man not easily discomfited or overcome by adversities, moved outside the town limits and applied for a new license. The townspeople were not to be so easily outmaneuvered; they saw to it that his petition was rejected by the state.

Sergeant Black still has his cabin in the town of Eagle across from the post office, adjacent to the open fields which were once Fort Egbert. He does not live there, but he has the last word, echoing Carruthers' censure in 1898, with a bit of doggerel, which he has painted in red and blue letters on a white background covering much of one side of the cabin:

Our Town Eagle

It is mostly a bunch of tumbled down huts
    And the place is overrun with Indian muts
And most of the grub comes packed in tin,
    But it is a damn good town for the shape it is in.

The weather is cold, damn cold I'll say,
    And the long winter lasts from October to May,
And most of the shacks have a roof fallin in,
    But it is a damn good town for the shape it is in.

The people all gossip and knock to beat hell
    And must be excused for the wild tales they tell,
And to do as they do is an unpardonable sin,
    But it is a damn good town for the shape it is in.

The town is divided into two social lots,
    Those that are in it and those that are not,
And knocking each other they raise a great din,
    But it is a damn good town for the shape it is in.

Carruthers may have been reporting fact, Sergeant Black may have his justification, but the last line of his doggerel is truer than the preceding three lines. Eagle was and is the loveliest town on the Yukon.

9

Circle, the End of the Road

THE EARLY HISTORY OF CIRCLE CITY[1] is a peculiar mélange of fact and fancy, of hope and greed and discovery of something that had probably never existed. It started in 1862 with the Reverend Robert McDonald and a story of gold and culminated in 1893 with three young Bostonians who accidentally stumbled on the reality of myth.

In 1862 the Church of England sent Robert McDonald to Fort Yukon.[2] McDonald had a flair for the exotic in travel. The assignment appealed to him more for the lure of the vast wilderness to be seen than for the hope of saving savage souls. He loved the rugged challenge of the bleak country, living his life as he wanted, in the frugal splendor of the land.

Although McDonald became an archdeacon and a renowned scholar whose translation of the Bible into local dialect is still used along the Yukon, he was not an administrator or an established church man. He spent as little time as possible at headquarters, preferring to take the essence of Christianity and medicine to the Indians where he found them, rather than waiting for them to seek him out. He had slight interest in personal comfort or the means of acquiring it. By dog sled, by boat, and by foot he ranged hundreds of miles up and down the Yukon and along its tributaries, seeking those to whom he might bring spiritual and physical help. He developed an empathy for the Indians rare among frontiersmen of the day and was most contented when he was on the trail experiencing God's arctic power and beauty. He was a mystical man, who liked to share the beauty he saw with those who would listen; and on his return from trips would gladly describe the great salmon runs he had seen, the countless caribou migrations, the many moose swimming the Yukon or placidly nuzzling in the shallows for the tender subaqueous grasses. He would tell of encounters with bear, of shores white with molting ducks that ran into the brush upon his approach because they could not fly, of beaver, otter, fox, and of streams that glittered like the midnight skies with the sparkle of gold.[3] The potential fisheries, the furs, the gold suggested no material wealth to him; arrd if he exaggerated what he saw, it was merely with a storyteller's whim for the dramatic and not for self-importance.

One of those who listened to the missionary's accounts and who liked to color his own prosaic existence with the words of others was a young clerk of the Hudson's Bay Company at Fort Yukon, Robert Campbell. In a letter dated October 2, 1864, he wrote his father in Ontario and, having little to narrate of his own dull existence as a clerk at a trading post, told of the "preacher's" travels and recounted what he had heard of the "preacher's" creek with gold so plentiful it could be scooped up with a spoon. One day, he assured his father, when he had time from his duties, he would go to the "preacher's" creek and gather his fortune in gold.[4] Whether this was only a youthful fancy which was forgotten as soon as written or whether Robert Campbell never found time from his duties is unknown, but the letter was published in Ontario and subsequently was picked up by American papers in the East, where it created only a passing flurry of excitement during the Civil War.

But if the titillation of war news dulled the story in 1864, the glamor and promise of wealth were still remembered by the three Bostonians who set out to find gold in 1893. By that time, Alaska had changed from Russian to American territory, and the Hudson's Bay Company had withdrawn from Fort Yukon back up the Porcupine to Canadian jurisdiction.

In late May of that year two men seeking Jack McQuesten entered his store at Forty Mile. One was a barrel-chested, heavy-thighed trapper by the name of Cherosky. His father, he said, had been a Russian trader on the lower Yukon. It may have been true, but if so, his father had bequeathed him only the name. The disheveled brown-black hair, the swarthy complexion, the epicanthic eyes, everything about him was Indian. The other man also claimed a Russian father, Pavlov, and went by the name of Pitka.[5] Unlike the former, he had dirty blond hair and was a head taller than his companion, and his blue eyes were an anomaly in the swarthy complexion.

Cherosky and Pitka had a familiar story to tell. It had been a bad winter. The animals had been scarce. A wolverine had robbed the traps. McQuesten waited quietly through the story of hardship and hard luck. It was an oft-repeated story of almost impossible adversity; so he was more relieved than susprised when, instead of asking for an advance against next year's trap line, the two men said they intended trying their luck gold mining on the Too-whun-na and wanted a grubstake.

To the traders of the Yukon, judicious grubstaking was not a gamble, but a reasonable business venture. There was enough gold around so that there was always a chance of a handsome return for food and clothing. More important to a farsighted man like McQuesten was the possibility of obtaining information. In a country largely unexplored, any report from gold miners on a new stream helped fill in the large blank areas of the map and was intelligence of potential commercial value. A trader who gained a reputation of knowing the country would draw new prospectors better heeled than Cherosky and Pitka. And through grubstaking, a trader could gain early knowledge of a new strike so that he could move in first to a stampede area with whiskey and other essential specifics for separating gold from miners.

McQuesten knew of the Too-whun-na, or Birch Creek. He probably knew that it was about one day's pack west of the Yukon and that it paralleled the Yukon for a hundred miles or more before joining it below Fort Yukon. But this was all he knew. He did not know the terrain, the nature of the country, the best way to reach the Too-whun-na, and most important, he did not know if any color had been found on the stream. Accordingly he acceded to the request and authorized the men to draw what they needed while he prepared the necessary papers for them to sign.

At the same time the three Bostonians were departing for Alaska, Cherosky and Pitka quit Forty Mile. Familiar with the limiting confines of time in the Yukon, they knew prospecting was a summer job to be carried on during the few brief months between snows. June was upon them. Before October, they must find gold, if it was to be found. They must stake their claims. They must record those claims. They must build a winter camp and sink a shaft that could be worked during the winter. In the Yukon there is never enough time to do what must be done and too much time to do nothing. They loaded the flatbottomed boat they had built from handsawn planks and caulked with melted tallow and rope. It was a cumbersome boat, but it would carry two men and their supplies downriver with ease. Using paddles instead of oars, they pushed out into the muddy current. In the first day they swept past Belle Isle and Boundary or Eagle Bluff. They entered the Upper Ramparts and camped near Calico Bluff.

On the third day they came out of the Upper Ramparts into the beginning of the Yukon Flats, where the river widens and the country opens into a monotony of level land stretching away to the northern mountains of the Brooks Range. They pulled into a deep inlet several miles wide on the west bank and un-loaded. Here they had decided to cache their boat and go overland to strike the Too-whun-na on its upper reaches.

No account remains of their trip to the Too-whun-na, but it is known that they found the stream as expected about a day's trip to the west and subsequently discovered gold on the Masto-don, a tributary. They staked claims, each running five hundred feet along the creek, and headed for the nearest American record-ing office. Claim-jumping was rife and a prudent prospector wasted no time in legalizing his find. There were too many lonely prospectors who had delayed, thinking themselves safe from publicity, only to discover upon arrival at the recording office that rumor had preceded them and prior claims had already been filed on their diggings.

The nearest American recording office was at Tanana, nearly four hundred miles downriver from where they had cached their boat; so Cherosky and Pitka made for Tanana. Here they met Jack Gregor, Pat Kennaley, and Jonathan Pemberton, the three Bostonians, who had crossed the United States by rail to San Francisco. From there they had taken a steamer to St. Michael, where they transferred to a riverboat. They had been in Tanana for several weeks, canvassing the saloons and boarding houses[6] in search of someone who knew of Preacher's Creek, only to learn that it was a name long since forgotten in Alaska, or when recalled, remembered but dimly as a myth unrelated to the realities of the Yukon. In frustration, they had decided to try the Koyukuk. The three were looking for a guide to lead them there, when Jonathan Pemberton had a chance meeting with Cherosky in a waterfront saloon, which restored their belief in Preacher's Creek.

Normally, Cherosky would have been uncommunicative, but having legalized his strike, he had no hesitancy about telling of the claim on the Mastodon. Indeed, he was eager to do so. Miners are a greedy lot, but not stupidly greedy. Cherosky and Pitka had claimed as much as they were legally entitled to and more than they could work. Now there was no objection to others' sharing in the find. They were welcome. A rough but largely just law followed the mining camps. While a lonely prospector might be in danger from an unscrupulous band, a member of a mining camp was protected by the need of all for security.

Cherosky had told anyone who would listen about the gold on the Mastodon and with each telling had downed a glass of whiskey. He had exhausted his available audience when he saw Pemberton, a slight man with glasses and a scant stubble of beard grown in an attempt to gain a patina of frontier respectability. Even through an alcoholic haze, Cherosky recognized a cheechako, one who would gladly listen to an account of gold. "Have a drink," he invited, dropping his poke on the bar, and over the drinks he narrated again the story of his strike on the Mastodon, with embellishments fit for a cheechako's ears.

To Pemberton, unfamiliar with the ways of miners and stampedes, yet to wash his first pan, the account was even more brilliantly hued than intended. To him the Too-whun-na was Preacher's Creek. It had to be. He dragged Cherosky away from the saloon to meet his partners and repeat the story, and Cherosky let himself be led away willingly with the promise of a new audience.

The three partners were agreed, this must be Preacher's Creek. Without real reason, they had formed the impression that the fabled creek was north or east of Fort Yukon, but they admitted it could just as well be south and west. The location had never been defined, and the Mastodon and Too-whun-na were within the area of McDonald's travels. The stream was of the size they had pictured, and the gold was the clincher. The very fact that in two weeks they had found no one who had ever heard of Preacher's Creek proved that the name was not important. It could have been lost or changed with the withdrawal of the Hudson's Bay Company from the territory.

With Cherosky, the three Bostonians searched out Pitka and proposed that they hire the two men to lead them to Preacher's Creek. Pitka, who was sober, immediately saw the advantage in the offer. If he and Cherosky had to pole back up river against the swift Yukon current, several weeks of precious summer would be lost. Whether the Americans came or not was unimportant, for others would soon arrive. What was important was to return to the claims as soon as possible, and neither he nor Cherosky could afford the steamer fare. He accepted the proposal for himself and Cherosky and promised they would be ready to leave when the steamboat, *Arctic*, left two days later.

The return trip up the Yukon was uneventful for Cherosky and Pitka, who spent their days sitting on the limited deck space smoking in silence and watching the familiar pattern of desolate banks dropping slowly astern the tiny boat that was nearly all engine and storage room. To the three Back Bay adventurers, it must have been a voyage of utmost excitement. Each mile was taking them farther from civilization, each curve of the river was bringing them closer to Preacher's Creek, a mirage which had been growing dimmer and dimmer as they had neared it, until in Tanana it had all but disappeared. To Cherosky and Pitka, the return upriver was wonderfully swift compared with what it might have been by flatbottomed boat. To the three white men, it was excruciatingly slow, each stop for wood a regrettable delay, each pause to drop off supplies a personal harassment.

When they reached the point from which Cherosky and Pitka had started for Preacher's Creek or the Too-whun-na, or Birch Creek as it is now listed on maps, summer was well into its last phase. Already there were several hours of near darkness during the nights. At last, the three men, each with his privately held dream, were faced with a reality of that dream—a debris-littered shingle sloping into a shallow mudbank, a sparse forest of emaciated spruce stretching in flat monotony to distant hills. Within this bleak scene lay their dreams of fortune. To this unlovely reality each sensed an irrevocable commitment.

Willing hands hastily dumped equipment on shore, anxious to get the steamer on its way. Silently the men watched as the *Arctic* backed into deep water, swung upstream and with a shrill whistle and clouds of smoke slowly pulled away, gradually disappearing behind a promontory to the south, stretching thinner and thinner the umbilical cord tying the men to home. With the last sight of the boat, it snapped. They were suddenly alone, abandoned in the wilderness they had struggled to reach. The excitement and the thrill of expectation were replaced by a dreary sense of loneliness.

With the help of Cherosky and Pitka, Gregor, Kennaley, and Pemberton made up packs that would tax to the limit their physical capacities. The remainder of their supplies they cached in a tree out of the reach of curious bears. As there were still several hours of daylight remaining when they had completed their preparations, they started their trek to the west with the hope this would make for an easy hike the second day.

Within two hundred yards Pemberton was soaked in sweat, which seemed to attract a myriad of invisible gnats. The perspiration ran into his eyes and dripped from his hands. The gnats flew into his ears, nose, and mouth when he gasped for breath, biting his hands and face and neck. He was in agony, but ashamed to admit it. Somehow he had never visualized the need of packing when daydreaming of the Preacher's Creek and gold; somehow he just got there, finding himself without intermediate steps on the banks of a clear, rushing stream, scooping gold off the sand bars. Now the creek seemed farther away than it had in Boston. There were miles of this ordeal ahead of him He had to call a halt and collapse in exhaustion. Then a half mile and stop and a quarter mile and stop. They made less than five miles that day and not much more the whole of the next day. It took five days to cover a distance Cherosky and Pitka would have completed in one day. When they finally reached the Too-whun-na, the Bostonians had had it; and when Cherosky and Pitka said their claims were further upstream on a tributary, they parted company. As far as Gregor, Kennaley, and Pemberton were concerned, they had reached their creek. They would go no farther. They would try their luck where they were, rather than submit to another day pushing through dense willow thickets, climbing over the welter of down-timber, working around bogs and over gorges.

The Bostonians never found gold in the quantities pictured in the news story which had incited them to the trip, but they did find sufficient to justify filing claims. They built a cache on Preacher's Creek to store their mining gear and some food; then with lightened packs they started the return trek to the Yukon. Conditioned by the rigors of camp living and the physical drudgery of mining, they were surprised to find how much easier the trip was than they remembered it. They were more surprised upon reaching Tanana to find how changed was their perspective. The dismal frontier camp seemed now a teeming metropolis, the dusty streets were broad thoroughfares, the squalid bars, palatial establishments, the limited menus of moose meat, potatoes, stewed fruit, and pies were epicurean delights. They had thought they would be interested to learn the news of Boston, what their kin were doing, how the war with Spain progressed, only to find their interest in metropolitan affairs lost in the domed vastness of the arctic world. The fulminations of civilization lacked significance compared with the importance of how much flour and bacon remained, or the concern about getting a caribou or moose or bear with the last of the fresh meat gone, or compared with the decision to take time from the constant excitement of the next wash of a pan to try for a mess of grayling for dinner, or the worry about the state of one's boots. Strikes in Pennsylvania, conscription in Boston, or political news from Washington had little reality in Tanana. They found themselves far more interested in talking with other miners about gold strikes, new stampedes, and mining techniques.

They spent only as much time in Tanana as necessary to file their claims and catch the last boat up the Yukon, driven by the fever-fired delirium for gold. But a new surprise awaited them on the wilderness banks of the Yukon nearest Birch Creek. News of the Cherosky-Pitka strike had reached Forty Mile, as well as Tanana, and when Gregor, Kennaley, and Pemberton arrived, they were greeted by McQuesten and over a hundred stampeders who had gathered to try the new gold field. McQuesten had left Harper to run the post at Forty Mile, while he joined the stampede to the new locale, bringing with him supplies of miners' grub, boots, parkas, shovels, picks, crowbars, pans, and all the basic stores which men must have and for which they would pay dearly where competition did not exist, and a million-dollar find might be lost while a person caviled over a few extra dollars.

It was now nearly October, and McQuesten, from two decades of experience on the Yukon, warned against setting out for the back country in the threat of winter. Better, he advised, to build log cabins and winter on the Yukon. Winter in the interior would be grim and lonely for those unaccustomed to the arctic, and prospecting would be virtually impossible during the months of freezing weather.

The admonition made sense to Pemberton and his partners, who already had their claims. They were now familiar with the difficulties of mining under the good conditions of summer and were hesitant to pit themselves against a hostile nature alone in the long nights.

There were those who could not wait, for whom eagerness and ignorance combined in an irresistible drive for gold. They openly ignored McQuesten's experience or secretively packed up and set off in the dark with the hope of locating claims and staking out their finds before the best sites were taken. A few of these managed to last out the winter, but most straggled back to the Yukon to seek a miserable protection in hastily constructed lean-tos, while others were never heard of again. Most of the stampeders, however, stayed and started felling and dressing trees for the rough log cabins, which would afford protection from the northern blasts that were soon expected.

McQuesten showed the cheechakos how to build their cabins with sod roofs. "Don't worry if it ain't watertight," he said. "Just get it built fast. There ain't much rain anyways and if a little summer air comes in, it don't do any harm. Come winter, the snow will pack the roof and if you feel a draft coming through the logs, splash a pail of water over the spot and the crack'll be froze airtight with a sheet of ice."[7] He may also have given the advice tendered by other sourdoughs: "Build close to water. Toting water gets mighty tiresome. The old Yukon is muddy now and ain't fit drinking until it's set long enough to settle, but come winter, it'll be clear. When the glaciers stop melting and the river's froze solid so as the banks don't keep caving in, why you can saw yourselves a hole in the ice, and sink a barrel in the hole to keep it open, and have all the clear water you want. It's the only thing good about winter, that and no mosquitos."

That was the winter of 1893–94. It was before the big rush started, when all types of men from all walks of life, in all conditions of preparedness or unpreparedness, started streaming into the Far North. Unlike the Klondike stampeders, these early miners were fairly well-equipped, and what they did not have McQuesten could supply. Later the great rush was to outstrip his logistical planning, but at this time he had plenty of what miners needed. He had baking powder, soda, flour, sugar, coffee, bacon, shortening, syrup, rice, beans, canned milk, and dried fruit. He carried mackinaw coats, wool shirts, flannel underwear, wool pants, fourteen- and twelve-pound blankets, mittens, sox, wool caps, epsom salts, tincture of benzoine, turpentine, soap, and mosquito netting. He had nails, hammers, axes, saws, rope, picks, shovels, pans, quicksilver, candles, buckets, matches, and skillets. A lot of things he didn't have, but he did have a good supply of drinking liquor, and on a slab-sided shelf just beside the entrance to his store was his trademark, the McQuesten barometer, consisting of four small bottles. One was filled with quicksilver, one with whiskey, one with kerosene, and the fourth with Perry Davis' Painkiller. A notice nailed beside the shelf advised that when the quicksilver became solid a man should not plan to be on the trail overnight. When the whiskey solidified, he should not leave camp. If the kerosene froze, he was admonished to stay close to his cabin. But when Perry Davis' Painkiller froze, it wasn't safe to step away from the fire.[8]

It was an uneventful winter, except for some big blizzards that left each cabin isolated from its neighbors until the men could dig their way out. And there was always some excitement when a lone miner or a group from the number who had refused to heed McQuesten's warning stumbled back into camp with accounts of the horrors of trying to live in primitive shelters, with the placer gravels frozen solid, and no water to wash a pan of dirt if you could chip it out and melt it in a fire. The men griped and dreamed and went over and over their equipment, preparing for next season. And they would visit back and forth, swapping stories of other gold-mining fields and fabulous discoveries. They liked, most of all, to gather at what they called "Boston House," and talk with the three partners who already had their claims staked

and discuss where would be the likeliest places to prospect—
whether they should go downstream, following the wash of gold,
or head upstream toward the mother lode, where them half-
breeds probably were. There was some talk about the half-breeds
maybe not being Americans and so not having any rights to stake
on American soil, but the consensus was that there was plenty
up there for everyone without people getting greedy.

It may have been during this winter that a group of the men,
sitting around the fire at McQuesten's store, could have decided
they ought to give a name to the cluster of cabins along the river.
Precise details were not recorded but the general process of naming
can be surmised. New Boston, Preacher's Dream, Nugget, Gold
City, Hell were suggested and rejected. During a lull in the discussion, an old sourdough pointed out that they were inside the
Arctic Circle. "The line marking it runs just south of here," he
said. "When it's light enough, you can see the line. It starts out
on the promontory just up river and runs through the trees back
towards the mountains." McQuesten nodded seriously and allowed as he had seen the line himself and had wondered what it
was. Whereupon a young cheechako said they ought to call the
camp Arctic Circle City, and the sourdough agreed that was a
fitting name. But the name was too long and the final vote was
for Circle City. This was the founding of the town, named for
a sourdough's joke, but which might more appropriately have
been given a name commemorating Archdeacon McDonald; or
Robert Campbell and his Preachers' Creek; or McQuesten who
grubstaked Cherosky and Pitka; or Cherosky and Pitka, who discovered the gold on the Mastodon and led the three Bostonians
to Birch Creek and the reality of their dreams.

The next three years saw a rapid growth of the community.
More miners came down from Forty Mile and Sixty Mile. They
came upriver on steamers from Tanana and the coast, from Washington, Oregon, and California. Some say it reached a peak of
five hundred, some say five thousand. Probably both are correct.
It must have had a permanent population of at least five hundred, and a transient population of several thousand as miners
drifted into town to sit out the winter. It was the queen city of
the Yukon, the golden town of Alaska, the American metropolis
of the North, which would never decline but only continue to
grow.

Circle City, like Dawson, Forty Mile, and Eagle, was a symbol of man's desire for adventure within a socially acceptable framework. Man has always struggled against the confining strictures of his social pattern. His thrust across the oceans, pushing beyond the fixed perimeter of towns and trade, was a response to his need for greater freedom of movement. As a whole, however, except for the few in any time who manage to escape the law of social gravity, men can find their escape only in ways socially acceptable.

In the 1890's only Alaska remained as an adventurous escape, but to take off for Alaska for adventure alone was not socially acceptable. To go in search of wealth, to find a fortune in gold, was acceptable. In a period when the United States was suffering a prolonged financial recession, to abandon one's family, quit a promising career, or throw over a paying job to search for gold in Alaska could be done without fear of social stigma. Gold was a justification any man could give himself for succumbing to the drive for adventure. Many could delude themselves into thinking the justification was the reality. The irony is that, in making their escape, men must always take with them the blueprint of their prison so that they may reconstruct it in their freedom, building a new prison from which to seek escape. They must build new communities structured on known patterns; draft laws; elect committees; erect libraries, hospitals, churches, stores, meeting halls—the whole fabric of the abandoned society must be repeated as a subconscious proof that an escape was not intended.

So in Circle a library was started. The men pooled their skills and idle enthusiasm to build a two-storied opera house. Another store was opened, as well as saloons and gambling halls. Churches were built and a hospital. A debating society was organized, and a miners' committee was elected to resolve disputes and administer survival justice.

A young woman who had recourse to Circle City justice appealed to the miners' committee to compel a dance-hall fiddler to marry her and pay the expenses for a child, the issue of her misplaced reliance on the man's promises. The miners met and elected a judge and a sheriff. A warrant was issued and the fiddler brought before the court. The plaintiff told her story, and "the defendant was heard in ominous silence." The verdict was prompt and simple, "Resolved, that defendant pay plaintiff's hospital bill of $500 and pay plaintiff $500 damages and marry her as he promised to do and that he have until five o'clock this afternoon to obey this order; and Resolved further, that this meeting do now adjourn till five o'clock." When the court reconvened at five o'clock, the committee reported satisfaction of judgment. Whereupon the court, led by the judge and sheriff and escorted by the jury, adjourned to the nearest bar to congratulate the happy couple.[9]

A jail was built, with a grim warning posted on the door, "Notice: All prisoners must report by 9 o'clock P.M. or they will be locked out for the night"—a warning not to be ignored by men who had experienced the sub-zero weather of the Yukon.

"Dutch" Kate Wilson, the first white woman to cross the Chilkoot Pass,[10] arrived in Circle City and soon moved upriver to open an inn, a vantage point from which she shot at every boat that dared pass along the Yukon without stopping at her place of business for a meal or overnight lodging.

"Hootch" Albert, for the price of a pencil and a piece of paper to write a promissory note, bought up a shipment of potatoes that had spoiled. He devised a still and was soon selling raw potato whiskey, parlaying a few tons of rotten potatoes into a pile of gold dust that would have tempted cheechakos and sourdoughs alike to the frozen gates of hell. He went on to even greater business success in Fairbanks. To this day there are those who insist the name "hootch" for rotgut liquor comes from Circle City as a questionable memorial to "Hootch" Albert. Others, more accurately, put it the other way around. Hootch was a common Alaskan synonym for raw whiskey long before "Hootch" Albert got his name from the stuff he served over his bar, which was as raw and vicious as that made by a tribe of Tlingit Indians known as the Hutsnuwu, prounounced "hoochinoo" by the sourdoughs, or "hootch" for short.

By 1896 the growth of Circle City showed no signs of slackening. Miners continued to arrive with every steamer. A few, exhausted by the effort to get this far, frightened by the barren, desolate prospect of the wilderness beyond the town, remained in Circle, taking what jobs they could find or returned downriver by the next steamer. The rest shouldered their loads and joined the crowd on the trail for Birch Creek, which reached its production peak of $700,000 that year. To these, as one miner re-

Circle City, May 27, 1904.   (L. C. ROBERTSON)

Circle City fire department.   (E. A. HEGG)

minisced years later, "It seemed like all that wonderful clear air and mountains and sweet snow without wind and knowing we was going to get rich was something a fellow could hug to his heart and hold forever." Some remained just long enough to run a lucky streak of poker into a small fortune, like John McLernan, who won $25,000 one night at Bob English's Monte Carlo and left by the next steamer on request, or in response to a fortuitous sense of timing. He may have been lucky or a good poker player, but he apparently thought it wise later to change his name to Jack Kearns, when he promoted Dempsey to some of the biggest gates in fight history.

By 1897 the United States government considered Circle City important enough to deserve a postmaster; but the postmaster, with more sense than honor, remained in San Francisco and drew his pay where he could spend it more comfortably. The assistant postmaster was fired for drunkenness. It did not matter, however, as there was no mail to be delivered; the government had not considered it necessary to issue a contract to move the mail beyond St. Michael.[11]

An estimated thiry thousand stampeders crossed the Chilkoot Pass or White Pass in 1897–98. Another fifteen thousand tried to reach the Yukon via the all-Canadian route through the Peace River country. Thousands more took the longer but easier route to St. Michael and up the river by steamer. A few of the men were experienced and well-equipped, but most were strangers to mining with no preparation for the rigors of frontier living. They had the wrong supplies or not enough. Some were physically incapable of coping with primitive life; others were unable to adjust psychologically to the realities they found. The transportation companies had rapidly expanded their fleets but still could not cope with the traffic. Prompted by the mercantile law of demand, they loaded barges with whiskey rather than food. Those who struck it rich wanted liquor and luxuries. Those who did not could hardly afford the staples, such as beans and bacon and flour. So the boats carried what brought the greatest profit, not what was required. Gerstle's letter of 1886 was forgotten.

Reports of starvation and famine, exaggerated by the press and excited relatives, stirred to action a Congress that for thirty years had shown little interest in Alaska. Sheldon Jackson was commissioned to bring reindeer to Alaska from Siberia.[12] Captain

P. H. Ray of the Eighth Infantry was ordered to Alaska with instructions to investigate reports of starvation among the miners.[13] He left Lieutenant W. P. Richardson at Fort Yukon and proceeded up the river. Ray intended to go as far as Dawson, surveying conditions in the mining camps, but ice conditions stopped him at Forty Mile and forced him to return to Fort Yukon, from which post he filed a series of reports fluctuating between alarm and optimism. At one time he reported that there was not, or likely to be within the next year, adequate or efficient means of supplying people then in Alaska or the North-West Territory. He wrote that hundreds of miners were scattered along the river destitute of food, clothing, and money.[14] Two months later he wrote that there was sufficient food in Dawson with no danger of starvation. Circle City had adequate supplies. Fort Yukon had more than enough to meet all demands, including those of the neighboring Indians.[15]

His vacillation may have resulted from the conflict between a personal desire to magnify the importance of his mission by emphasizing the darkest aspects of conditions in the Yukon and a recognition of the need to placate the anxieties existing in the States for the welfare of the men in Alaska. Undoubtedly he wanted recognition for his work and honestly believed that Alaska needed martial law, preferably under his command. In one communication, after narrating a harrowing experience in which only his courage and prompt action prevented a mob of determined miners from seizing all the supplies in Fort Yukon, he concluded, "I only hope the President and Congress will sustain my action and treat me with charity should I be found in error."[16] It was rather pompous language from a captain with many command levels between himself and the President. He added that experience confirmed his earlier opinion that some radical steps were necessary to give protection to life and property along the Yukon. To support his statement, he cited the case of O. E. Weymouth and the unfortunate results of miners' law in Circle City.

Weymouth showed up in Fort Yukon early in November of 1897. He was destitute, or so he claimed. This was no surprise to Captain Ray, who had several hundred destitute miners on his hands. Some were provided with supplies against notes payable in Circle, so that they could return to mining. Those who had no mines were provided work cutting wood for the transportation companies in return for food. However, as there were not enough tools to go around, many men had to be given help without any expectation of reimbursement. Weymouth claimed to be a prospector and under oath stated that he was without food, money, or credit. Accordingly, he was issued provisions sufficient to feed him until June 1, 1898.

Apparently Weymouth was not destitute. Instead of heading for the mines, he set out for Circle City, and ten miles up the trail contracted with a freighter to haul his goods to Circle for twenty-five cents a pound. Upon hearing of this, Captain Ray had Weymouth arrested for obtaining goods under false pretenses. Weymouth was put in jail in Circle and his provisions impounded. The idle miners in Circle protested the arrest. They may have had good reasons, or at least reasons satisfactory to themselves; but Captain Ray's report is the only available account, and according to that report the miners were a bad lot—ignorant of mining, unable to take care of themselves, shiftless, lawless, and untrustworthy. The miners broke open the jail, released Weymouth, and returned his provisions to him. Weymouth then auctioned off his outfit to the miners who had released him, gambled away the proceeds of the sale at faro, and set off for Dawson.[17]

If Captain Ray's reports were inconsistent, it is a matter of no surprise. He was but a single man under instructions to report on an area covering thousands of miles with no telegraph and his only means of transportation during the winter a dog sled. Under the circumstances, he had of necessity to rely upon reports from travelers passing up and down the Yukon. These reports were perhaps colored by the bias of the traveler. The transportation companies and the trading posts were anxious for a greater military control in the Yukon. From their viewpoint, the absence of law was a danger because they had the goods and the means of movement, large investments to be protected. To the miners, the transportation companies and the traders were scoundrels. They wanted to see more food, more competition. The traders who were there already, having a monopoly of business, forced the men coming into the territory to be wholly dependent upon the stores for supplies and at the prices set by the stores. The transportation companies would not carry freight for traders not connected with them or for private parties. Under these circumstances, it is understandable that the truth was seen in different ways, and so reported by Captain Ray. Indeed, there were those who made a business of false reports for their own benefit.

An unauthenticated memorandum which reached the Acting Secretary of War, February 1, 1898, illustrates the venality of the situation. George M. Pinney had been a clerk in the Naval Paymaster's office in San Francisco, where he was involved in the issuance of fraudulent certificates by which he mulcted banks in San Francisco of half a million dollars. He was not apprehended and showed up later in Washington, D. C., where he promoted a bill for the appropriation of funds to relieve miners in "Klondyke, Alaska." His associate in this scheme was one Pierre Humbert, Jr., who had been involved in a forgery case in the office of a San Francisco attorney. The memorandum listed his present occupation as mining sharper and promoter. The two men and their associates were engaged in furnishing false news from Alaska, "scheming to get appropriations for that region from which they hope to get large returns by means of contracts."[18]

Captain Ray's reports reflected such rumormongering, as well as the conflicting claims of the companies wishing military protection and those fearing the effect on prices if government supplies were sent to the Yukon. Reports from some traders, perhaps fearing the effect on prices of government aid, insisted there was no problem in the Yukon. Food was in adequate quantities and there was no prospect of starvation or destitution. At the same time, the North American Transportation and Trading Company painted conditions in the gravest manner. In a letter to the Adjutant General, John Healy, manager for the company in Alaska, wrote that the mining industries of the American portion of the Yukon valley would be seriously crippled, if not entirely paralyzed, because it was not safe to run steamers and land supplies at any of the mining camps along the river. "The great rush of people to the Yukon makes it probable," he asserted, "that armed raiders will hold up the steamers and loot the stores of their supplies; consequently the merchants and the transportation companies will be obliged to confine their business to the Canadian side of the Yukon valley, as the North-West Mounted Police offer protection to life and property."[19]

The key to the problems of the Yukon was Circle City. It was the big American city on the river. Even after the stampede to the

Klondike, Circle continued its preeminence as the American gold camp. Samuel C. Dunham, writing from Circle City for the Department of Labor in May of 1898, considered this area to have greater promise than even the Klondike. He predicted that two miles of ground on the Mastodon in the Circle City area would eventually produce as much gold as any successive ten miles on Bonanza. The ten claims on Mastodon from 4 Below to 5 Above Discovery, he estimated, would prove as productive as any ten claims on Eldorado. Furthermore, Dunham stated, the even distribution of the gold in the Birch Creek District, of which Mastodon is a part, and the output extending over a longer period of time and employing larger numbers of men would be an incalculably greater economic benefit to the community than the more phenomenal production of the creeks in the Klondike District. He also considered the gold found in the Birch Creek District to be of a higher quality than that of the Klondike. He put the average value at $17.20 per ounce compared with less than $16 per ounce for the Klondike area. The Eldorado gold, containing much silver and base material, he reported as being worth only $15.25 per ounce.[20] Despite his sanguine report, Dunham admitted that the miners were working only long enough to get a grubstake before taking off for the Klondike.

In 1898 Circle City was still the most exciting gold town on the river. The miners from the Klondike on their way out stopped there to have their first fling on American soil. There were the saloons, the cribs, the gambling halls, as well as the libraries and churches, a hospital, debating societies, roadhouses, restaurants, and stores, even one run by Jack McQuesten himself. It was a city of hanging gardens where every sod roof, heated from the living quarters below and warmed by the sun of the lengthening days above, burst into luxurious bloom each spring.

To this town Lieutenant Richardson, in the absence of Captain Ray, moved the military post in June of 1898. Almost immediately upon his arrival in Circle, Richardson attempted to inject his sense of military orderliness into the community. Although he and Captain Ray had been sent to Alaska under instructions only "to investigate and report on the conditions of affairs," both officers exceeded these orders whenever and wherever they felt justified. They seized stores, issued food, provided for the welfare, and arrested men as they felt necessary. They constituted themselves the law. There is no question that this took courage without back-up support or authorization and, at times, prevented unfortunate developments. It also created resentment and open hostility. In his report of February 13, 1899, to the Adjutant General, Richardson wrote:

> The old miners and pioneers of Circle have been so long accustomed to settle all their affairs by so-called "miners" meetings, which more properly might be called, in most instances, mere mob gatherings, that they viewed the advent of troops at Circle with open disfavor, in which feeling they were strongly supported, naturally, by the element of toughs and idlers in the town. I noticed this feeling upon my arrival . . . and made it my endeavor from the first to overcome it among the better class, and to separate the law-abiding from the lawless, and to initiate a sentiment in the community favorable to the establishment of some simple form of town government or administration suitable to the needs of the place.
>
> In pursuance of this policy I requested the citizens and others having business interests in the town to meet me on November the 29th for the purpose of considering the subject of protection against fire, and for the discussion of other matters pertaining to the general welfare of the community.[21]

Although he was interfering in municipal affairs not rightfully his business, Richardson (now Captain Richardson) no doubt congratulated himself on his foresight when a month later the Alaska Commercial Company store caught fire. Circle, unlike Dawson, did not have sophisticated pumps and fire engines. An old iron bell was the town's tocsin. Its fire-fighting apparatus consisted of ingenuity, homemade materials, and volunteer teams. A primitive wagon with buckets, five-gallon tins, and ladders was the fire engine, powered not by steam or horses but by the willing brawn of the first men to respond to the call. According to an extra edition of the *Yukon Press*, the Circle Hook and Ladder Company, under the leadership of President Selden, responded promptly to the ominous clamor of the bell. Soon the entire able-bodied population of the town was gathered at the waterfront conflagration. Captain Richardson was on hand with all available troops. Mrs. Crane, who lived nearby, promptly hung out a hastily scribbled notice inviting all fire fighters to have coffee and food at her place.

Judge Crane, unable to participate in the physical exertions of the bucket brigade, nevertheless brought his own bucket filled with whiskey and, in the parlance of the times, passed around the dipper.[22]

A fire was a social affair bringing the town together, arousing the best in people and for the time erasing petty differences of opinion. Despite the whiskey and the fact that some took advantage of the Judge's generosity to get drunk, the Circle Hook and Ladder Company remained true to its high purpose. The following day, Manager Wheaton of the Alaska Commercial Company presented President Selden with a bottle of good drinking whiskey "for not touching a drop during the fire although it was available for those who needed it and many who did not need it but took the occasion to get drunk."

Encouraged by his fortunate choice of subjects for his first meeting, Richardson called a second meeting to consider raising money for the expense of certain necessary sanitary measures, such as opening drains and removing garbage, and also for the care of destitute citizens. But he had gone too far. At a third meeting, the town turned out in force. By majority vote, they rejected, as Captain Richardson plaintively reported, "not only the plan submitted, but all other plans which might have for their object the establishment of any form or phase of town government whatsoever; one of the opposition remarking that they had entirely too much law and government in the town already."

Circle was the way the stampeders liked it, a town adjusted to individualism. It was a typical American frontier mining town in which law was not taken too seriously. Not that law wasn't respected, and not that it wasn't enforced even more stringently at times than under the Mounties in Canadian territory. It was only that the American miners did not take law with the same serious intent as Canadians. They did not accept law as something handed down from a higher source in which all authority was vested. It stemmed from them. It existed for their benefit and would benefit them only so long as they made it work. So they made it work, but it was a familiar process, nurtured in their hands, with which they were at ease.

American sourdoughs coming from Dawson looked forward eagerly to visiting Circle City, a real American town. After a year or two spent in Canada, kept in line by the Mounties, badgered by

Canadian laws and regulations, being treated as foreigners by Canadian officials, it was like coming home to land at Circle and not see any Mounties around or have to check in with Canadian officials or pay Canadian taxes. It was an American city, where a feller could have fun and get drunk and be a mite boisterous among his own people, who understood that kind of thing. It was an American city that took the side of an American against Canadian officialdom. Even a robber laden with gold dust stolen from the Klondike mines was made to feel welcome, and every opportunity provided the truant to divest himself of his gold.

Senator Lynch was robbed in Dawson by his cook, who turned up shortly in Circle City. The Canadian police followed him, were able to identify the robber, and prove his guilt. Since Senator Lynch was an American with some influence in Washington, he managed to recover some of his gold dust, but Circle City officials refused to extradite the cook, who was allowed his liberty without penalty as an example to others who might wish to bring gold to Circle in this manner. Another robber brought $40,000 in gold dust, which he gladly squandered in the gambling saloons and dance halls, while the Canadian police were rebuffed in their attempts to recover either the gold or the culprit.[23]

Neither Ray nor Richardson, trained in military conformity, could ever appreciate the psychology of the stampeders. To them, these miners were an unruly mob to be viewed with suspicion. Newcomers from the outside, disenchanted Klondikers who had found all the best diggings staked and had come downriver to Circle, old-timers from Forty Mile on the drift, hangers-on in the whiskey wallows, the girls, and the miners' meetings with their raw gusto of life were viewed by Ray and Richardson as anarchy to be controlled. To them, an affair like the case of Carolina May was an anathema. It represented all that was wrong with the Yukon.

May was a black girl from South Carolina with a quick temper and a strong sense of personal dignity. Falling out with a stampeder who had been sharing her bed and board, she kicked him out of the house with instructions not to return if he didn't want his throat cut from ear to ear. Not content with this, she then brought a suit against her former paramour, demanding $2,200 for boarding his dogs and for bodily services. The miners, as was customary, met and elected Mr. McConnell as judge. McConnell was a man of great gravity, who took his position with deadly seriousness. Indeed, so much authority did he invest in his elective office that during the brief course of his appointment he gave American citizenship to three French-Canadians for an ounce of gold each. The trial went into session. The jury was chosen and arguments heard. At the end of the presentations by the two sides, the jury retired to the back room of a saloon, where the members proceeded to get gloriously drunk. In this mellow mood they reached a verdict, and staggering back to the courtroom, the foreman announced it as the will of the jury that they found for the plaintiff but that the amount claimed was excessive. The defendant should be fined but the plaintiff should be assessed the costs of the case, including the expense of alcohol consumed by the jury. In the glow of Solomon-like self-righteousness at the delicate balance of equity struck, they retired from the scene of their deliberations to a neighboring saloon, where they continued to celebrate their judicial achievement. Sometime that night and many rounds of whiskey later, an idea occurred to one of the jurors, which was put to vote and approved unanimously. The idea was simple and one which commended itself to the humor of the times.

There were three things mighty scarce in any mining community—candles, windows, and stovepipes. Probably stovepipes were as scarce as anything because of their bulk and weight. The idea as it occurred to Charley Mower, a member of the jury who could barely stand without hanging onto the bar, was that if they could create a kind of friction, like, for example, making it appear that the judge was trying to steal May's stovepipe, why then May, being the hot-tempered critter she was, might take off after the judge and give him what-ho without his knowing why. The prospect at any time would have appealed to the miners' sense of humor. Under the conditions of alcoholic myopia, it was positively hilarious. The twelve men staggered out into the night, found themselves a long pole, and managed somehow to get themselves to May's cabin. A couple of them hanging onto one end of the pole struck the stovepipe on top of the cabin, while others yelled, "Come down off there, Judge. Don't steal May's stovepipe." After doing this sufficiently to make sure May got the message, the jurors retired with a warm glow of accomplishment. Sure enough, come morning, while the judge was still in bed, May rushed into his cabin and started beating the hell out of him, all the while berating him for a scoundrel and a thief, who not only denied a woman her just demands in court but then would turn around and try to steal her stovepipe at night.[24]

Women were usually treated with more consideration, as in the case when the appointed clerk of the town called a miners' meeting as the sole legislative, judiciary, and executive body in the community. The hurriedly convened body met in front of Jack McQuesten's store on the banks of the Yukon. A chairman was selected. He then demanded of the clerk the reason for the meeting. The clerk explained that an occasion had arisen which allowed him no alternative. Someone had settled on a piece of land set aside for town purposes. He, the town clerk, acting in accordance with the miners' law had warned said person several times to vacate the land. Despite such warnings, said person, with full knowledge, was proceeding to erect a log house. A tall stampeder with a voice of authority asked for and was given recognition by the chair. He proceeded to argue with logic and quiet reasonableness that since the person had acted in defiance of the rules adopted by the miners' meeting, which were the accepted laws of the community, the meeting had no alternative but to invoke punishment suitable to the crime. He proposed that to set a good example in the establishment of law and order the person should be either fined or put aboard a boat and set afloat on the river. The clerk tried to get the attention of the chair unsuccessfully. The process of miners' justice set in motion was not to be stemmed. The motion was put to a vote and adopted. Only then did the clerk manage to be heard. "I should add," he said, "that the person in question is Kitty Brown."

In the silence that greeted this turn of events, the tall miner with the commanding voice again addressed the meeting, pointing out with obvious rationality that no one wanted to quarrel with a woman and anyhow there was plenty of land for public purposes. To his previous motion, he offered an amendment that Kitty be let alone. The amendment was carried without dissent and the meeting adjourned.[25]

The worst crime that could be committed on the Yukon was robbery. Murder might be justified. Other crimes could be condoned. But thievery was unforgivable to every stampeder who had worked his way into the country, carrying a thousand or two thousand pounds of equipment over every foot of exhausting trail. A sign nailed to the dining cabin near Circle City epitomized the normal attitude:

NOTICE

To Whom it May Concern

At a general meeting of miners held in Circle City it was the unanimous Verdict that all thieving and stealing shall be punished by WHIPPING AT THE POST AND BANISHMENT FROM THE COUNTRY, *the severity of the whipping and the guilt of the accused to be determined by the Jury.*

SO ALL THIEVES BEWARE[26]

Oddly enough, in a country where drinking was generally accepted as a necessity, the selling of whiskey to Indians was probably the second most serious offense. As previously noted, in Forty Mile the miners passed a decree of banishment or execution by hanging of anyone caught selling liquor to an Indian. But extenuating circumstances could save a man, as they saved Thomas Davis, an Australian, who traveled from Lost Preacher Creek to Circle. He wrote later:

I wanted to reach Circle as soon as possible and had to leave Lost Preacher Creek alone. It was nearly fifty below and the trail was known as a roundabout way, although there was one straight trail only known to the Indians. For the first hundred miles I traveled all alone, passing several fellows who would not go on fast with me. When about one hundred miles out, I met two Indians who were fighting. I calmed them down and, as they had a fast dog team, asked them to take me to Circle assuring them that I would give them anything they asked for if they did. They were out hunting and did not want to go back to Circle, but I told them I would give all the whiskey they could drink if they would take me in. Finally I got them to take me and the next morning I started out with the Indians and team but we had to break trail all the way for the Indians were taking me the shortest way and incidentally the one least used.

When about two days out from Circle there came some unusually cold weather and threatened to freeze us all. The Indians slept at night, but I would not trust myself and tried to keep awake all night. Some time in the night I went to sleep for a short time and my parka caught fire and left me just the head piece. Such was the way I had to travel the next day and the thermometer was down near sixty below. The next day and night by using all the furs, clothes, etc., I could find I managed to get through the night without freezing. The next day they told me we had just thirty miles to go. We had come to the big trail again and I was acquainted here. I told them I would go on ahead and have a supper ready for them and so I did. On arriving in Circle I ordered a big supper for three and true to my promise I got several bottles of whiskey. The Indians arrived when the supper was ready and we all had a big and deserving dinner. When we were through I showed them the whiskey and they each took a bottle and disappeared. Later on in the hotel, the Indians came back, the whiskey gone, and feeling kind of good. They were followed however by big Ed Wickersham, Marshal of Circle. I did not know about the law of giving liquor to Indians and the Marshal kindly informed me what I meant by giving liquor to Indians, that it was against the law. However, I gave him a sad story of how the Indians had saved my life from sure freezing to death and starvation. He balked around a while and then advised me that next time he would soak me good.[27]

Hatless Bob Truesdale almost got into serious trouble over allegedly selling liquor to Indians, and would have, except for a legal technicality. He was accused of selling whiskey to Indians. A jury was impaneled and his trial set before the commissioner. A bottle of whiskey which had belonged to Hatless and found in the possession of certain Indians was the principal evidence. After the jury retired, they called for the bottle of whiskey to check its contents. Each juryman sampled the bottle to satisfy himself that it was what the prosecution claimed. When the test was completed so was the whiskey. The bottle was empty. The foreman of the jury then called on his peers for a verdict, which obviously had to be, "guilty." But one of the more technically minded jurors objected. "On what evidence?" he wanted to know.

"Why, on the evidence of this here whiskey," the foreman said.

The objecting juror shook his head. "The evidence is missing," he pointed out. "There just ain't any. I move the accused be acquitted for lack of evidence." The simple truth of the point was obvious to all and so the accused was acquitted for lack of evidence.

If the hospitality of giving liquor to Indians was a crime, other forms of hospitality and generosity were so commonplace as to be considered a way of life, not a virtue. The latchstring was always out, literally as well as figuratively. The latchstring is a piece of rawhide, usually attached to a latch on the inside of a cabin door. It passes through a hole in the door so that it hangs outside, acting in lieu of doorknobs, which were unknown in the primitive cabins. A pull on the latchstring released the latch and opened the door. If an occupant of a cabin did not wish to be disturbed, he simply pulled the latchstring inside and the door was barred; but this was never done. A lonely man on the trail could always pull the latchstring on a cabin, knowing he would be welcome if the occupant were at home, or he could make himself a fire and build a meal with what was available if the owner should be away.

Slaven was a possible exception. It was not that he did not observe the rule of the latchstring. He did. But he was not known for his generosity. He was tight. Slaven ran a roadhouse between Circle and Eagle, and for two dollars served a meal with surly reluctance. A rabbit stew at Slaven's could be expected to be stretched to the point of tastelessness with the repeated addition of water. When he came to Circle for supplies, he complained bitterly of the high prices and bargained over every cent he spent.

One day he came into Circle, where he stayed at Mrs. Olsen's roadhouse. Breakfast was fifty cents, but Slaven felt this was entirely too much. He took such a charge as a personal affront. Someone was trying to take him and he wasn't about to be took. Mrs. Olsen finally said, "All right, Mr. Slaven. I'm out of bacon. If you will go to N. C. Company and get me a pound of bacon, I'll give you breakfast for twenty cents."

Grumbling that this was more like it, Slaven went off for the pound of bacon. She thanked him and gave him his breakfast for twenty cents. When he asked for the money he had spent for bacon and heard that the bargain was breakfast for twenty cents and a pound of bacon, his blood pressure hit an all-time high, which was not helped by being the butt of the hilarity of other people present.[28]

The *Yukon Press*, in its first regular issue in March 1898, listed five general stores in Circle, two jewelers, two physicians, two dentists, and a hospital to be opened in the spring. The editor was Sam Dunham, poet laureate of Alaska, statistical expert of the United States Department of Labor, and special agent for the twelfth census of Alaska. He got out the paper with the help of the Outcast Club and its honorary member, Joaquin Miller, who had been sent to the Yukon to do a special series for the *San Francisco Examiner*. By the beginning of 1899 Circle's white population was 625, including 65 soldiers, 32 women, and 7 children. There were 26 Indians.[29]

When the steamer, *Yukoner*, arrived on June 14, Circle City was still the largest log-cabin city in Alaska, but its decline had set in. The Nugget Saloon had its faro table, roulette table, and blackjack table, but they were covered with canvas to protect them from the dust. Behind the blackjack table, the legend informed players, "Dealer stands on 17 but draws to 16." But the dealer had gone to Dawson. The row of log cabins were still occupied by young dance-hall girls smiling from open windows, but the visitors were becoming infrequent. However, to the crew of the *Yukoner*, which had wintered a thousand miles downriver in an isolated side stream, Circle was a lively and exciting place. Visitors from the town were entertained aboard the ship. Eugene Schmitz, a musician from San Francisco, who had joined the steamer at Fort Yukon, composed and sang a parody of *On the Banks of the Wabash*, which he called *On the Banks of the Yukon:*

> Oh, there is a river in Alaska called the Yukon,
> About which some fool author wrote a song,
> But he surely must have been dreaming,
> Or else his imagination proved him wrong.
>
> Why the water in that river is so shallow,
> The fish stand on their heads to swim,
> The mosquitos are so thick along the Yukon
> You have to wear an armor made of tin.
>
> Oh, the midnight sun shines bright along the Yukon,
> Upon its banks there is never ending day.
> Through the pine trees the never setting sun is gleaming,
> On the banks of the Yukon, far away.[30]

No doubt the verse was mercifully forgotten before the lyricist became mayor of San Francisco two years later.

The summer of 1899 saw the growth of Eagle at the expense of Circle. Despite Captain Richardson's report that Circle was the most important town in the American Yukon and would continue to be for some time because of the neighboring gold fields, he was

instructed to move the post to Eagle and start work on Fort Egbert. When this move was completed and with the return of
Major Ray at the end of July, Eagle became the military command
post for North Alaska. With the selection of Eagle for the headquarters of the Third Judicial District of Alaska and the customs
station, the prominence of Circle was doomed. By September 15,
1899, the white population of Circle was down to fifty-five.

Circle City has changed little since then, except it is quieter,
smaller. But there are still those who recall its days of glory. Petite,
attractive Mary Warren, who, with her husband, runs the restaurant, store, post office, gasoline pump, and tourist cabins, is the
great-granddaughter of the first woman in Circle, half-Russian and
half-Indian, who left the gold discoverer, Cherosky, to marry Dan
Callahan. Her grandfather was a Dane from Wrangell, who
bought all the saloons in Circle when prohibition went into effect
in 1918, so that he ended up with the largest stock of liquor in
Alaska. One of his purchases, the Principal Saloon, is the present
store. Her great-great aunt, Helen Callahan, a daughter of Cherosky, is still around, a charming and delightful spinster, who was
baptized by Archdeacon McDonald. She moved to Circle when it
was founded, but spoke only Russian and Indian until she went to
the mission school at Forty Mile. A spritely eighty-seven or so, she
looks as though she had never had a sick day in her life, but she
admits to having been a sickly child. She recalls the medicine men
and the women who would come when she was sick. They would
sing and lay their hands on her feverish brow or on a spot that hurt
and take away the sickness. She had seen the medicine men, after
making their incantations, draw something small and wiggly from
a person's body, thus exorcising evil. There were no doctors then,
she says, we had no choice. We had to believe in the medicine
men, and we did believe, and we were cured.

Circle City is little more today than a period to the road Captain W. R. Abercrombie was commissioned in 1883 to map from
Valdez to the Yukon; it was not completed until 1927. Staked in
the mud shore of the Yukon is a large sign. In the center of the
sign is a map of Alaska, and beneath the map is lettered, "The
End of the Road." This is the road Abercrombie never built from
the coast to the Yukon, the all-American route from the ocean to
the gold fields. Across the top of the map is "Welcome to Circle
City."

Most visitors, by the time they reach this welcome, have passed through Circle City and, if not alert, would not know it. There is little left to mark Circle except this sign, a few desultory buildings, and an outhouse fronting on the river. Of the boisterous, hopeful, or frustrated thousands who passed through Circle, there remain but a few score. Gone is the dream of metropolitan greatness when Circle expected to surpass New York; forgotten are Cherosky and Pitka, the golden fable of Preacher's Creek, and the three Boston adventurers who started the stampede to Birch Creek. No evidence remains of Captain Richardson's post, of Leroy Napoleon Mc-Questen and his famous barometer, of "Hootch" Albert, or the golden-hearted girls who peopled the little cabins. A single store, a few houses, and a sawmill line the bank like debris left by the spring flood when the ice breaks in the Upper Ramparts. Even the name is now meaningless, the Arctic Circle is ninety miles north of Circle City.

10

Nome, the Most Exciting Stampede Town

THE LAST STAMPEDE included strikes from one end of Alaska to the other. Gold was found on the slopes of the Brooks Range above the Arctic Circle and on the southern coast of the territory along the Gulf of Alaska. It was found on the creeks spilling across the eastern border out of Canada and on the westernmost peninsula that reaches into the Bering Sea to within a few miles of Asia. About the same year Archdeacon McDonald is supposed to have seen gold on what was to become Preacher's Creek, Daniel B. Libbey, an American, found gold on the Seward Peninsula. Like McDonald, Libbey was not looking for gold. He was involved with digging postholes for a telegraph line to be strung across Russian America two years before the American acquisition of the territory. Thus the antecedents for two of the major strikes in Alaska—strikes leading to the founding of Circle and Nome—occurred while the country still belonged to Russia.

The telegraph line was the dream of Perry McDonough Collins, who envisaged a global communications network connecting Europe, Asia, North America, and South America. Because of the repeated failures to lay a cable under the Atlantic, Collins proposed to the Western Union Telegraph Company that a telegraph line be run from California across British Columbia, down the Yukon, through Russian America to the Bering Strait, under the water of this narrow gap to Siberia, and on to the capitals of Europe. Feeder lines would reach down to the trading centers of China, and later to India, and southeast Asia. A subsidiary company to the Western Union, known as the Collins Overland Route, was formed to develop this project. Treaties were negotiated with Great Britain and Russia to allow the construction of the telegraph line across western Canada and through Alaska. Russia was to construct the trans-Siberian section of the line.

Daniel Libbey was a member of the initial party of men sent north to lay out the line eastward from the Bering Strait to the Yukon. It was while he was on this assignment in 1865 that he found traces of gold along the Niukluk River. He mentally microfilmed the knowledge and filed it away in his mind to be used thirty years later.

With the abandonment of the Collins Overland Route in 1867 and the withdrawal of the crews, little was heard of the Seward Peninsula until 1888. That year two men, reported simply as King and Green, panned fine gold on the bars of Fish River, between the Niukluk and the beaches of what was to be Nome. Failing to find any good prospects, they operated a silver mine before drifting on. Six years later a Norwegian by the name of Johannsen, anglicized to Joe Hansen, prospecting along the old Collins Overland Route, found good color on the Niukluk. And another two years found Libbey back on the Seward Peninsula. He was a man of mature years now. He brought partners and equipment. They organized the Eldorado Mining District, and before the Niukluk froze that year he had mined $75,000 in gold. This was 1896, and $75,000 was far more than Carmack took out of the Bonanza that same year. If it had not been for the large numbers of men in the upper Yukon to develop the Klondike area so dramatically during the first year, the great rush of 1897-98 might have been to Nome, instead of Dawson. But there were few men near the Niukluk or on the Seward Peninsula, so that it was nearly three years later before Nome came into focus. When it did, as a city it was bigger, more exciting, rowdier than Dawson. The gold harvest was not as great, but it seemed to be everywhere. A newcomer stepped ashore and he was up to his gumboots in gold-bearing sand.

The country was different, but men were the same. Writers who described the upper Yukon as grim and inhospitable never saw the Bering Sea coast. The upper Yukon is mountainous—with forests, sparkling streams, lush fields of grass and flowers—and cold, but a dry, still cold. Along the Bering Sea, the cold damp of the arctic sifts in from the ocean across an overcast land. It is a barren, open country with no apparent soft, seducing qualities. But seduce men it did with its very challenge. The loners, the adventurers, the individualists found what they sought, or enjoyed what they found. The deep cold when food froze between plate and mouth was considered remarkable, not horrible. Storms and parties were of equal interest, as they were to George Russell Adams, who, like Libbey, was a young crew chief in the employ of the Collins Overland Route. To him, Christmas in camp in 1866 was a feast—"Vegetable soup made from preserved vegetables boiled all day. Grouse stewed and accompanied with a delightful gravy. Stewed tomatoes and peas. Two noble puddings as large as water pails and weighing from fifty to seventy-five pounds made from flour and dried applesauce tied up in a bag and boiled with two pounds of sugar." Christmas called for a little extravagance; so in addition to the puddings, they had a huge berry pie. However, having used so much of their scarce sugar in the puddings and believing the berries would be sweet enough, the cooks used no sugar in the pie. Adams, normally a good trencherman, wrote: "Each person ate but one mouthful. Know now what an alum or vinegar pie would taste like."

In his diary account of the year spent with the Collins Overland Route, Adams foresaw that the extravagance of the Christmas feast would mean future shortages, but he did not realize how soon he would feel the pinch. By New Year's Day short rations caused him social embarrassment. A paradox of the North is that where there is apparently no life, there is life. A stark ice floe will house seals or a bear. The desolate tundra is a mass of small flowers, insects, and birds. Along the lifeless coast of the Bering Sea are Eskimo villages, and one of the villages was near the camp of the telegraph crew. The Eskimos had already learned from the Russians that New Year's Day was a special occasion when calls were made and hospitality tendered. As crew chief, Adams had to receive callers and provide something from his limited larder. The camp cook suggested giving guests bread, since that was one item they still had in some quantity. Another advised providing a dish of molasses as something sweet and sticky, which the Eskimos were bound to like. Adams set out both. After three callers had refused the hospitality and left obviously disappointed, Adams asked and was told that bread and molasses was a poor substitute for the pieces of seal fat given to callers by the village chief. Mortified by his inability to provide something better, Adams abandoned his social post. He wrote later, "I hung an empty nail keg to the door knob for cards and left."

But the food shortage became more critical by the end of the month. The crew was down to bean soup twice a day, with a little bread and weak tea. Once a week a ham or canned beef was issued. The spurned molasses was finished. All sugar, coffee, canned vegetables, applesauce, and desiccated potatoes were gone. In a country where men required twice as much food as normal to maintain energy because of the cold, Adams noted that his men instead of double had barely half normal rations.

Inadequate food supplies remained a constant problem throughout the winter, but despite this, George Adams' diary is a sanguine account of an interesting life. When the thermometer registered fifty below zero, he entered in his diary, "It is pleasant weather to travel in." A week later he enters as an interesting commentary rather than as a complaint: "I could not get near the fire to eat supper. As the result, my beans were frozen before I had half eaten supper. The tea was frozen tight." To young men who had signed up of their own volition to work in Russian America, fifty below zero, bean-freezing weather when boiling tea froze into a solid block before it could be sipped, was not a tragic circumstance. It was all part of the adventure which brought them into the country. Storms, gales, and blizzards were also a part of the reality of the North.

On February 7, 1867, a storm which had been threatening Adams' crew for some days broke. The fine snow whipped into their faces with the blinding force of a sandstorm. Visibility was less than ten feet. Adams ordered the men to close ranks as they broke trail toward the point where they planned to make camp. Each man was to walk close enough to touch the next man. If a person faltered, he was to hit the man ahead and so down the line alerting the group to stop immediately. Without this precaution, a man who fell back would be lost. As they were muffled to their eyes and with the wind screaming around them, any attempt at oral communications was impossible; and outside of the ten-foot radius a man was invisible, his tracks immediately obliterated.

Fortunately, they were almost at their destination when the storm hit, and soon, more by instinct than reason, Adams led his party into the small Eskimo community where they had planned to make camp. He ordered the men to fall out and gather spruce bows from the spindly trees growing in the area. But they refused, numbed to the bone, and afraid of getting lost in the swirling white shroud. Instead, they accepted invitations from the Eskimos and crawled into two small huts, where they collapsed on the earthen floors. George Adams, in an attempt to project his authority, refused to accept hospitality. Building a rude shelter in the snow, he made his own camp outside; but after two days of continuous blizzard, even he felt that the need to preserve his position was not as important as seeking shelter. He crawled into a small house which, though only ten by twelve feet in size, housed sixteen Eskimos and eleven dogs.

One night was enough for him, and by this time his men also had had enough of the Eskimo quarters. They emerged into the storm that had abated only a little and under Adams' supervision completed a camp of their own. It was not much of a shelter, only a lean-to three feet high and twenty-four feet long by twenty-four feet in depth. Made of spruce boughs, the protection was not complete, but the ventilation, after the reeking conditions of the Eskimo houses, was welcome.

With such primitive quarters, the blizzard still screaming across the open countryside, enforced inactivity, and scant rations, one would have expected serious morale problems. Such was not the case. These men had come north for adventure, and this was adventure, not a hardship. In these conditions, Adams still maintained his diary; and it was not the roar of the wind, the cold, or the constant presence of hunger that made the task difficult as he wrote this entry: "All the boys in good spirits. All laughing and singing and making so much noise that I can hardly write. Clark is teaching Lunchy English. Charley Pease joking about our living conditions said, 'Wish I had my uncle Lem's pig sty up here to live in. I would have better quarters than any in this country.' "

But they had a job to do, and they could not remain inactive long. With the first break in the weather they were back in the countryside. The snow had to be scraped from the ground and holes chopped into soil frozen as hard as granite. Poles iced to the snow had to be pried loose and manhandled into place. Despite

Gold was on the beaches of Nome. Step ashore and start digging.
Women as well as men could do it. (E. A. HEGG)

Valdez is the northernmost ice-free port of Alaska. The new
town was built on rock instead of alluvial fill after the
1964 earthquake.

these working conditions peculiar to the subarctic and despite the few hours of daylight, they managed to set nearly a half-mile of poles a day.

As they moved ahead, they could see behind them a line of dark poles etching a streak across the white landscape, and they took pride in their accomplishment. They were achieving a first in history, connecting the civilization of the Western Hemisphere, connecting their own great United States with the older civilzations of Europe. It was their job and their accomplishment. It was a personal thing, not the achievement of the Collins Overland Route. By April 26 Adams wrote: "Most men unable to work. Hard work no grub. We are almost completely out of provisions, only a little tea and bran is all we have to live on." Somehow, they went on, working in a void of silence, accentuated by the constant presence of the mute telegraph poles. They had heard nothing, knew nothing of what was happening outside. With neither ship, nor mail, nor courier, they remained ignorant of two important events that had occurred. One was to have a personal and immediate impact upon them, the other would have a less immediate impact but would be more dramatic.

Not until June 26 were they to learn of these events. On that day, their camp was set up on an inlet near the coast. The sun had just dipped below the horizon to mark the night which by now was like daytime. Adams' friend, Dennison, came running up to his tent as Adams sat writing. He was in a state of extreme excitement. The bark *Andrae* was out on the bar. It was low tide and she could not get in until the next day. Dennison wanted to row out immediately, just for the fun, he explained, in an attempt to conceal his youthful excitement. But Adams was equally excited by the news. This was their first contact with the outside world since their arrival.

The two young men hurried to the shore and pushed off in a rowboat. As they climbed aboard, they were met by Mr. Bean, the company storekeeper at the St. Michael supply depot. There Bean had been the recipient of news; now he was to be the purveyor, and he relished the occasion to its utmost. Instead of coming directly out with what he had heard, he backed into the news. "You fellers are all through," he said. "Yup, you're to pack up and come aboard."

The first thought of both Adams and Dennison was that they

had been fired. The company was dissatisfied with their efforts. The line of poles that they had worked so hard to set up under such terrible difficulties was unappreciated. They were both downcast and angry. Without being given a chance to explain how much they had done and under what conditions, they were to be replaced by some newcomers unacquainted with the country or the methods of work required.

Having given his simple statement a chance to have the required effect, Mr. Bean explained that the steamship *Clara Bell* had arrived at St. Michael from San Francisco. It seemed that after five unsuccessful attempts, a cable had finally been laid under the Atlantic. The Collins Overland Route was no longer needed. The company had suspended all operations. The work of the young men was for nothing.

Then, to compensate for this bad news, Bean pointed to the mast of the *Andrae*, where it was customary to fly the flag of the host country when in port. "What do you think of that?" he asked.

Puzzled, Adams said he didn't understand.

"No Russian flag," Bean said. "We're in American waters. The United States has bought Russian America."

"Bought it?" Adams was incredulous.

"Yup. Lock, stock, furs, and Indians."

"Let's get ashore and tell the men," Dennison said. Adams was equally anxious to break the news, but first he got a sack and filled it with bacon, coffee, sugar, canned milk, and real potatoes, not desiccated ones.

That night, after the excitement had died down, after they all had had their fill of potatoes and bacon fried together and washed down with cup after cup of coffee loaded with sugar and milk, Adams and Dennison sat on the gentle slope overlooking the inlet. It was sometime between midnight and dawn. There had been no darkness and wouldn't be for another couple of weeks. They recalled shared experiences from the past winter—the time they had been lost in a snowstorm, how great they felt the day they planted seventeen poles in two hours—and they talked about going home, San Francisco, where they would eat the first night and what they would have. Perhaps, Adams thought, he would come back after a visit home now that this was American country. He would like to go up the Yukon, or Kwikpak, as he knew it. There was supposed to be gold up there. A couple of the boys, Ketchum and Labarge, had been sent up the river on a survey mission. He might see them at St. Michael or on the boat shipping out and find out about the country from them. Dennison's reaction was more prosaic. It was California here I come, and he was not going to leave it again.[1]

Dennison did not come back, nor did Adams. Labarge did, and Bean stayed on. Both became traders along the Yukon and its tributaries. But with the end of the Collins Overland Route, Seward Peninsula was forgotten, except for the occasional prospector, until Libbey returned with his remembrance of gold on the Niukluk. With his return, the stage was set for the drama that was Nome.

H. L. Blake was one of the men associated with Daniel Libbey. After the summer operations on the Niukluk were completed, he decided to make an exploratory trip to Cape Nome to see if other good prospects could be located. With him he took Nels C. Hultberg, a Swedish missionary at the Eskimo village of Cheenik. The trip was a success, in some ways too successful. Blake found gold and, as a result, is credited with the discovery of gold in the Nome area. Hultberg also found gold—heavy, gravel-rich deposits—on Anvil Creek, which was to Nome what Bonanza Creek was to Dawson. And he did not tell Blake, though why he did not is not clear. There was Hultberg's version of the trip and his difficult relationship with Blake, and there was Blake's version. The two differed in many respects. Whichever version one accepts, the truth is that Hultberg did not tell Blake of the great potential of Anvil Creek which was a sin in the prospectors' code, inducing Blake to refer to his former companion as that sly, crafty, avaricious, God-fearing, Eskimo-loving missionary.

Whether Hultberg was motivated by personal dislike of Blake, whether he wished to keep the resources of the country for its native people, or whether he had some other conscious or subconscious reason for dissembling, he did subsequently reveal the rich potential of Anvil, the original name of Nome, to three fellow-countrymen, Eric Lindblom, John Brynteson, and Jafet Lindeberg. Lindblom was a former tailor from San Francisco. Brynteson had worked in coal and iron mines in Michigan before reaching Alaska in search of coal. The youngest of the trio was twenty-one-year-old Jafet Lindeberg, who had come to Alaska as one of the men in charge of the reindeer imported by

Sheldon Jackson to augment the food supply of the country. The three men, known as the Three Lucky Swedes, formed a partnership and went up the Snake River, at whose mouth today is the city of Nome. They staked claims on Glacier, Anvil, Snow, Rock, Dry, and Dexter creeks. Under the name of the Pioneer Mining Company of Seattle, they consolidated their holdings.

The Lucky Swedes did not depend on luck. They were lucky to be on the Seward Peninsula in 1898, and they were lucky to know Hultberg, but there the luck ended. They employed cunning, guile, and shrewdness—not always ethical but still shrewdness. And they stuck together, helping each other and themselves in turn. Together, they were instrumental in organizing the Cape Nome Mining District, incorporating in the rules of organization permission to locate claims by power of attorney, which made it possible for them to gain control of most of the rich areas in the district. They filed forty-three claims in their own names and forty-seven others through powers of attorney. They took practical steps to gain support for these lax rules. They saw to it that the commissioner at St. Michael and the commanding officer of troops stationed there had between them one hundred claims obtained through powers of attorney, thus assuring that the civil and military authorities would be prejudiced in favor of preserving the status quo.

Miners, who arrived too late to participate in organizing the Cape Nome Mining District, became angry when they found all the best claims staked by the Lucky Swedes. At first they decided to seize the claims by force and restake them, but subtler minds prevailed. They would call a miners' meeting and invoke the law of the land. According to the law no aliens could stake claims on American soil. The Scandinavians had not taken out papers or declared their intention of becoming American nationals. Although there was no court or legal representative in the area before whom such a declaration of intent could be made, the law was the law. A group of claimless miners was stationed on Anvil Hill, eight miles from the proposed meeting place and adjacent to some of the richest claims belonging to the Swedes. The plan was to make a motion that Lindeberg, Lindblom, and Brynteson as aliens had improperly staked claims on American soil. All claims held in their own names or through power of attorney should be declared illegal. As soon as the motion was passed, a huge pile of firewood stacked outside the meeting place would be ignited. When the men stationed on Anvil Hill saw the fire, they would restake the claims.

The luck of the Swedes seemed about to run out, but their shrewdness in involving the military saved them. Lieutenant Spaulding, using his troops with fixed bayonets, broke up the meeting and ordered the miners to disperse, advising them against trying to take the law into their own hands.

Fortunately for the peace of the area, soon thereafter gold was discovered along the beach at the mouth of the Snake River. Anyone with a shovel, a bucket, and a rocker could get gold, easy gold, lying there in the sand of the beach. All thoughts of claim jumping were forgotten. Two thousand miners were soon at work on the beaches. In little over a month more than a million dollars worth of gold was taken from the sands along the waterfront of what is now Nome.

News of these strikes was at first discounted. Rumors of stampedes were rife throughout Alaska. People had become suspicious. Walter Curtin, on his way to Dawson with his father, was frozen in along the Yukon during the winter of 1898–99. In February his father received a letter from the United States marshal in St. Michael, an old Montana friend. The marshal said he had heard of a gold strike at Cape Nome, but thought it a fake. Walter's father didn't believe there was any way of prospecting at this season of the year. To be on the safe side, however, he sent his old friend some powers of attorney, so that if the strike should prove true he could take up some claims for the Curtins.[2]

By september of 1899 there were no doubters. Lieutenant Wallace M. Craigie, writing from St. Michael to the commanding officer at Fort Gibbon, admitted to mining on the side and hoped to strike it rich. He expected thirty thousand people in Nome by the next spring.[3] No mean entrepreneur apparently, Lt. Craigie proudly reported how he augmented the company funds at the expense of the civilian government. There was no jail in St. Michael, and he kept the marshal's prisoners in the army stockade. For this service, he charged the marshal $1 a meal per prisoner. Since he fed the prisoners on pork and beans, of which he had a surplus, he made a nice profit.

Historically, 1898 invokes mental images of the Chilkoot

Pass, the Klondike, and Dawson. Tens of thousands were heading there. But that same year thousands were also making for the Seward Peninsula. On June 12, 1898, a dozen ships were anchored in Dutch Harbor in the Aleutian chain, waiting for reports that the seas and ports to the north were open. The revenue cutter *Bear* was there to make reconnaissance, give assistance, and enforce law where necessary. On a calm evening the buglers of the cutter would give a concert for the passengers of the anchored ships. It was a winy atmosphere, tingling with the expectation of gold and adventure. A young man who was in Dutch Harbor that day wrote: "It is a beautiful scene. The water is still as mercury. The people are all on deck singing and playing music. The buglers from the Revenue Cutter *Bear* gave a concert. With the snow-covered peaks in the background and sun shining on them, it is a memory a man must always carry with him."[4]

The young man was Maurice Hartnett, who had joined the stampede to the west coast of Alaska. He and his party spent the winter on the Kuak River at the northern base of the Seward Peninsula. Winter comes early there. By October 13 the river was full of floating ice, and two days later it was frozen solid. But mining was not just drudgery and hardships to young men of adventurous spirit. They found pleasure where they could find it. Hartnett and his companions took an old whipsaw and made themselves skates, he records in his diary, and on October 16 they skated all day. Nor was it lonely in those days in this region just under the Arctic Circle, when more people were there than there are today. Guests would stop by the little log cabin Hartnett and his partners had built on the banks of the Kuak. One visitor, who spent the night with them on October 23, while getting dressed the next morning, dropped a revolver from his pants and shot himself in the hip. "There will be a guest," notes Hartnett, "for some time longer."

For Thanksgiving the young men planned a celebration feast. A crowd of Indians came in, and they sang and danced the night before Thanksgiving. But as in any group of men, each must take his turn as cook while others mine, and this was Hartnett's week. While the others slept, exhausted from singing and dancing, he had to stay up to get the pies and the cakes ready for the next day.

After the feast, which was probably not unlike the one eaten by Alden Smith on the Klondike, the boys decided they would

like to get weighed. Today that would be an impossibility on the
Kuak, but then there were more amenities in the wilderness. Five
of them took off down the river to visit the schooner *Riley*
that was frozen in. It was twenty below zero, but they had their
skates; they were young, and life was a lark. And Hartnett weighed
a hundred and seventy pounds. They returned up the river shouting and yelling, throwing snowballs, and challenging each other
to races in which anything went—tripping, bumping, tackling—
laughing until they were breathless, as they rolled each other in
the snow like a litter of puppies.

There is nothing in the diary of hardships and discomforts,
of unhappiness with their lot. In an area which would seem to
be one of the most isolated in America, the Hartnett camp had
a constant stream of visitors, guests, and parties. Typical is a
December entry which tells about a number of Eskimo girls who
came to the cabin and played cards all night. Nor was weather
a cause for complaint. A week after the card party with the
Eskimo girls, Hartnett writes of ten degrees below freezing
weather as being so mild they were able to sit in their cabin without a fire and be comfortable.

For these young stampeders it had been an exciting year, and
the new year held promise of being even more exciting. So in
true mining camp style, when the hands of the clock pointed to
twelve midnight on the last day of 1898, all the young men and
the Eskimos who had gathered at the cabin went outside and
fired revolvers in the air. Although Hartnett doesn't mention it
in his laconic recording of the event, they probably also yelled,
howled, beat pans, pranced in the snow, kissed the Eskimo girls,
and ended by joining hands and singing "Auld Lang Syne."

The Kuak is not a long river, and yet in the beginning of
1899 the mail carrier, who took the mail by dog sled to the
miners along its course, reported 769 men there; and with a census
taker's mind for figures or to justify his job, he added that there
were 260 cabins occupied and 37 unoccupied. Men in that country
of harsh winters built a cabin immediately upon staking a claim.
If it then proved a bad claim, they moved on, abandoning the
cabin. Other men might move in and frequently did. There was
more than one cabin at the Hartnett site, and they were occupied
by different people during the winter. A strike at Alashook was

reported that winter, but Hartnett notes that it was started maliciously by men on the river who wanted to leave and had extra provisions they wanted to sell.

These young men on the Kuak were not the rough miners one thinks of as peopling the wild mining camps of the West or the Far North. They were like the young men found in Forty Mile, on the Klondike, along the Stewart, or in the Circle Mining District. They were the kind of men who on March 1, Hartnett writes, had a meeting in the cabin to read Henry George; he adds what must be a blow to scholars. "We exploded the Malthusian theory."

Hartnett and his party did not hear of the gold strike at Cape Nome until April 12, 1899. Considering the report to be of summer diggings of no permanent importance, they paid no attention at first. But news of the Nome strike was percolating up and down the river. The lure of greener pastures, with summer coming on, proved irresistible. Sam Colclove stopped by the cabin on his way from Ambler and talked about the Nome strike. Frank Hertzer came in from the Kotzebue camp on his way to Selawik River to trade for dogs. If he could get them, he said, he was going to Cape Nome. On April 19 Ambrose headed out. A week later seven men passed by on their way from Hunt River. They too were going to Nome. And another party of six from Riley Camp. On April 30 two other parties passed Hartnett's cabin on their way to Nome. A stampede was under way.

Early in May the captain of the schooner *Riley*, sensing the feeling of the men along the river, hired an agent to go up the Kuak advertising that the schooner would be leaving for Nome. Hartnett, who was skeptical of the reports, was not easily stampeded. Instead of abandoning the Kuak, he took off on a prospecting trip up the river. For five days he hiked up and down the headwaters of the Kuak but found nothing worth claiming and returned to his cabin. Having satisfied himself that the Kuak was not a good river for mining, he too was now ready for the *Ka'beruk*, the Eskimo name for the Cape Nome area.

He and his partners packed their belongings. For the last time, they quit the little cabin where they had spent so many pleasant evenings, the little cabin on the Kuak filled with memories they could never share with people on the outside, for only those who had experienced it could understand the happiness to be found in the simple life of a seemingly remote miner's camp, the warmth of companionships based on shared hardships.

With nostalgia mixed with excitement, they set off for new adventure. They made first for the schooner *Riley*, but it was already booked to its last available space. It did not matter. There was the schooner *General McPherson* with available space, and no ships were leaving Kotzebue Sound yet. North of the Bering Strait, summer does not come early. The ice in the bay traps the ships until late in the year.

As they waited for the ice to free the ships, more and more miners arrived from outlying camps. On July 3 twenty-five boats came down the Kuak River. The embarking sites were alive with excitement. Not only was there the thrill of a stampede, but the next day was July 4, and the young men intended a big celebration. The day was opened with shooting and the firing of homemade firecrackers. There were foot races, wrestling, boxing, tug of war, blanket tossing, blubber-eating contests, jumping, and boat races. Hartnett noted that the only excitement was provided during a sailing race when "Burt, Pat, and Herb turned over in their homemade dinghy trying to round a buoy too sharply." The best part of the July 4th celebration, according to Hartnett, was a literary program at two o'clock.

On July 20 the schooner *General McPherson* was at last able to weigh anchor and sail out of Kotzebue Sound bound for Nome. In addition to Maurice Hartnett, who had earned his passage selling tickets, the ship carried sixty paying passengers and fourteen others. When they were three days at sea, the revenue cutter *Bear* hailed them; and when they hove to, came alongside. The commanding officer of the cutter came aboard, placed the captain of the *General McPherson* under arrest for piracy, and put one of his men in charge of the schooner. Unfortunately, there are no further entries in Hartnett's diary concerning the *General McPherson* or its captain. Hartnett was not interested in the troubles of others; his interest was in reaching the Cape Nome District, which he did on July 26, having traveled less than two hundred land miles from his cabin on the Kuak in over two months.

The excitement on the beach was a far different thing from the quiet life on the Kuak. The intoxication of gold was a vital factor of daily existence. As far as the eye could see, men were shoveling and washing sand. Every device conceivable to the ingenuity of man was in use or, having been tried and proved a failure, lay rusting on the beach. No complicated claim procedure was required. A man found a vacant spot on the beach and started digging. Hartnett and his partners wasted no time. They hiked along the beach until they found an empty stretch of sand. They pitched their tents. Within three days of arrival, they panned their first gold, a fine, flour gold, unlike the coarse gold of the stream. In two hours Hartnett made 50¢, not much, but it proved gold was there. The young men chipped in and bought an old rocker for sixty-five dollars. Shoveling, rocking, and carrying water in turns, by August 3 they were getting six to seven ounces of gold a day. On the sixth, they made $154, figuring gold at $10 an ounce. The next day, they made $100, then $80, and $135. This wasn't fabulous wealth, it was not the path to being a millionaire, but it was good money and, more important, it was gold. There is something about gold that triggers the emotions. Of all minerals, only gold, and especially placer gold, can be taken directly from the ground to the bank. It can be put in a poke and used as a medium of exchange.

With experience, Hartnett and his partners improved their take. The richest sands were near the mouth of the Snake River itself, but there was no space there for latecomers. However, for fifteen miles the beach was rich in gold. Gold was found principally in ruby sand, but it was also found in ruby sand mixed with black sand; the richest concentrates were at bedrock, which was only four to eight feet from the surface; but from the water line to the edge of the tundra, stretching from fifty to two hundred feet, any place a man might stick a shovel, he might find gold. All types of machinery could be seen along the beach, but most of it was worthless. A shovel and a rocker were still the most practical means of extracting the gold from the sand for the average man. Only the big combines with financial backing could afford the machinery necessary to make big profits. But they also took big risks. It was a gamble of the total loss of machinery against the need to handle large quantities of sand and earth in the short summer period of one hundred days when mechanical mining was possible. There was the constant peril of storms hurtling in over the Bering Sea. A dredge or unwieldy machinery would be quickly destroyed, unless it could be withdrawn into the shelter of the river by cables or pulled above high-water mark. But with each storm also came fresh concentrates of gold.

One of the partners became sick and took a ship for the outside. Two others, feeling the pangs of homesickness, also decided to go. Hartnett began to experience the pinch of loneliness; the crowds of strangers were no compensation for old friends. And there were thousands of strangers. This was a stampede in which anyone could participate, for here was gold that could be reached with no hardships. There was no Chilkoot to cross, no whipsawing of timber to build boats on Lake Bennett, no Miles Canyon, Whitehorse Rapids, nor hundreds of miles of river to be navigated to reach Dawson, no Valdez trail over glaciers, no Dalton trail stretching hundreds of miles through wilderness, no prolonged trip up the Yukon with the constant threat of being stranded on a sandbar or being frozen in for the winter. A person had only to board a ship in San Francisco or Seattle and disembark on the beach of Nome, and the gold was there ready to be dug. Missing here were the hardships which tried men and made for lasting friendships among those who overcame them. Instead there was squabbling over every inch of the beach, suspicion and jealousy and distrust. A man couldn't urinate where he pleased but had to pay ten cents to use a public latrine. There was no timber along the bleak stretch of coast, and the supplies brought in were inadequate for fuel or building. Tents were erected anywhere and everywhere. An Anvil City council was formed, and the name of the tent town changed to Nome. But little could be or was done about the confusion created by the influx of miners and supplies. Ships anchored off shore and tons of freight were lightered to the beach, where they were dumped for two miles along the water's edge. Machinery of all sorts, supplies of hay, grain, lumber, hardware, provisions, liquor, tents, stoves, sewing machines, mirrors, bar fixtures, and other goods were dumped, and the ships pulled out, steaming south under forced draft for new loads.

With the partnership broken up and old Kuak friends leaving, Hartnett found no appeal in the prospects of another winter in Alaska. The boisterous tent city afforded a poor substitute for the easy friendships and life of the Kuak—visiting among the camps along the river with the warm-hearted Eskimo girls and men, card playing and dancing and singing, and the ice skating. In

Nome pleasure or amusement had a price tag. Dancing was a retail item. So with the end of summer Hartnett also packed and headed outside.

But more came than left, and among the new arrivals on August 23, 1899, were three Australians.⁵ There was Dingo, a small, mean-faced man with a great beak of a nose in his narrow face and a wart on his left ear. His eyes were closer together than they should have been, giving him a tight, sour appearance, but he was actully a kind and generous-hearted person who would give a down-and-outer his last crust of bread or pinch of tea. There was the Swag Man, a huge, dark man with a great bush of black hair and a scar that ran from his scalp to jaw line down the right side of his face. It was rumored to be an old boomerang scar or the result of a spear thrust he had received in Africa, but more likely it was a battle scar from a saloon brawl, for he was a robust, fighting man who enjoyed nothing more than a good free-for-all. When not in fighting mood, he was a hard worker and as gentle as a baby koala. The leader of the trio was Jock, a heavyset, blond man with an open countenance and a broken nose and with more gold in his mouth than in his pockets. He was a humorous man who loved to joke and sing with a group around a campfire. The three men had been together for more years than they would admit. They had met on the stampede to South Africa. Later they had pooled their resources and prospected the Australian gold strike and had done time in the New Zealand gold fields. Now they were in this Godforsaken land, once more following the call of gold that respects neither nationality nor color nor creed and wondering why they had come to this bleak desolation. But they were not men given to unnecessary introspection. Within twenty-four hours of hitting the beach, they had contracted a lay for a piece of beach property, had set up a rocker and were busy with their shovels. They were soon known up and down the beach as "the Diggers." Instead of trying to distinguish between the three, people just called them, "Hey, damn Digger."

The Diggers knew their business and gold mining was their business. They didn't expect great riches. They had been at this too long. They knew that gold mining was hard work, and the man who worked hard could at least make a living. With luck, and they discounted luck because they never had it, he would strike it rich. But no miracles were in their lexicon. By the end of the beach season, when storms drove men away from the shore and the salt water of the Bering Sea froze, they had accumulated enough gold to tide them over the winter and give them a little nest egg for the next year, in case something interesting presented itself.

In the winter when a few men sank holes through the ice near the shore to recover the sand from the sea bottom but most men holed up in their tents, the Diggers were not idle. Geologists had found there was not just one beach, there were other beaches, prehistoric beaches farther inland, a second beach and a third beach, each seemingly richer than the one before. The first inland beach was discovered less than a quarter of a mile from the shore. But the whole of the tundra lying between Nome and the foothills, they said, was mineralized and full of gold being constantly washed into the sea. The Diggers decided to take a walkabout and see the country for themselves. In a cold, gray drizzle, they set out on a swing to the creeks and other gold-mining areas in the region. They went to Council and Teller, looking for an unstaked place that had signs indicating it would be worthwhile to burn a hole down through the frozen tundra. They visited Solomon, the Big Hurrah, Bluff, Iron Creek, Golovin, Omoluk, Haven, Dime, a name which the postal authorities were to reject as an improper use of a monetary unit. They saw Aurora, Candle, Tin City, Asses' Ears, Not River, Dry, and Ophir. But they found nothing. In June when the wash-ups began, they met an old miner who had driven a shaft down on beach number two, and though he had no color to show for his labors, he had not abandoned hope. However, he had injured himself during the winter and needed money badly to take a trip outside. He offered the Diggers a twelve-month lease, but the price would take half their remaining capital. Should they keep their money and go back to the beach for another year or should they take a flyer?

The Swag Man said, "What the hell; we'll never get rich on the beach. What's money for? You take it out of the ground; you put it back."

Dingo agreed. "The old man needs the money. We ought to help him. Maybe we help each other."

The clincher for Jock was Ophir. The mine was near Ophir. Every gold-mining district has an Ophir, a name rich in appeal to miners with its ring of the Arabian Nights, of oriental magnificence. But the name had special significance to Jock. Like many miners, he picked up bits of esoteric information without regard for their authenticity, and in South Africa he had heard that the very name "Africa" had evolved from the Carthaginian "Afur," a corruption of the Hebrew word "Ophir." He had heard, and was willing to repeat as fact, that Ophir was a fabled country in the Zambezi region of central Africa from which came gold and precious stones and rare trees for King Solomon. He would swear as gospel that between the Zambezi and the Sabi rivers in Rhodesia were thousands of old mines and, scattered over seven hundred fifty thousand square miles, ruins of cities, fortresses, and temples bearing evidence of the ancient worship of Baal Ashera and of the civilization that characterized the Himyarites of southern Arabia. One of the dominant features of the country was a mountain called Fura, a name taken by the Portugese from Arab traders who, like the Carthaginians, corrupted it from Hebrew "Ophir." Accordingly, Jock considered it a good omen that the mine was in the vicinity of Ophir.

A deal was made. The Diggers took the lease, bought an old boiler, a set of steam points, and hauled the equipment out to the mine. They purchased fuel and made arrangements for water so they could get up a good head of steam and, with the points, thaw out the face of the drifts below ground.

For nine months the Diggers toiled in their mine, taking turns at the three operations. They would set the points at night and fire the boiler, and during the day one man would tear at the thawed face of the drift, a second hauled the thawed dirt to the mine shaft, where he put it in buckets. The third man, above ground, worked the windlass to haul the dirt to the surface, where it was dumped in a pile. Each night they washed a pan of sample dirt and each night they found little to encourage them.

At the end of nine months their money was running low. They had barely enough left to get out of the country. The Swag Man and Dingo were for leaving. Jock said, no. They had come this far. They had worked this long. They couldn't give up so easily. As usual, Jock's word was the decision. They returned to the mine and continued for another month. Still no sign of pay dirt. Both the Swag Man and Dingo had had it to the teeth. They began talking of pulling out and leaving Jock by himself. But already their funds were too low even to get out of the country. They had barely enough to buy fuel for another thirty days of operating the boiler.

Jock continued to counsel work, but Dingo and the Swag Man said, screw it. So they drew cards. The man with the high card would decide, a decision-making method which gave Dingo and the Swag Man a two-to-one advantage over Jock. Jock preferred it this way. If fate was to be determined by chance, then it was best done against the odds. It had been a hard year. To conserve money for operations, they had skimped on food. Not once since going down in the mine had they knocked off for so much as a day to go into Nome for a blow. This was particularly hard on the Swag Man, who was spoiling for a free-for-all. He was itching to tie one on, go on a real bender. And Dingo had cabin fever bad. He liked people. He reveled in the saloon atmosphere, the loud talking and jostling at the bar, the warm glow of a half-dozen shots of Green River whiskey at the Board of Trade Saloon, where he knew a thirsty man could buy the stuff for 12½¢ a drink. Jock missed all this too. He would have liked to go on the town—the whole lot, from a hot bath, a restaurant-cooked meal, to a real old-fashioned toot. But he was less subservient to his emotions than were his partners. As leader, he knew that now was no time for reason. His partners were in no mood to accept logic, but a decision based on luck would be acceptable.

Dingo drew first—a four of clubs. He swore, a string of harsh, scatological oaths. It was just his luck and only went to prove what chance they had of finding anything in this frozen country.

But the Swag Man drew a king of diamonds, and a big grin displaced the usual frown. "Hot damn," he said. "We're getting out of this place right now. I've had my last of clawing at the damn face down there."

Jock said nothing. He drew a card and flipped it quickly—the ace of spades. "We stay," he said. And stay they did. Somehow the very fact that Jock, the leader, had the luck of the draw gave them fresh hope.

On the twenty-ninth day they had just enough fuel for one more firing and still no show of pay dirt. Jock himself could feel the gloom. It looked as if this was it. But they fired up the boiler for the last time and placed the points for the night. On the morning of the thirtieth day Jock and Dingo went below. It was

Dingo who was working the face, and with the first pick, he let out a great yell. Jock hurried to see what had happened, fearing perhaps there had been a cave-in; but it wasn't that. Dingo was kneeling on the floor of the tunnel, sand and gravel cupped in his hands, sand and gravel glittering with gold. They had found the old beach and pay dirt. Or was it? Maybe it was just an isolated pocket.

Jock grabbed up the pick Dingo had dropped and started hacking away feverishly at the solid earth, but it was no longer just muck. It was sand and gravel with the glitter of gold apparent even without washing. Dingo accompanied Jock back to the mine shaft with the filled wheelbarrow and helped him dump the contents into the square wooden box. They fixed the rope handles over the pigtail, jerked on the rope, and stepped back while the Swag Man hoisted the laden box to the surface. They could hear him swearing as he worked the windlass. It was a heavier load than usual. Dingo and Jock grinned at each other in anticipation of the shout that would greet the contents of this much-cursed load when the Swag Man dumped it on the wash-up pile. Nor were they disappointed.

"Gold." It was hardly more than a whisper. Then a shout, "Gold, gold. Holy Jesus," and the great, shaggy black head appeared at the top of the shaft. "Did you cobbers see that load?" he yelled. "It's almost solid gold. Fair dinkum. Ever-loving, bloody gold."

They yelled back and forth at each other, neither listening nor hearing, venting their excitement. Finally, the Swag Man yelled, "Stand back. I'm lowering the bucket. Get your fat asses in and I'll haul you both out together."

"Not yet," Jock shouted up. "We'll take out enough to make damned sure we have a real pay streak; then we head for town."

Back to the face they went. But it was no longer drudgery. Every pick loosed a cascade of glittering sand. Never had either man seen such a rich digging. They had heard of them; now here it was and it was theirs. Dingo picked up a nugget as big as his thumb and handed it to Jock. "That's yours," he said, "for drawing that ace of spades."

When it was certain that this was not just a freak pocket but the main stream bed, they dropped their tools and headed for topside. The Swag Man was cavorting around like an unleashed sled dog. "That damned town ain't never seen a blow like its going to see tonight," he exulted.

Jock grinned at his big partner and grabbed him around the waist in a bear hug, lifting the bigger man clear off the ground and swinging him around. "Goddamnit, Swag," he said, "you've earned it." Then the light went out of his eyes. His face became serious.

"Oh, no, you don't," said Dingo. He could read the signs. "Not this time you don't Swag is right, goddamnit. We owe our selves a blow and you ain't stopping us."

"Who said anything about stopping you?"

"I can see it in your goddamn face. Me and Swag ain't falling for any of your fast talk this time."

Jock picked up a handful from the dump and watched it glitter as it sifted through his fingers. "You deserve a blow," he said. "We all deserve a blow—," he paused, "but we have just thirty days to go on the lease. What we get out is ours. What we leave down there goes back to the old man. Now if we go on a blow now, first thing, we have to wash up this pile to get some gold for the blow. That'll take us a day. Figure a day for the blow, and then about a week, if we're lucky, before Swag gets out of jail. Why give that gold to the old man? What I say is, we take some of this sand and gravel into town with us. On the strength of that we can borrow enough to buy more fuel and perhaps get another boiler and some more points. While I do that, you two go around and hire all the men you can get. Offer them anything you have to— $5 a day, $10 a day, $15 a day if necessary, and then we get back here and work like we never worked before for thirty days. Then we have a blow this town will never forget."

Dingo and the Swag Man did not like this counsel, but they knew Jock was right. Grudgingly they agreed.

They followed Jock's plan. Money was readily available against the rich pay dirt. An old boiler was found they could rent for a month, and more points. They hired every able-bodied man they could find quickly. Shifts were set up to work around the clock. Two new shafts were sunk over a projection of the beach. Points were doubled and tripled. The boilers were kept fired twenty-four hours a day, moving the points from one face to another while the men below ground cleared out the thawed sand and gravel.

Twenty-four hours a day, seven days a week, the three Diggers drove their men constantly and drove themselves even harder. They cooked for their crews. They fired the boilers. They kept constant watch to see that no one goofed off, that no nuggets were being high-graded. And at the end of thirty days, a great pile of sand and gravel at the mouths of the pits untouched, unwashed, the three Diggers, red-eyed and exhausted, surrendered their lease. "Now," Jock could hardly speak above a hoarse whisper, "Now you sonsobitches, have your blow. I'm going to sleep." And he stumbled into their shack and fell onto his bunk, sweaty, filthy, booted, and slept.

The Swag Man looked at Dingo. They had both gone beyond physical endurance, driving themselves on nervous energy, but the Swag Man did not want to give in. Jock had said now, and by gawd now it was. "Let's go, Dingo," he said. But Dingo just shook his head. The Swag Man summoned up one last burst of energy. "You little ha'penny welsher," and he took a mighty swing at Dingo. Missing, he collapsed on the ground and slept.

Twenty-four hours later Jock came out of the shack to find his partners still asleep on the ground. He kicked them awake. "Rise and shine, you millionaire bastards," he shouted. "Let's have us some bannock and a billy of tea. We'll wash us up a poke of gold apiece and head for that blow."

They paid off all but five of the most trustworthy men with promissory notes. After washing up enough for three pokes and leaving the five remaining men to continue the wash-up, the three headed for Nome. Old-timers may still recall the day of the Digger dance. They started with the self-promised hot baths. Next they laid in a solid supply of provisions at the best restaurant in town— real beef and ham and eggs, pie and stewed fruit, and potatoes and more meat. Only then did they head for the Board of Trade Saloon and Green River whiskey. "I'm first," Jock insisted as they walked in, and with that he threw his poke on the bar and said, "Set them up and don't stop until that is gone."

That was a day to remember, and a night too. They shouted and sang and danced, and finally at the end of it all, they fought— the Diggers versus all comers. No one was angry. It was a fight for the pure animal pleasure of it, the release from a long year of work and frustration and privation.

It took another month to wash up. It was going to be rich,

but how rich they did not know until the last bucket of gravel had passed through the sluice and the sluice box cleaned out. The total, an impossible $413,000 worth of gold. The three Diggers had finally made it. Jock's superstitious association with the fabled wealth of Ophir was vindicated.

In the same year Captain E. W. Johnston came to Nome, where he was to repeat the experience of the Diggers. Captain Johnston started life on the Great Lakes. As a boy, he made money selling bait to Chicago fishermen. When old enough, he shipped before the mast as a sailor on the lakes. When the gold rush started, he went to Seattle, where he bought a small launch, sailed it to Dyea, and engaged in lightering. In two years he made nearly one hundred thousand dollars. When Dyea ceased to be a principal port and the docks of Skagway made lightering unnecessary there, he moved on to Nome in 1900. There the launch that had served so well for two years began to give trouble. When he met a man who offered to trade a mining claim for the launch, he was receptive. However, the Captain was an honest man and felt it necessary to advise the miner that the launch was acting up. The miner with equal honesty admitted his claim seemed a blank, but he knew something about machinery and might be able to make the launch run. The trade was made, and Captain Johnston became the owner of Number 8 Cooper Gulch. He sank several holes to bedrock but failed to strike a pay streak. By 1905 the mine was still a blank and Johnston's money had about run out. In the fall of that year, discouraged and nearly broke, he turned over the operation of the mine to his father-in-law, J. L. Pidgeon. Pidgeon put down a new shaft on the lower end of the claim. Immediately he hit a pay streak. Within a year the mine yielded $900,000 worth of gold. The next year over $600,000 in gold was taken out, despite labor strikes during the winter.

It became customary for visitors to Nome to include Number 8 on Cooper Gulch in their itinerary, for so rich was the mine and so inexhaustible seemed the gold that every visitor was invited to help himself to nuggets. The only way in which they were expected to return the Captain's generosity was to listen to him philosophize. He liked to expound on the dignity of labor and the philosophical aspects of gold mining. "There is one unquestionably honest method of accumulating much money," he liked to tell visitors, "a method which injures no one. It does not take money from another. It is the cleanest money that anybody can obtain. Mining. A man may have socialistic tendencies and yet not begrudge the miner all the gold he has been lucky enough to find."

Captain Johnston retired with his fortune and built a home on the eastern shore of Lake Washington in Seattle. Like the millionaires' homes of his day, it was a showplace with reception room, dining room, den, cold storage, billiard room, conservatory, and even a shooting gallery. True to his original profession, he carried the nautical theme throughout the mansion. The conservatory was like the inverted hull of a five-hundred-ton schooner.[6]

Not everyone was as lucky as the Lucky Swedes, the Diggers, and Captain Johnston. It is proverbial that God looks after drunks, and it often seems true. It seems equally true that His back is frequently turned on His servants. Carlson, head of the Unalakleet Mission, staked a claim at Number 15 Ophir. When he was offered five thousand dollars, he quickly concluded the sale on behalf of the mission. He felt indeed he must be acting under divine guidance. He had done better than many an experienced miner and had five thousand dollars to prove it. The next year the claim produced $1½ million; and if there were a tithe given, it was not to the mission but to the saloons of Nome.[7]

With gold came civilization. In 1900 the first automobile was brought to Nome to establish a service between Nome and Solomon. An Eskimo by the name of Alapah Emuk witnessed the first run of the car. He saw men pour benzine into the automobile and then it fired up with a great roar and moved off down the road. Alapah Emuk, meaning cold water, was given his name because he adhered to the mission teachings against drinking whiskey. He drank only water. But when Emuk saw the miraculous results obtained from pouring the benzine into the red vehicle, he was determined to try this powerful liquid. He bought a bottle of water-that-make-dogless-sled-on-wheels-move and proceeded to an Eskimo gathering on the beach east of the Snake River. There he gave a great speech, telling of the power of this new ingredient he had in the bottle. It made dead thing like red wagon go like northern lights. Pour this into man and he can outrun reindeer. He can even go faster than flying ptarmigan. It give a man strength to kill polar bear. Climaxing his speech, Emuk poured a large drink down his throat. With a great roar, he leaped into the air and started to prance, emitting shrieks and cries that rent the air. One after another, the Eskimos took a great swig of this potent elixir, and each in turn jumped into the air and started prancing and screaming. Thus developed the red-wagon dance.[8]

If benzine corrupted the native dancing, gold corrupted the white man even more. Nome became the most lawless town in Alaska. Exploding from a few hundred to over twenty thousand people in a year, it outstripped in size and crime every city in the territory. With no dedicated police force, such as the Mounties in Dawson, the venality of Nome was worse than that of Skagway under the domination of "Soapy" Smith. The legally constituted authority openly plundered the mining districts. Gangs operated freely throughout the crowded streets. Repeatedly they started fires so that they could rob in the confusion of fire fighting. Nothing was too small, to large, or seemingly inconsequential to escape their attention. The entire city's butter supply was stolen and resold to the stores at inflated prices. Fifteen caribou were stolen and retailed from the rear door of a building, while police officers were held at bay at the front door. A house was jacked up and was being moved from the lot, when its absent owners, two women, returned and drove the thieves off at gun point.

Worse than the lawless depradations, however, were the legal crimes committed in Nome, giving it the questionable distinction of having one of the worst records in the history of the United States for flagrant refusal to recognize the lawful rights of individuals. With the influx of thousands of men unaccustomed to the discipline of miners' meetings and miners' law, claims were jumped and re-jumped. Claims and counterclaims were filed. Nowhere in the North was the recording system so chaotic. Lindeberg, Lindblom, and Brynteson probably were largely responsible. They had engineered the Cape Nome Mining District and had proposed the rules which permitted a miner to stake more than one claim. Between the three of them, they held ninety claims. Many of the claims lay idle, unworked. Whereas in other mining districts claims had to be proved and worked each year, in the Nome district there were no such provisions. Confronted with this condition, the stampeders who arrived in Nome in 1900 were resentful and bitter. They felt, as American citizens, they were being cheated by the cunning of the dumb Swedes. Men started to jump vacant claims. Even working claims were not safe from seizure. Law, such as it was, challenged by disgruntled stampeders, came into disrepute. The situation was chaotic, the time ripe for unscrupulous men.

Three local lawyers saw in this chaos an opportunity to establish their fortunes.[9] They went to Washington with a scheme that for its open cupidity is almost without parallel in American history. They approached Alexander McKenzie, a leader of the Republican party in the days when Mark Hanna dominated President McKinley. With his support, the backing of several senators and congressmen was solicited. The Alaska Gold Mining Company was organized with a capitalization of $15 million. The plan was simple and almost foolproof in the nation's capital, where Nome was just a distant name with no reality or political heft.

The first stage of the plan called for obtaining title to several rich claims which had already been jumped. With the help of the senators and congressmen involved, it was hoped to have an act of Congress establish the company's right to the claims involved. If this move failed, and it did, they would have a district court established at Nome with a judge selected by McKenzie. If rightful owners should then contest confiscation or if any claims were presented before the court for litigation, the mines would be placed in the hands of a receiver. The receiver, of course, would be appointed by the judge. While cases were under consideration of the court, and decisions could be postponed indefinitely, the receiver would operate the mines. The gold extracted would be sent to New York to substantiate the $15 million capitalization of the Alaska Gold Mining Company. Against this evidence of extractive capacity, stock in the company would be sold. Since little money was needed for exploration or operating going mines, the money from stock sales was certain to enrich all involved, even if the company eventually failed.

At McKenzie's suggestion, Arthur E. Noyes was appointed judge at Nome. No sooner had Noyes arrived and the first litigation been presented to his court than he appointed McKenzie as receiver to operate the mine in question until such time as the court should reach a decision. Case after case was tied up in court with mines being turned over to McKenzie to operate and milk. The situation became so critical that miners no longer filed claims for fear they would be contested and turned over to McKenzie as receiver. Gold that was mined was smuggled out of the country for fear the "Noyes gang," learning of a rich gold mine, would jump the claim, throwing the mine into receivership during litigation.

All seemed to be going well for the gang until a group of indignant miners, receiving no satisfaction in Nome, went to San Francisco and presented their case to the Court of Appeals there. The court ordered McKenzie to desist, but he refused. The court then ordered Noyes to appear in San Francisco, and he also refused. Two marshals were sent to Nome. McKenzie, Noyes, and the court clerk were arrested and brought to San Francisco. All three were convicted of contempt of court, but only the clerk was to serve time for the crimes of the gang. Judge Morrow, of the Court of Appeals, heeding an entreaty from President McKinley, acquitted McKenzie and commuted Noyes' sentence. McKenzie returned to Washington to resume his position of high leadership in the Republican party, ending a period of legalized embezzlement.

Judge Wickersham was sent from Eagle to Nome to clean up the mess.[10] He did his best, but was soon replaced by Alfred S. Moore at the request of Matthew Stanley Quay, political boss of Pennsylvania. Moore was little better than Noyes, but at least the blatant confiscation of claims and placing them in receivership to be exploited was ended.

But there are two sides to the record of Nome. All was not avarice and corruption. There was G. L. "Tex" Rickard, for example, and his famous Christmas dinner. "Tex" was a sourdough before arriving in Nome. He had been in Dawson and Circle City. He had crossed the Chilkoot Pass. On leave from his elected office of city marshal of Henrietta, Texas, he had visited Juneau in 1895. While there, he met Al Mayo, whose stories of the Yukon, the gold, the moose and caribou, the great runs of salmon, and the raw beauty of the country excited the pioneer instinct of the young Texan. He mailed his resignation to Henrietta, bought an outfit, and headed for Dyea. With a small party, he pulled a sled over the Dyea trail in April of 1896. Like most of the men going inside that year, he made for Circle City, where he staked a claim on Deadwood Gulch in the Birch Creek District. The claim was poor, so when news of the Bonanza reached Circle, he set out for Dawson. Pulling his sled three hundred miles up the frozen Yukon in February of 1897, he arrived too late to stake a claim on the Bonanza or the Eldorado, but he did manage to buy a half-interest in Number 3 Below on Bonanza. The young Texan, more of a businessman than a miner, sold his interest in Number 3 Below for twenty thousand dollars. With part of his profit, he bought an interest in Number 4 Below Discovery, which he turned around and sold to an English syndicate for thirty thousand dollars. With his pyramiding capital, he invested in three claims on Eureka Creek, all of which turned out to be rich. He bought a cottage in Dawson near Tammany Hall, where the Rickard southern hospitality became a byword.[11] Restless, searching for new adventures, he set off down the Yukon in 1898 and eventually reached Anvil City, where he opened a saloon. Combining a natural generosity with a flair for publicity, he cornered the turkey market, hired a restaurant and orchestra, and on Christmas, 1900, gave a turkey dinner for everyone in town. If there was ever hunger in Nome, it was not on that day, for no one was turned away. Meals were served in shifts, the orchestra played, and people sang, "For He's a Jolly Good Fellow," until the last person was glutted and the turkeys were reduced to soup bones.

For his hospitality or his marshal's background, or because he was a tall, clean-shaven movie version of the Texas lawman, he was elected to the first city council when Nome was incorporated in April of 1901. This was the same Tex Rickard who in 1906 opened The Northern Saloon with eighty bartenders in Goldfield, Nevada. There he first became interested in boxing when, to increase business in his saloon, he promoted the Gans–Nelson "Battle of the Century" for the lightweight championship of the world. Later, with the Jim Jeffries–Jack Johnston match in Reno, he became established as the leading fight promoter in the country.

Nome was a ribald, boisterous town, which did not take its lawlessness or itself too seriously. Fighting was a way of life. If guns weren't handy to settle a dispute, fists always were. Under the heading, "Early Morning Eruption in the Tenderloin," the *Nome News* of February 20, 1903, gave this lighthearted account of a fight:

> Two well-known citizens engaged in strenuous exercise that disturbed even that neighborhood. William Austin, erstwhile candidate for Chief of Police, and Charley Johnson became involved in the parliamentary rulings of Mayor Pearson in a free and easy lump in the hurrah block. Fearing that the heat of their debate might set

the place on fire, the two gentlemen retired to a large heap of garbage and empty beer bottles in the rear; and there, locked in each
others' arms, they finally landed in the stockade. Officer Harris, the
old sleuth, heard the battle cries of the two gladiators from afar, and
leaving his glass of untouched liquor on the bar, hurried to the
scene of strife. The officer hurled himself into the center of skirmish.
But who should loom up before him like a lump taken out of a
salted mine but councilman Mather, chairman of the police committee and ex-jailer for Jack Jolly. The ex-policeman wished to
exert his authority and not allow the two combatants to be thrown
into the bastille, but officer Harris said they will come along with
me and if you interfere, I will take you along too. Harris took the
two men into the city boarding house and there they were released
on bond.

Although the Klondike captured the imagination of the world,
Nome, if not as rich, was wilder and more exciting. Its gold fields
seemed inexhaustible; new strike after new strike was recorded.
There was no apparent end to the wealth to be found under the
tundra. In 1907 the *Alaska-Yukon Magazine* in an article on the
Seward Peninsula predicted there would never be any permanent
setback to Nome: "It is certain to become the capital of the richest
mining center in the world. In every way Nome shows it is on the
high road to civil dignity and wealth."[12] That year, although
labor strikes throughout the winter had limited production, $11
million in gold was shipped out of Nome.

Gold is still in the air of Nome, in the empty lots filled with
rusting boilers and old mining equipment, and along the shoveled
beaches, littered now with cans and bottles and refuse washed up
by the tides and storms, where gold can still be panned. Offshore,
scientifically equipped ships have located a new beach under the
sea and men are waiting only for an economical method to mine
the submarine bonanza. But the frenetic period of the Lucky
Swedes, the Diggers, the Noyes gang, and Tex Rickard is gone,
replaced by a paradoxical languor that contrasts oddly with the
bleak landscape. An almost tropical lassitude pervades Nome.
There are taxis and tour buses and a few cars and trucks, but they
must share the dirt streets with the children and dogs. Still lacking
are regulations and harsh signs demanding patterned conformity.
A person may wander where he wishes and camp on the beach
where stampeders rocked gold out of the ruby-sand concentrates.

Nome, the Most Exciting Stampede Town

In the gray twilight of night with a fine rain sifting out of the Bering sky, he may build a fire for warmth or cooking, or retreat to the shelter of an old shack without fear of molestation.

Nome has that singular dichotomy of remote communities in which a person may either escape the interference of society or seek the warmth of personal relationships. He may be a hermit within the town or exhibit eccentricities for which he would be censured in places where a man may not be his own keeper. On the other hand, in Nome he is not a nameplate on an apartment door, a forgotten social security number. He is known to everyone. If he does not appear in public within a reasonable time, someone will look in to see if he is well, and if he needs help—a bowl of soup, a doctor, or the sound of friendly voices.

It is a town of cheechako, sourdough, and Eskimo. The latter frequently represent the best of many bloods—the strong independence of pioneer adventurers combined with the staunch conservative experience of the local people. Laura Johnsen is one. Dressed in stretch pants, parka, a pillbox fur hat set jauntily on her glossy black hair, she drives a taxi. Her grandfather, Tetaworph, crossed from Siberia when the Bering Strait was frozen. He married her grandmother and they moved to San Francisco, where he was shanghaied and died in Liverpool. With a son, the grandmother returned to the North, married again, and settled in Sitka. But the son, Laura's father, was drawn back to the Seward Peninsula, where his father had first reached American soil. He taught school and mined and married.

Still young and attractive, Laura recalls her childhood when they followed the Indian way of life her father loved. Each year they repeated an established pattern, gathering food. First they would collect roots and eggs from the nesting birds at White Mound. They put the roots in a gunnysack and buried them in the ground. In the winter the roots froze and became sweet. Next they would go to Six Mile and trap salmon, which they put down in salt or smoked for the dogs. From Six Mile, they went up Fish River with the dogs pulling the skin boats. There they fished for dog salmon and the humpies, which they sun-dried. Then on to Council to gather salmonberries, blueberries, blackberries, and cranberries to put down in barrels. At the end of the season there was hunting for squirrels and the occasional porcupine. These also were sun-dried or salted. After the ice formed on the river, they would fish for whitefish, and in November they butchered reindeer.

Nor is the past in Nome merely a closed chapter recalled. As Laura reminisced over a heavy mug of steaming coffee, the phone rang. After answering it, she laughed at the coincidence. "That was my cousin," she said. "She wanted to know if it wasn't about time to go squirrel hunting and were we going this year."

To the seaward of Nome is the gray and forlorn Bering Sea. Inland, the treeless tundra fades into low, featureless hills. But it is a warm, friendly, relaxed town with the most colorful and exciting past of any place in Alaska.

11

Valdez,
the Forgotten Stampede Town

I N THE LEXICON OF THE LAST STAMPEDE, Valdez was a synonym
for impossible. It was popularly believed that anyone who attempted to reach the Yukon via Valdez would go crazy, starve,
or be permanently crippled. In the April 1, 1898, edition of *The
Klondike News*, describing the routes to the Klondike, the editor
wrote:

> We warn our readers against any attempt to reach the Klondike
> country by the way of Copper River [Valdez was the gateway to the
> Copper River country.] No living man ever made the trip, and the
> bones of many a prospector whiten the way.
>
> In the first place it is almost impossible to ascend the Copper
> River. There are trackless mountains to cross, by the side of which
> the Chilcoot Pass trail is a boulevard, and rapids that would make
> the White Horse dry up and quit business.
>
> Certain unscrupulous parties operating steamboats up that way
> are issuing gaudy pamphlets with nicely worded directions of how to
> travel over a country that white man never set foot in. This is worse
> than murder, and such crimes deserve to be punished to the full
> extent of the law. We would suggest that they be hung, drawn, quar-
> tered and fed to a pack of hungry Malamute dogs.

In 1898 four thousand prospectors landed at Valdez and
crossed the glacier headed for the Yukon. However, Valdez is
little remembered as a stampede route. Discredited by early reports

of the horror of the glacier that had to be traversed, it was later ignored or forgotten by the elite of the sourdoughs, the Yukoners, the Klondikers who came via the Chilkoot and White Pass. It was not on the circuit of the dance-hall girls or theatrical troupes. It attracted no "Soapy" Smith, no Noyes gang. It produced no millionaires, no headlines in the press of the world. And yet Valdez was definitely a part of the last stampede.

The recorded history of the Valdez area begins before that of any other stampede site, before the Klondike, or Forty Mile, or Circle, or Nome, or Fairbanks. It antedates the nineteenth century. Despite the presence of the Russians, or rather because of it, the Spaniards are credited with the discovery of Valdez Bay.[1] Disturbed by reports of Russian encroachment on the west coast of America, the Viceroy of Mexico sent successive expeditions to explore the northwest coast. In June of 1790 Don Salvador Fidalgo, under orders to explore and to plant the standard of Spain where he found the coast unoccupied, sailed through a narrow channel and found himself in a relatively small but beautiful bay. A nautical man, he first noted that it was completely free of ice and the waters of great depth. As a Spaniard, he then observed the beauty of his surroundings, the sheltered waters tightly ruffed by a high range of mountains, snowcapped and cradling dozens of glaciers. Approaching the eastern extremity of the bay, he made special note of a glacier that poured out of the mountains to the north, spreading across the alluvial plain almost to the water's edge.

In accordance with instructions, he rowed ashore and took formal possession of the land in the name of His Most Catholic Majesty. Being a naval officer first and a Spaniard second, on June 16, 1790, he named the harbor for a celebrated Spanish naval officer, Antonio Valdes y Basan. Captain Vancouver adopted the name on his maps in a subsequent survey of the Alaskan coast. And so it became confirmed as Port Valdez.

During the Russian period, the Indians from the interior, along the Copper River, crossed the Chugach Mountains to Valdez Bay to trade their furs. They may have had copper instruments and a few gold nuggets, but not enough to interest the Russians in mineral development, since they were principally concerned with furs. However, there must have been some hint of the mineral wealth of the country, for the peripatetic American miners were there within five years of the purchase of Alaska. In 1884 Captain William Ralph Abercrombie of the United States Army, on an exploring expedition of the Copper River, surveyed a portage route from the interior to Port Valdez.[2] If an overland route should be opened from the coast to the interior of Alaska, Valdez, the northernmost ice-free port, seemed the logical terminal. The glacier noted by Don Salvador Fidalgo in 1790, which by 1884 had receded several miles, provided a broad and gradual ascent to the summit of the Chugach Mountains.

When Forty Mile was the only town on the Yukon, prospectors were fanning out from Port Valdez, chipping away at the glaciated ravines of the Chugach Mountains, cautiously edging their way up the glacier first marked by Don Salvador Fidalgo in 1790, and penetrating the Copper River valley. In 1893 eighty-three claims were recorded in the Valdez area. That same year Cherosky and Pitka discovered gold on the Mastodon, the three men from Boston filed claims on Birch Creek, and Circle City was started. It was three years before a single claim would be filed in the Klondike region or Libbey would return to the Niukluk to prepare the way for the Nome stampede.

Captain Abercrombie returned to Valdez in 1898 in command of a survey party that successfully blazed a trail from the Gulf of Alaska to the Yukon via the Copper River, across the Tanana, and down the Forty Mile and Sixty Mile rivers. With the establishment of the military command of North Alaska at Fort Egbert, Abercrombie was directed to lay out a military road to Eagle. In addition to its military importance, the road would provide stampeders with an overland all-American route to the gold fields of the interior. It was not completed for a quarter of a century.

Despite the early presence of miners and the early interest of the military in developing a route from the coast to the interior, Valdez has been forgotten as a stampede town, except in the fearful words of Captain Abercrombie's report of 1889, echoing the sentiment of *The Klondike News*, but in more personal and grisly terms.[3] Perhaps to aggrandize the part he played in bringing relief to the distressed miners, Abercrombie accentuated the situation he found when he returned to Port Valdez on April 21, 1899. Or perhaps he did honestly report what he saw, but the unfortunate cases of distress he objectively recorded so distorted his subjective conclusions that a balanced representation was impossible. There was scurvy in advanced stages; some prospectors were crowded fifteen and twenty to a cabin; and men were frozen trying to cross the glacier to reach the interior. Abercrombie recorded the physical suffering he saw and the reports of mental derangement resulting from glacial madness he did not see. He summarized the horror of crazed men in the story of a huge Swede who told of the Valdez glacier demon which had strangled his son. The man had been pushing his sled across the ice pack while his son hauled on the front rope when the demon sprang out from behind a hummock and killed the boy. Subsequent writers, letting their imaginations take up where Abercrombie's report stopped, told of thousands of men being blinded by the snow and going mad on the Valdez Glacier. Those who survived and managed to get back to Valdez, it was said, died from starvation or were crippled for life by scurvy before they could be rescued.

Abercrombie blamed ignorance for most of the trouble. He concluded that the men who came to Valdez seeking a short route to the interior had no idea of what to expect. Three-fourths of every outfit in 1898 had turned back, he wrote. Those who did not turn back were to decide later that they were foolish not to have returned. Disease and false rumors aggravated the situation. During the winter of 1898-99 the story was circulated that the War Department had withdrawn its representatives from Alaska. No help from that source would be available, and no relief could be expected. In the ensuing panic to escape the scurvy that was already setting in, Valdez was deserted. Two-thirds of the people attempting to cross the Valdez Glacier were frozen to death.

With the conscientiousness of his military training, Abercrombie categorized the causes for failure of the stampeders to survive the rigors of the north. First, advanced age. The average age of the stampeders was over forty-seven years. Second, lack of mining experience. They had no knowledge of indications of mineral deposits. Third, no business qualities. Ninety-five percent of the men, he notes smugly, were already business failures who hoped to make good in the gold fields. How a man who could not succeed in business in the comparatively easy circumstances of civilization could hope to succeed in the more difficult task of mining was beyond Abercrombie's imagination. Of the four thousand persons he estimated stampeding to the Copper River country in

1898, not a man had economic experience in the development of minerals after discovery.

This pedantry sits oddly on the pages of what should be an objective report. He does not indicate what economic experience is applicable to pocketing placer gold or spending the yellow dust. There is no reason offered why these men should fail, while men with a similar lack of experience succeeded on the Klondike. Perhaps he did not believe what he wrote. Certainly, he did not offer the miners a course in elementary geology or economics or prohibit older men from attempting the glacier. He addressed his authority only to a minor evil not mentioned as one of the causes of disaster. He found the local agent of a steamship company selling liquor and conducting gambling operations. He declared these acts illegal and forbade the only successful business operation in Valdez which offered a supply to meet a demand.

There were other men in Valdez at the time who had crossed the Valdez Glacier to the Copper River country, prospected for gold, and returned, who wrote from firsthand experience and did not retail secondhand stories and half-baked theories from the relative comfort of a command tent. Neal D. Benedict was one of them.[4] He crossed the Valdez Glacier in the early spring of 1898, prospected the Copper River country, and came out before the following winter. His account, while not minimizing the hardships, presents a picture radically different from the calamitous canvas painted by Captain Abercrombie.

Benedict agreed with Abercrombie in one particular; he too said four thousand men crossed the Valdez Glacier early in 1898. But he reported no instance of a glacier demon attacking any stampeder. There were dangers, but they were natural dangers, not fanciful ones. Early in the winter deep crevasses were only loosely concealed by snow, posing a constant threat to men grown careless with fatigue. He recommended waiting until late winter when the heavy snows formed solid bridges over the fatal fissures. The loners joined groups or banded together in companies for mutual assistance and protection in crossing the glacier. There was CATCO, the Connecticut and Alaska Trading Company, and the Zagelmeyer Company. The Chicago Company hauled a fully equipped yawl over the glacier and put it together on Lake Klutena.

From Valdez to the summit of the glacier was twenty-three miles, just a little farther than the distance from Dyea to the summit of the Chilkoot Pass, and it took about the same time to negotiate the route, two months of slow, back-breaking toil. Each day, the men would load their sleds with as much as they could pull, and, with men hauling on lines ahead and others pushing from behind, they would work their way upwards for one to two miles before making a new camp. Then back to the old camp for another load, relaying four or five loads a day. This would be repeated day after day until the entire camp with all its provisions and supplies had been moved to the new site. In addition to the food and equipment they would need when they reached the interior, they had to carry enough wood to last the trip on the glacier. With dehydration a major problem, wood was an absolute necessity. Food, if necessary, could be eaten cold. Men could huddle in their tents, wrapped in their sleeping bags for warmth; but at the end of a sweat-slogging day, bodily moisture had to be replaced. Ice and snow had to be melted for coffee or tea. It seemed they could never get enough liquids.

Days would be lost when a camp was immobilized by a blizzard. Then more days would be required to dig out equipment before another move could be made. Dark glasses were a must for all who crossed the snow and ice fields of the glacier, but they were also a nuisance. Fine snow like grains of dust, whipped by the winds pouring off the mountains, stuck to the glasses. A man with his hands wrapped around a pulling line or pushing on a load waited until his vision was blinded before wiping his glasses. He hated to lose the scant momentum of the sled so arduously gained. Most men soon discarded the dark glasses brought from the States and carved for themselves Eskimo goggles, thin pieces of wood with narrow slits that fit over the eyes. They cut the glare even better than glasses, and snow did not adhere to the wood or block the scant openings.

At the foot of the summit, in April 1898, was a camp stretching over a half mile, similar to Sheep Camp near the base of the Chilkoot Pass. Here, however, there was no hospital, no restaurant, no post office, and no telephone service as at Sheep Camp. The stampede to the Copper River country, unlike the more publicized Klondike stampede, did not attract the capital or entrepreneurs to build a powered cable to haul equipment over the pass. The last rise from the camp to the summit was four thousand and nine hundred feet of frozen snow and ice. Sleds had to be worked up the steep incline with block and tackle. Each company that was properly equipped brought along eight hundred feet of rope plus block and tackle for this final assault.

For six days the camp was closed in and all traffic stopped as a blinding storm cut visibility to less than two feet. For six days men stayed in their sleeping bags day and night for warmth. The storm dumped seven feet of snow on the unprotected camp, so that scarcely a tent or supply dump could be seen when the sun came out on the seventh day. Many men were still in their blankets on April 30, when an avalanche roared down from the summit and swept over part of the camp. The fortunate ones grabbed shovels and started digging. Twenty-four of twenty-six missing people were freed before a second avalanche struck, and only those two died before they could be rescued.

Even there on the bleak desolation of the glacier, where mere survival was a constant struggle and the drive to cross the summit was a constant goad, men still observed the niceties of society and the legal conventions with which they were familiar. A coroner's jury was impaneled and a verdict rendered that the deaths were accidental. A report was duly written and certified by the coroner and physician. As both the deceased were Freemasons, fellow members collected their personal effects and the cash derived from a sale of their share of provisions, which were sent to the relatives of the dead men. And despite the difficulty of the last leg of the trip over the glacier, both bodies were hauled over the summit to the Klutena valley, where they were buried in a grove of poplars.

With the storm, the avalanches, the rescue operation, and digging out, nearly two weeks passed before Benedict's party could start on the final mile to the summit. It then took them five days to move their fifteen tons of equipment to the top. Once over the summit, it was easy going, the first stop being Twelve Mile Camp, twelve miles from the summit. Then there was Saw Mill. Then Seven Mile Camp and Eight Mile Camp, both named for their distance from Twelve Mile Camp. As Lake Bennett was the beginning of the water route for the Yukoners, Lake Klutena was the beginning for those who came over the Valdez Trail. And by 1898, in addition to the yawl brought in by the Chicago Company, there was the Schooner *Manhattan* already on the lake and a small steam launch belonging to Dr. Ottaway. The half-humorous, half-ambitious conceits which characterized the American pioneers gave the name of Klutena City to the miserable collection of tents and huts at the lower end of Lake Klutena, and the principal street of Klutena City was Mosquito Avenue.

Contrary to Captain Abercrombie's report of the failure of men to make it across the glacier, there were several thousand in the interior of the Copper River country when Benedict reached it in the spring of 1898. There were tent cities springing up all along the trail and at river crossings. Between Valdez Glacier and Copper River were ten camps. At Twelve Mile there were over a hundred tents when Benedict arrived. When he returned, September 1, there were only thirty, but there was an established restaurant. At Three Mile, or Saw Mill, there was a cluster of tents, and also at Seven Mile, although it was never large and was completely deserted by July. There was Peninsula City with one hundred twenty-five tents, Amie's Rapids, Cox's Landing, Copper Center, and Copper Ferry. There was an established mail service. Jackson, the squaw man, delivered letters for $1 a month per man. He brought in as many as two thousand letters a trip. There were women who made it over the Valdez Glacier in the summer of 1898, two single women and thirteen who had accompanied their husbands. Benedict wrote: "Every woman is treated with respect. The slightest wrong would be resented by every man in the country as a personal grievance. The two unmarried women were cheerful and helpful to everyone and everyone realized they would have done as well as the best in the case of any rich strike."

Frau Freiherz, a German woman, ran a restaurant at Eight Mile Camp, where she provided dinner, supper, breakfast, and sleeping accommodations of sorts for $1 a day. Supper was perhaps not much, but it seemed wonderful to men who had been cooking and eating their own concoctions. The night Benedict spent there, she served "hot biscuits and johnny cake, baked and boiled beans, fried evaporated potatoes, bacon, dried salmon, and hot coffee." Not a great selection but plenty of what there was.

From Valdez to Twelve Mile Camp was thirty-five miles, and though it took Benedict and his party two months, Jim Stewart, a well-known trail guide, made the same trip with an eighty-pound pack in twelve hours. Many of the thousands of stampeders on the trail that year hoped to reach Circle City. The plan was to follow up the Copper River, cross the river at Copper Crossing, and head for Millard Trail, which had been laid out by members of the Wisconsin Company and Great Northern Party. That trail, beginning from Klowosinak River, runs north past Mt. Drum and Sanford to the Tanana Mountains, on the north side of which Benedict says they expected to strike Forty Mile River, which they could follow down to Circle City.

The route is easier on paper than on the trail. Although Lieutenant P. G. Lowe, under Abercrombie's orders, reached the Yukon that summer, few stampeders who crossed the Valdez Glacier in 1898 ever saw Circle City or the Klondike. Having made it to the Copper River country, most were content to prospect the streams in that area. Benedict was one of those who spent the summer prospecting the Klutena and the creeks along the Copper River. He soon learned, as did other benighted stampeders, that gold could not be scooped from the gravel bars by the shovelful, as the newspapers reported in San Francisco and Seattle. Gold mining required intelligent prospecting and hard work. He could have told Captain Abercrombie that it was not a matter of business experience or economics, but of sweat and some knowledge of mineralization. Talking with old-timers in the interior, he learned what to expect if a man wished to have a reasonable chance of finding gold—winters spent in a frozen world of ice and snow, summers plagued by constant swarms of mosquitos, food and supplies to be hauled over the Valdez Glacier. He did not believe the potential reward worth the effort, and in September he headed back over the trail. With a light pack, he crossed from Twelve Mile, over the Valdez Glacier, to Valdez in two days to find the tent city he had left nine months earlier replaced by log cabins and board buildings. The misery which confronted Abercrombie struck Benedict as the opulence of civilization. This was the beginning of Valdez.

Valdez was never a gold town like Dawson, Forty Mile, Circle City, or Nome. Although it started with gold, its primary importance was as a stampede port. Most of the men who were drawn to Valdez came in search of a short route to the Yukon. Captain Abercrombie had instructions to construct a military route from Valdez to Fort Egbert. Oscar Rohn, accompanying Abercrombie, drew up a report on a route for reaching the interior gold fields of Alaska and Canada, but no road was built to the Yukon until 1927.

However, there was a trail from Valdez to Eagle, and Lieutenant William "Billy" Mitchell constructed a telegraph line between the two towns. Tanana Crossing, or Tanacross, where the trail and telegraph line crossed the Tanana River, led accidentally to the founding of Fairbanks, which in turn had a greater impact on the growth of Valdez than did any of the towns of the Yukon. With the rise of Fairbanks, Valdez became the principal port of the interior of Alaska, and a road that had previously only been considered soon became a reality.

Valdez' senior citizen, Billy Quitch, arrived there in 1906. Within twenty-four hours he had a job on a road gang clearing trees for a road to Fairbanks. Within a year crews, working from both ends, had cleared a right-of-way over three hundred and sixty miles. A horse and buggy could, and did, then travel from Valdez to Fairbanks. Horse-drawn sleds in the winter and coaches in the summer were regularly used on this route between the coast and the interior.

Even before the road and Fairbanks, Valdez was the accepted port for the interior. When Fairbanks was Barnette's Cache, a single trading post, Barnette and his wife came by dog sled over the Valdez Glacier to Valdez to take their furs outside to sell.

In addition to being the port for the interior, however, Valdez had gold. It was not necessary to cross the Valdez Glacier to reach the gold fields as so many did. There was gold in the streams entering Valdez Bay and quartz gold in the mountains ringing the port. There was the Gold King and the Ruff and Tuff and the Gibraltar Mine. On a hogback ridge running into the Columbia Glacier, a prospector had stumbled on a quartz ledge stretching from one side of the mountain to the other. Weathering had crumbled the face of the ledge, scattering $40,000 worth of naked ore at the foot of the outcrop. In the steep mountains, the mines were difficult to operate and the season short. More sensational placer deposits in Nome and Fairbanks attracted the men and capital. With the prohibition on gold mining during World War II and the influx of military spending and high wages, the gold mining of Valdez died. But for a few years at the beginning of the century it was one of the most important cities in Alaska. Its churches, its houses, and its hotels were among the grandest in the territory. The main hotel may have had eight beds to a room, but it was a two-storied, luxurious establishment. Indeed, many houses and buildings in

Valdez were two-storied. In a country where packed snow lay deep in the winter, a second floor with its own door was a great advantage. During the summer months the ground floor was used; but in the winter, when the snow lay ten feet on the level, second-floor doors would be used to enter and leave houses. Lacking second floors, tunnels were dug across streets to connect buildings. In the coldest months the streets of Valdez became a warren of tunnels. So deep were the snows and so long did they last that the miners working in the mountains noted the coming of spring by the appearance of the green roofs of Valdez poking through the snow. Bodies of the dead were kept until summer for burial. The gayest spot in town was the Morgue Bar, so named because when it opened for business there were two frozen corpses stored in the back room awaiting the spring thaw.

Valdez might have gone on to be the principal city of Alaska, but for chance and the cantankerous nature of man. With the discovery of rich copper deposits in the Copper River valley, Valdez was the natural choice for a shipping point. As noted earlier, Bill McPhee from Forty Mile built the Keystone wharf to handle expected ore shipments. A railroad was to be built connecting Valdez with the copper mines, but bad blood and fighting halted the project. The Guggenheim interests claimed a right-of-way along the only practicable route. A second company, known as the Reynolds group, maintained that the right-of-way had lapsed and tried to move in.

Billy Quitch was working for the Guggenheim faction at the time. Work had been started on a tunnel through Gravel Hill. Guards were stationed to hold off any attempt by the Reynolds' men to interfere with the work. Two deputy marshals had been posted at the camp to see that the law was not broken. At three A.M. one summer morning, when Billy Quitch was going off duty, he saw what looked like an army of men coming up the canyon. He aroused O'Neil, the manager, and soon the entire camp, which numbered only nineteen, was gathered behind a log barricade that had been erected across the trail. Billy counted two hundred fifty of the Reynolds' group, but there might have been more. Many were mounted on horses. O'Neil went out to remonstrate, but the Reynolds' men were in no mood to talk. They seized O'Neil as a hostage and continued toward the barricade. A man by the name of Hesy in the Guggenheim camp started shooting in the air, but when that didn't stop the Reynolds' group, he lowered his aim. Three men fell. As the Reynolds' men were unarmed, they retreated with their wounded.

Open warfare was threatened and must surely have ensued if the United States marshal had not taken prompt action. He arrested Hesy and withdrew the two deputies from the Guggenheim camp, since their presence had proved more of a provocation than an assurance of law and order. Hesy was first tried for murder, one of the wounded men having died; but as the jury felt the punishment would be too severe, he was acquitted. He was then tried for assault in the case of another man who had not been injured fatally. Although the evidence was identical in the two cases, the jury returned a verdict of guilty for the second offense, and Hesy was sentenced to five years.

Open fighting had been avoided, but trouble continued. Harassments and intimidation were routine. Finally, neither group having gained complete dominance, the route was abandoned, and the railroad project moved to the town of Seward, which existed before Anchorage was started as a railroad construction camp.

The old town of Valdez, which never recovered from this struggle, was finally abandoned in 1964, a year remembered in Alaska for the Anchorage earthquake. However, the epicenter was near Valdez. Because the Valdez Glacier furnished the shortest route to the interior, the town was built on the glacial-silt deposits left by the retreating glacier. On the day of the earthquake, a ship was tied up to the main dock discharging cargo. Workmen and the idle curious were standing on the dock, either working or watching. With the first tremor, a huge section of the glacial silt along the waterfront slid into the depths of the bay. The dock, the people, and the ship disappeared from sight. No body and no wreckage of the ship or dock has ever been found. A tidal wave swept in through the narrow entrance to Valdez Harbor. Blocked, like a wave in a tub, it washed back and forth across the bay, sweeping each time through the city of Valdez. Houses, stores, hotels, warehouses, churches, schools, business and municipal establishments were destroyed or left mud-filled shambles. The city could have cleaned up, foundations could have been reset, houses rebuilt, but the reason for the site was gone. The Valdez Glacier was no longer a route, and the glacial deposit would always be dangerous in an earthquake country. The town in its entirety moved five miles to higher and more solid ground. New schools, a new hospital, new churches, a new dock, motels, restaurants, stores, and houses were built. Old Valdez stands deserted as a vacant memorial to the last stampede.

The new Valdez—or the Mineral Creek Subdivision of Valdez, as the purists call it—has no great concern for the past and little for the future. For people living on what must be considered one of the most beautiful harbors in the world there can be only enough time to enjoy the present. It might have been the Juneau of Alaska if the quartz gold that is surely in the mineralized mountains around the bay had ever been discovered; but who wants the political problems of a capital. It could have been the Anchorage of the state, if fighting over the railroad right-of-way had not driven the copper companies to seek an alternate outlet to the sea; but who wants to be an Anchorage when it can be a quiet fishing town without urban problems. With the opening of the oil fields on the North Slope and pipelines and trucking routes projected to the northernmost ice-free port in Alaska, Valdez is again threatened by destiny. With luck, it may again fail to achieve commercial greatness and just remain the exquisite harbor Don Salvador Fidalgo discovered in June of 1790 and formally possessed for His Most Catholic Majesty, King Charles IV of Spain.

12

Fairbanks,
the Last of the Last Stampede

BOUT SEVEN HUNDRED MILES from where the Yukon emp-
ties into the Bering Sea, it divides into two apparently
equal rivers. The one entering from the south is known as the
Tanana and was once believed to be the main branch of the
Yukon. Three hundred miles up the Tanana River, the Chena
Slough enters from the north. In itself, this is unimportant, but it
is part of the coincidence of nature which led to the founding of
Fairbanks.

Fairbanks is both the hub of the richest gold fields in Alaska
and the geographical center of the state. It dominates the great
interior valley. Backed against a wall of low mountains to the
north, to the south it faces the vast Alaska Range tumbling away
from the highest peak on the continent which the Indians called
Denali, the father of all mountains, the great one, the home of
the supreme spirit.

Named unimaginatively as a political gesture for a respected
Senator who was to become an anonymous Vice President, Fair-
banks is circled by names more meaningful to its history: Pedro
Dome, Cleary, Olnes, Wickersham Dome, Happy, Goldstream
Creek, Livengood, Fox, Big Eldorado Creek, Moose Creek, Spin-
ach Creek, McCloud, Murphy, Keystone Creek, Fortune Creek,
Nugget Creek, Hard Luck Creek, Hattie, Eureka, Windy, French-
man, Last Chance, Iowa, Uncle Sam, Niggerhead, Montana,

Idaho, Colorado, Rusty Gold, Captain, Pilot, Sargent, and Our Creek. These are names of the hopes of the time, the frustrations, the success, the nostalgia. Here, entirely by chance and unwilling accident, E. T. Barnette in 1901 established a trading post to be known first as Barnette's Cache and later as Fairbanks, when the Tanana strike precipitated the final rush of the last stampede.

The beginning of the Tanana gold strike goes back several decades before Barnette. Like the history of most of the Yukon gold strikes, it starts with McQuesten and Harper. In 1876 Mc-Questen went three hundred and fifty miles up the Tanana trading with the Indians. According to his own statement, he was the first white man to penetrate that part of the country. The next year Bob Bean, the same Mr. Bean who had been storekeeper for the Collins Overland Route project and had told Adams of the American purchase of Alaska, arrived at the mouth of the Tanana. He was married now and had a child. He proposed going up the Tanana to open a trading post. McQuesten tried to dissuade him. Although he had been well treated by the Indians on his trip up the river, he felt they were untrustworthy. Bean was adamant and took his family seventy-five miles up the Tanana, where he built a cabin. It was an unfortunate venture for a man whom McQuesten considered an Alaskan old-timer.

Bean was a close trader. He wanted to leave the country and intended to make as much as he could out of this last venture. Accordingly, he demanded more for his trade goods than Mc-Questen charged. The Indians had little choice. If they needed what Bean had, they must pay the price or travel seventy-five miles downriver to McQuesten's post at the mouth of the Tanana. They paid the price, but they were unhappy. In September of that first year two Indians appeared at the post to trade some fish. It was a routine transaction, and as McQuesten later wrote, "They done their trading and Mr. Bean and wife sat down to dinner. Mrs. Bean was sitting with her back to the door. Mr. Bean was sitting opposite to her. The door was open. One Indian stood in the doorway talking to Mr. Bean. The other Indian placed his gun under the man's arm and shot Mrs. Bean in the back. She fell over dead."

The Indian shot again, trying to get Mr. Bean, but the gun misfired. Bean dashed for his gun, but the Indians had disappeared into the forest before he could get in a shot. Afraid that they might return with reinforcements, Bean seized his child and a small girl living with them and shoved off in a canoe. In his agitation, he did not see a barely submerged snag which, catching the canoe, capsized it. Bean was able to swim to shore, but the overturned canoe swept downriver with the two children hanging on to it. Fortunately, an Indian woman was coming upriver at this time in a canoe and rescued the children. With the help of the Indian woman and her canoe, Bean made his way down to the Tanana Station. Harper happened to be there at the time, and with three Indians he went back to the cabin and brought away Mrs. Bean's body. That was the end of the first white residence in the Tanana valley.[1]

Although the traders did not attempt to apprehend the murderer, for they were the only white men in the entire middle Yukon-Tanana area, it would have been unnecessary. The Indian punished himself. He was a shaman who had believed that by killing a white man he would placate spirits inimical to his people. After the shooting, he learned that instead of benefitting his tribe, he had hurt them. The white man with his trade goods left the Tanana, so that the Indians had to go far for trade goods instead of having the trade goods brought to them. The shaman fled up the Tanana into a wilderness area north of the Chena Slough, where he lived for a quarter of a century in self-exile from which only death could free him.[2]

For two years no one ventured up the Tanana; then in 1879 McQuesten and Harper went together in the company's small steamboat. But where canoes could go a steamboat could not. The shifting channels, the sandbars, the hidden shallows made navigation treacherous, and they turned back after only one hundred miles.

Now that Harper had seen the Tanana as a trader, he would not be content until he saw it as a prospector. Two years later, back on the upper Yukon, he decided it was time to take a better look at the Tanana country. Leaving McQuesten in charge of the store, as usual, he and a companion set off up the Forty Mile to its headwaters, crossed over the divide into the Tanana valley. Here he built a moosehide boat and descended the Tanana to its mouth. Harper prospected everywhere he went, but he found the Tanana poor gold country. There was very little gravel along the river, the banks were low and muddy, and the bars nearly all sand. That was 1881.[3]

During the following two decades traders made occasional forays up the Tanana and a few prospectors passed through the country, but no records were kept and no one cared. In 1888 Frank Densmore, John Burke, and George Carry found gold on the Tanana, but not in paying quantities.[4] The same year, Marion B. Carey and his wife of less than a year prospected along the Tanana on their leisurely way to the town of Forty Mile via Chicken and the north fork of Forty Mile River.

Eleven years later the Tanana was still ignored. In April of 1899 Lieutenant George H. McManus attempted to reach the Tanana from Circle City in anticipation of opening a trail to the Tanana and beyond to Valdez, but he turned back fifty miles short of the river because of a shortage of rations and the knowledge that the absence of a trading post on the Tanana River made re-victualing impossible.

To prospectors the lack of trading posts was a hardship, but just one of many. No sourdough would turn back from a prospecting trip for that reason. Felix Pedro, who would be to Fairbanks what Carmack was to Dawson, arrived in Circle City in 1895. He worked Birch Creek, Mastodon, and Miller Creek before going over the hill to the Tanana. He tried the Tanana, the Chena, and creeks north and east of the Chena. He would prospect until his supplies ran out, then return to Circle City for more supplies. It was a three-hundred-mile roundtrip, but the Tanana country kept luring him back. That there was no trading post nearby was an inconvenience, but he never thought of not returning for that reason.[5]

While the early explorations of the Tanana valley were taking place, the man who was to found Fairbanks, E. T. Barnette, was working a placer mine in the state of Washington. In the spring of 1885 he and his partner had washed out some $4,000 in gold. Barnette wanted to go to Seattle while his partner wished to take advantage of the summer months for further prospecting, so they agreed to separate temporarily. Feeling it unsafe to carry around so much gold, the partner asked Barnette to take both shares to Seattle, and Barnette agreed. Later, when the two partners met in Seattle, Barnette told how he had been robbed by Indians on the trek into town. All the gold had been seized. There was nothing the partner could say, but the story ill fit Barnette's new clothes and general appearance of well-being. Suspicious, he followed Barnette for several days until he caught him spending gold dust. The partner went to the police and filed charges against Barnette for stealing $2,000 in gold. Barnette was arrested, and after a brief trial, he was convicted and sent to the federal penitentiary.[6]

Five years later, out of prison, Barnette, now referred to as Captain Barnette, appeared in St. Michael with a Mrs. Barnette. He was no longer interested in gold mining. He was older and had learned that fools joust with luck, while wise men engage the sure thing. Gold was luck. Selling services or goods in a country where both are in short supply was a sure thing. In 1901 Barnette determined to open a trading post where need might prove greatest and competition least. A telegraph line had been completed the previous year from Valdez to Eagle. He understood Captain Abercrombie had been commissioned to lay out a military road connecting these two important communities. A trail already existed, which stampeders followed from Valdez to the Yukon; but when the road was completed, traffic could be expected to increase considerably. Therefore, the logical place for a trading post was where men and communications crossed the Tanana at Tanana Crossing, or Tanacross. Here he could trade for furs and run a roadhouse simultaneously, and between the two sources of income, he could only prosper.

Barnette's first setback was the loss of his steamboat, *Arctic Bay*, which he piled up on the rocks in St. Michael Harbor. He would now have to hire transportation to take his outfit up the Tanana River to Tanacross, and he was short of capital. Fortunately for his venture, he met James H. Caustin in St. Michael, who agreed to put a thousand dollars into the undertaking. Successful in raising capital, Barnette then had to find someone willing to take him up the Tanana. In this, he was only partially successful. He met C. W. Adams, owner of the steamer *Lavelle Young*, and entered into negotiations.[7] Adams doubted whether he could get the *Lavelle Young* beyond Chena Slough, less than halfway between the mouth of the Tanana and Tanana Crossing. After considerable discussion, Adams agreed to take Barnette and his outfit as far as the Slough, and on to Tanana Crossing for an additional sum. It was further specified that at the point beyond which navigation was impossible, Barnette would land and his goods be put ashore. The *Lavelle Young* was not the best craft for this voyage. It was not a shallow-draft boat, and the Tanana, even more than the Yukon, demands a shallow draft. The shifting sandbars and the changing channels make navigation treacherous and difficult even with high water, which they would not have in August. Adams knew this; so in making the contract he was adamant that both parties should have complete understanding that the *Lavelle Young* would take Barnette and his outfit to the Tanana Crossing if, and only if, that were possible.

On August 8, 1901, the *Lavelle Young* left St. Michael, heading for the Tanana Crossing, where E. T. Barnette hoped to establish a prosperous business. But they never reached their destination. The little steamer, with Adams and his crew, the Barnettes and their four employees, a dog team and a horse, as well as one hundred and thirty tons of supplies, was heavily loaded. As long as they were on the Yukon, this was unimportant. Adams was thoroughly familiar with the Yukon, and, with the constant traffic in steamers going to Circle, Eagle, Forty Mile, and Dawson, help was always available in case of trouble. Once they cleared the mouth of the Tanana this changed. Neither Adams nor Barnette had been up the Tanana. There was no traffic on the Tanana. This was wilderness country, and they could expect no help in case of getting stuck or breaking down. There were no woodcutters with cords of wood ready-cut for sale as there were along the Yukon. It was necessary to stop late each afternoon and cut wood for the boilers. They steamed slowly, feeling their way along a strange river. About halfway between the mouth of the Tanana and Tanana Crossing, they passed the Chena Slough. Eight miles farther, Adams tied up to the shore to consider the unlikely prospect ahead. The river had spread out into a maze of islands and channels, none of which was deep enough for the *Lavelle Young*. It was doubtful if even a shallow-draft boat could have gone farther upriver; certainly the *Lavelle Young*, which was not shallow draft and was carrying a heavy load, could not. Adams told Barnette this seemed to be as far as they could go. However, Barnette said he had been told by an Indian that it was possible to detour this bad spot by going up the Chena Slough to where it reentered the Tanana above this shallow maze of channels. After some discussion, Captain Adams agreed to try the detour.

The Chena Slough proved a poor alternative. Its serpentine channel was seldom over a hundred feet wide. For twelve miles

Adams pushed the nose of the *Lavelle Young* cautiously around bend after bend, ready to reverse engines immediately if a sandbar blocked the channel or if it should pinch out completely. He had no faith in hearsay Indian reports, but he sympathized with Barnette and was willing to go as far as it was possible to do so without jeopardizing his ship. This he did, but when he reached that point beyond which navigation was too hazardous, he again tied up to the shore. He told Barnette that this was as far as he could go. According to their contract, Barnette would have to unload his supplies here and establish his post. If he wanted to go farther, he would have to do so on his own.

For an hour they argued and debated. To Adams, the situation was already too dangerous. Without a steam winch, it would be difficult to come about if the slough became narrower. They couldn't even return to the Tanana. With the heavy load and with the current pushing from astern, working back down the Chena would be hazardous. As a compromise, Adams finally agreed not to insist on Barnette's offloading at this point. Instead, he would take Barnette back to a place where Barnette recalled seeing high ground with good spruce timber for buildings. Twice the *Lavelle Young* was almost stranded on sandbars in the six-mile trip downstream to the location Barnette had selected.

While Mrs. Barnette wept, the *Lavelle Young* was unloaded and the venture of Barnette got off to a sad start. He was many miles downriver from his destination. There were no Indians to trade with, and no road, no communication lines or mail route between Valdez and Eagle would pass anywhere near this location. There was no mining in the area. For a quarter of a century men had prospected the area, but gold in paying quantities had never been found. Here, in this unlikely spot, Barnette had to be content to build his trading post. What Barnette did not know, and could not imagine, was that the fate which had brought him to this desolate spot in the Tanana valley had also brought the Italian immigrant Felix Pedro to the same area, and the combination of the two would lead to Fairbanks.

Felix Pedro was born Felice Pedroni in Italy in 1859. He did not come to America until he was twenty-two. He worked for a while in the coal mines of Illinois. Then he tried his hand at hardrock mining in Colorado. Restless and adventurous, he moved farther west, into Indian Territory. He returned to coal mining in

Washington. In 1895, at age thirty-six, Pedro decided to try Alaska. He took the miners' route through Juneau to Dyea and over the pass to the Yukon, heading for Forty Mile. When he reached there, he heard of Circle and the Birch Creek diggings and went on to Circle City. Except for a brief side trip to the Klondike to satisfy his curiosity, he worked out of Circle. In 1899 he crossed over into the Tanana valley and prospected what were to be known as Pedro and Bear and Fish creeks, but with little success. Then he tried the headwaters of the Chena River. He got good colors, but not enough to justify his remaining there.

The bane of the prospector's life was the need to resupply from time to time. It was never safe to get too far from a source of supplies. For Felix Pedro, the source of supplies was Circle City. It was a long hike from the Tanana valley, over one hundred and sixty miles of mountain passes and flooded streams. On one trip he stumbled upon a rich outcrop, but he was out of food and had to push on to Circle. He returned again and again in search of the ledge, which remains lost to this day.

And so in August of 1901, while looking for the lost outcropping and prospecting the creeks, he was happy to see smoke from a steamer rising in the distance. He climbed an elevation to observe what was happening, and when he saw a steamer enter the Chena and come to an eventual halt, he and his partner headed for the smoke, hoping to get supplies. Here he met Barnette, who told Felix Pedro of his problem, expecting that Pedro, familiar with the area, might be able to suggest some solution. But Felix Pedro was not a riverman. He was not familiar with the channels and currents and with the windings of the Tanana River, but he did know that for him, and for others like himself, it would be helpful to have a trading post right where Barnette was at the moment. So he told Barnette of the colors he had found and his hopes of making a good discovery in the area.

It was not much upon which to base an operation Barnette hoped would make his fortune, but he had no choice. The next day, after selling some bacon and flour to Pedro and his partner, Barnette and his men started to cut trees for the trading post and houses.

Aside from the prospect of gold, the winter turned out better than Barnette had anticipated. Indians came with marten skins and the trading was good. In midwinter one of Barnette's men went out to Valdez and returned with Frank J. Cleary, Mrs. Barnette's brother.

Leaving Cleary in charge, the Barnettes left for Valdez in early March with a dog team and sled loaded with furs. They went up the Tanana valley to the Delta River, up the Delta to Isabell Pass, across to the Copper River valley, where they followed the trail to the Valdez Glacier and Valdez. From Valdez the Barnettes went on to Seattle to sell their furs and buy supplies for the next year.

While the Barnettes were gone, Pedro returned to the post and outfitted himself and his partner again. It is reported that since Pedro did not have sufficient gold, Cleary advanced the outfit against his own account. If true, it would explain why Felix Pedro, when he made a rich strike on July 22, 1902, reported it to Cleary, who was still in charge at Barnette's post. When Barnette returned to the Tanana, he was elated to learn of the strike. Following the normal pattern, it should lead to a stampede. It would probably not be anything like the Klondike or Nome stampedes, but it could be as big as the Forty Mile or Circle City stampedes. If so, the Chena location would prove to have been a far better choice than Tanana Crossing, though it had not really been a matter of choice.

To give the prospective stampede a favorable nudge, Barnette dispatched to Dawson, Jujira Wada,[8] a Japanese working for him. Wada had instructions to spread the word of Felix Pedro's strike in Dawson, and Jujira Wada did his job well. Hundreds of people followed him back to the Tanana.

Among the early arrivals were bunko artists, cardsharps, gamblers, men who depended upon a wealthy society with easy money to glean their living. Having missed their chance in Dawson, they were particularly impatient for the stampede to develop, for the gold to start flowing, before others of their peer group should arrive. Some eight hundred people were in the Tanana valley before Christmas, 1902. But the great outpouring of gold promised by Felix Pedro's strike did not materialize. Few heavy pokes appeared at Barnette's post or in the hastily erected saloons. Gloom descended on Barnette's Cache. A group of the more militant members of the community set out to lynch Jujira Wada, whom they blamed rather than Barnette for having falsely lured them to the Tanana. Fortunately, Wada was a good runner, escaped the temporary wrath of the impetuous, and lived to become a hero of the stampede.

By the spring of 1903 people were fed up with the Tanana and the miserable life along the Chena. Disappointed ladies and gents of leisure began to leave, spreading a tale of woe, warning people to avoid Barnette's Cache. With the arrival of summer all but one hundred people had quit the Tanana. Commercial companies planning to establish competitive trading posts reconsidered. Barnette, despondent as the stampede petered out and the first rush of people left, overreacted. Afraid of being overstocked, he failed to reorder enough for even the hard core of miners who remained, men willing to pay new gold for their needs. As a result, the winter of 1903–4 would have been one of extreme hardship if it had not been unusually mild with an early spring. Even so, there was critical hunger, and men spent a disproportionate amount of time hunting instead of burning holes in the ground.

What Barnette did not realize and those who departed so hastily did not appreciate is that gold is everywhere different. It is different in appearance. It is found differently. At Nome, it was found in the sands of the beach. On the Bonanza and the Eldorado, it was found in the banks along the streams, the gravel bars, just beneath the surface, as well as at bedrock. In the Tanana valley, Felix Pedro found gold near the surface, but most of the rich mines were one hundred or more feet under a worthless overburden. Gold did not gush forth from the ground, and the summer of 1903 produced a mere trickle of gold. But by the spring of 1904, after the wash-up, gold started to flow. From the $40 thousand of 1903, the output of 1904 jumped to $600 thousand, and the next year to $6 million, then $9 million. The stampede was in full swing.

Slow to start, Fairbanks was the greatest of them all, exclusive of the Klondike. Juneau, with over twenty years' head start, did not produce as much gold. Nome produced a little over half as much, and Circle, a mere fraction of Fairbanks. Valdez, Rampart, the Koyukuk, the Kuskokwim, Eagle—all put together could not equal Fairbanks. It never quite outtotaled the Klondike; but if comparisons are made from 1905, the year Fairbanks' production got into high gear, the Fairbanks' fields outproduced Dawson's. In 1905, 1906, 1907, 1908, 1909—each year the Tanana valley mines yielded more gold than the Klondike, and have ever since.[9]

The gold mining around Fairbanks took more patience, more capital, more equipment. There were not the easy placers that attracted stampeders by the tens of thousands as did the diggings around Dawson or on the beaches of Nome. As a result, Fairbanks did not mushroom from zero to twenty thousand population in two years as did the other two gold cities.

An ex-Klondiker by the name of George Anderson was there in 1905. He had crossed the Chilkoot with the Batavia party in 1898 and had mined with Alden Smith around Dawson. He found the prospecting in the Tanana both expensive and unexciting. In a letter to Smith, he says:

They have one very good creek here called Cleary Creek and several others that are good but spotted. The Klondike is now on the bum for a small miner but there is millions in it yet. Frank Moore came down here and bought in on Ester Creek and then sold out and has gone to a new camp called Kantishna between here and Mt. McKinley. There are a number of creeks here that some pay has been found on that are only in the prospecting stage. The pay creeks so far are Cleary, Fairbanks, Ester, Pedro, Gold Stream, Dome, Fish, O'Conner, Vault. The first three are about the only ones that have turned out anything. Dome Creek is believed to be good, but gold has only been found in one part of the creek so far. Some of these creeks are 100 to 150 feet to bedrock. So you see it costs money to prospect. We was prospecting about 120 miles from Fairbanks. The creeks are in the same zone as the Circle and Forty Mile diggings, as you get a map you can see. We was on what is called the Salt Schaket River, empties into the Tanana about 50 miles above Fairbanks. Fairbanks is about 300 miles up the Tanana. There is plenty of broke men here and I suppose there always will be so long as whiskey and gambling is on the go. I often wonder how some people live, but they do somehow. They get in a few hundred and buck the tiger or get on a big drunk and then are looking for another job. Well, old boy, I think you did the wise thing when you settled down. Money is not the whole thing by any means, although it is a good thing to be packing around.[10]

Fairbanks was different from the older stampede towns in other ways as well. Dawson serviced the mining camps up and down the Klondike and its tributaries. Forty Mile provided the miners along the Forty Mile and Sixty Mile rivers. Circle City was the home base for the miners on the Birch Creek and Mastodon diggings.

Nome was built along the gold beaches where the miners were rocking out the pay dirt. Fairbanks was more of a supply depot for other towns that sprang up. There was Cleary City, which supported seventeen saloons at the peak of the stampede. And Fox and Livengood and Olnes. There was the town of Chatanika and Pedro Camp and Golden City. There was Ester and Nenana and Chena. Some of these were never more than overgrown mining camps, while others were viable towns not dependent on a single creek or group of mines. Chena was even a rival of Fairbanks. On the Tanana, at the mouth of the Chena Slough, it had the advantage that steamers could unload or load at its docks without having to negotiate the narrow Chena. It might have been the principal city of the area if its developers had not been so greedy. They set exorbitant prices on land for anyone who wished to build in Chena. Barnette, with more foresight, offered free land to anyone wishing to build at his site. Thus, even though Chena was a better location, new companies and businessmen chose Barnette's Cache over Chena. The post office was located there. With the declining importance of the Yukon, Judge Wickersham moved the headquarters of the Third Judicial District from Eagle to the Tanana Valley. He too selected Barnette's Cache, which was renamed Fairbanks about this time.

Within five years of Barnette's arrival on the Chena Slough, Fairbanks was a thriving community with all the modern conveniences then available. It had electric lights and a water system; it had a fire department, hotels, schools, churches, hospitals, daily newspapers, and a telephone system that not only opererated within the limits of the city, but connected the town with the outlying camps and other communities. A railway connected Fairbanks with Chena, and extended out to the principal mining districts. Tour trains were run for sightseers who wished to visit the rich gold mines. But the Tanana Valley Railroad had a problem. Its rolling stock consisted of four flatcars. With this small capacity it could still return its builders a handsome profit, but it could not comply with Interstate Commerce regulations governing railroads. The specific rule that caused trouble had to do with the carrying of dynamite, a principal freight item of the TVRR. The regulation specified that dynamite could not be carried less than ten cars from a locomotive and TVRR did not have ten cars. Fortu-

THE ALASKA GOLD RUSH

nately for their law-abiding peace of mind, the builders of the TVRR decided that as an intrastate carrier, laws governing interstate traffic did not apply to it. The dynamite went through.

Fairbanks was different from the other stampede towns sociologically as well as physically. From its start, it was more of a family and home town than were the other communities of the North. Men who had pioneered the Forty Mile, Circle, Dawson, and Nome came to Fairbanks, took steady jobs, and settled down, giving the town a tone of comparative moral sobriety. Writers, more interested in the exotic and flamboyant that characterized Circle and Nome, ignored Fairbanks so that few people today recall it as a great stampede town. It had its wild frontier days, however. It had its red-light district, but the street of cribs was screened from public gaze by a fence, lest the women selling their wares offend the eyes of passing children and wives. It had its share of saloons. They tell of the night Oscar Nordale was drinking with a bunch of the boys in a sporting house. The common drink was whiskey and water. The bartender would pour out the whiskey and the patrons would dip themselves a cup of water from a handy bucket. By midnight, the boys were leaning on the bar rather heavily. Oscar, in particular, had reached a point where a trip out back to relieve himself was beyond his powers of concentration. Shortly after this, the madam noticed the boys were beginning to drink their whiskey straight.

"What's the matter with you stupid bums?" she demanded. "Trying to get so drunk you can't do right by my girls?"

"It ain't that exactly. It's Oscar," one of the men volunteered. "He had to go real bad, and the water bucket just seemed the likeliest place to him, and damned if we want to drink out of Oscar's urinal."

Fairbanks' women were as much a part of the growth of the community as the men. They mined and grubstaked and embezzled with the best of them. They handled their own affairs, settled their own questions of honor. Margaret Mulrooney and her sister, Mrs. Carbonneau, were of this breed. Mrs. Carbonneau had been grubstaked by Lorine Byrnes and a Mrs. Scouse. Having reneged on her grubstake agreement, a judgment for $7,000 was returned against Mrs. Carbonneau. She refused to pay. About the same time, her sister Margaret was being accused of embezzling $10,500 when she was cashier at Dome City Bank in 1907. Another former cashier, A. F. Ruser, questioned Miss Mulrooney's honesty. Enraged by this slur on her sister's reputation, Mrs. Carbonneau called on Mr. Ruser with a horsewhip and administered Alaskan justice. From the safety of Seattle, where she and her sister retired, she later told reporters: "I needed no help. Twenty friends of ours, all old sourdoughs of Alaska, begged to take the work off my hands; but it was a family affair. The man had besmirched the name of my sister, and I tended to it to the best of my ability. I horsewhipped him until he cried like a baby."[11] But Margaret Mulrooney's embezzlement, proved or not, was amateurish compared to what the founder of Fairbanks planned.

In 1907 Barnette's star was on the ascendancy. His trading post had prospered. He had good gold claims, staked in his name by his brother-in-law, Cleary. He was president of the Washington-Alaska Bank. He was a leading citizen of the community. But Barnette was incapable of doing anything with complete rectitude. As a result, he was always in litigation. He refused to honor the partnership arrangement with James H. Caustin, who had put up the money to hire the *Lavelle Young*. Caustin had to bring legal action against Barnette in 1908 to obtain satisfaction.

Barnette had grown older and more subtle since stealing two thousand dollars from his partner in Washington thirteen years earlier, but his thinking had changed little. In that case, he pleaded robbery by Indians; in the Caustin case, his defense was that Cleary had embezzled the profits of the company while in charge of the post. The court wanted to know why he had not brought action against Cleary. He could not, he said with indignant righteousness, prosecute his own brother-in-law. The court awarded James Caustin forty thousand dollars.

Barnette was involved in a second case that year, involving mining interests. As the newspaper reported, tongue-in-cheek, Barnette won this case also. It cost him $115,000 to settle, but it gave him control of mining interests worth far more. He was in the big time now, riding the gold tide at its flood.

In 1910 gold production fell off, and in 1911 there was a further drop. Barnette shrewdly decided it was time to leave Fairbanks. How much Barnette was worth at this time is unknown, but all indications are that he was well-off. With the wealth he must have accumulated, it is difficult to understand why Barnette could not have left Fairbanks with a clean record. But he could not; to the last, there had to be something shady. Exact probity was apparently repugnant to Barnette. He sold his controlling interest in the Washington-Alaska Bank, but he made his sale of bank stock to a man without assets. To enable the man to pay for the purchase, Barnette personally authorized a bank loan for the amount involved. The stock was then deposited with the bank as collateral for the loan. In effect, Barnette sold the bank to itself, paying himself with all the money in the vaults. The bank was bankrupt. Fairbanks was bankrupt. Scrip had to be issued in lieu of money. It took three years for Fairbanks to recover.

Barnette left the country; but for some reason, he did return briefly. In a public meeting with depositors, he disclaimed responsibility, insisted he was under no legal restraint, but added, "My sense of justice tells me to help straighten things out." He did not, nor did he explain why his sense of justice had permitted him to do what he had done in the first place. Instead, he talked about a fabulous ranch he owned in Mexico, which he was willing to put up to protect the depositors. However, no one would take a chance on his Mexican "banana plantation." It was, as the Fairbanks *Daily Times* of March 2, 1911, wrote, "hokum reading like get-rich-money-order material."

Having offered nothing more tangible than talk, Barnette left for southern California, where he was arrested on December 3. The Fairbanks *Weekly Times* ran a four-column headline, "BARNETTE ARRESTED FOR EMBEZZLEMENT. Secret Indictments Returned by the Grand Jury Saturday. Warrant Wired to Los Angeles on Monday—Arrest Made Yesterday—Accused Will Be Held Awaiting Extradition to Fairbanks." The enormity of the offense was indicated by the amount of the bail —a third of a million dollars. So, less than a decade after arriving on the banks of the Chena Slough, broke except for the money advanced by Caustin, the founder of Fairbanks left the city in economic ruin. Old residents of Fairbanks recall those difficult years, but do not know what happened to Barnette.

Bobby Shelden, many-time legislator in Alaska, who built his own automobile in Skagway from a picture about the time Fairbanks was established, says he doesn't mind the crookedest street in Fairbanks being named after Barnette, but why name a school after him? Fabian Carey, tough-minded Alaskan trapper and collector of old magazines and books, makes a hobby of loathing Barnette. "It just ruins your stomach to see him get any credit around here. Robbed his own bank. The only successful withdrawal was made by a determined depositor who followed Barnette out of town and got his money back on the trail at the point of a Winchester. The son of a bitch was always in court. Captain Andersen built Barnette a barn and he never got paid. So then Andersen went mining up on the Dome, and Barnette sent men out with Winchesters and drove Andersen off his own claim. Andersen took Barnette to court." This is the case Barnette won at the cost of $115,000.

With Barnette's embezzlement, the great days of Fairbanks were over, the days when gold poured into the banks and money and credit were easy. Those were the days when checks were cashed to the closest nickel. Neither the bank nor the person worried about the pennies. The banks were charging three percent a month and at that rate could afford risks. The president of one bank was, of course, Barnette, an ex-convict. The president of a second bank was a well-known gambler from Dawson who found three percent a month beat poker or faro. But not just the banks, the trading companies also extended credit from year to year. Tuffy, who charged everything at the Northern Commercial Company, came in from the creeks broke. This did not faze him when he got a wedding invitation. In those days a wedding was an affair of real importance. A man had to dress for the occasion and go well-heeled. Tuxedos and full dress were the usual attire at weddings or dances. A miner, who looked the part of a down-and-out bum the rest of the year, was sure to be dressed in the latest fancy gear for a wedding. So Tuffy marched into the N. C. Company store and demanded their finest suit of clothes. Dressed in his finery, he then told the salesman he now needed some money to put in his pockets. And the money was advanced. Tuffy always paid—eventually.

Not everyone paid his bills as well as Tuffy. There were always deadbeats or men who just never had the wherewithal. And this is where Waterfront Brown came in. As Igloo N. 4 of the Pioneers of Alaska put it in rhyme:

If you want a debt collected and the man is in town
Just slip your bill to Waterfront Brown.

He didn't always get his man, but he usually did. He had learned

from long experience at his profession that being on the waterfront when a steamer was about to leave was an almost sure way
to catch someone trying to avoid a debt in Fairbanks. So he was
called Waterfront Brown.

One day he stepped up to big Mike Shea, who was about to
board a steamer, leaving a sizable debt in arrears. Waterfront
presented him with a bill, demanding payment. "I'll pay ya,"
said Mike, "with interest." With which he landed a right backed
up by his two-hundred-some pounds on Waterfront Brown's jaw.
As Waterfront went sprawling, Mike sauntered aboard the
steamer. But Waterfront Brown was not one easily discomfited.
He got to his feet, brushed off his bowler hat and shrugged. "You
win some, you lose some," he said, and marched off for a beer.

The mining camps of the Tanana valley were founded partly
by chance, partly by superstition, as they were in other areas. A
slaughtered moose with a nugget in its hoof was the Alaska version
of the runaway burro who leads the prospector to a rich outcropping. Superstition took many forms and gave rise to many
stories. The rich Livengood district was staked and then abandoned before its riches were discovered because of superstition.

Two partners came into the Tanana from the Circle mining
district. One of the partners was known as Bear Grease Tom. He
was a short, stocky man with small feet and small hands and
balding, even though comparatively young. He was a great one for
practical jokes and was always laughing. His hands were extremely sensitive to the cold, and he used bear grease to keep
them lubricated in the winter and to prevent them from becoming
chapped and cracked. His partner was equally short and stocky,
but redheaded and freckled. An Irishman by the name of O'Brien,
he was called Pinky.

Pinky and Bear Grease had been together since before the
Klondike, when they had met up on Glacier Creek in the Sixty
Mile country. They hit it off and formed a partnership which
lasted all their lives. They were hard workers and good miners,
but they did not have that ingredient known as luck, and without
it no gold miner ever becomes rich.

When news of Felix Pedro's strike got around Circle, Pinky
and Bear Grease decided to have a try in the new area, so they
got their supplies at Jack McQuesten's in Circle and joined the
stampede over the pass. They prospected Globe. They tried the

Tatalina River. They made a strike on a tributary creek of the Tatalina which still bears the name O'Brien Creek. But it was not a rich strike, and they moved on trying one creek after another. They reached the Tolovana River, where they found some color. Hoping for something better, they followed up the Tolovana to Livengood Creek, which was then nameless, and there they staked a claim. The colors were good—maybe this time.

Their camp was selected as home base by a particularly larcenous camp robber. This bird is a member of the jay family, sometimes called a whiskey jack in the north. It is at any time an audacious and highly vocal bird. It knows little fear and will seize any food left lying around, a trait Bear Grease and Pinky did nothing to discourage, as the presence of a whiskey jack was supposed to bring good luck, and they were superstitious. Like other miners who worked hard but, lacking luck, did not find gold, they had to have some excuse outside themselves to explain failure.

The camp robber or whiskey jack, treated in such a friendly manner, became bolder and bolder. He took to swooping down on the table and grabbing food that was left there. One day when supplies were getting short, the camp robber made a particularly bold swoop and grabbed a pancake from the table. Bear Grease in his anger hurled a rock at the bird and by chance struck it. He called to Pinky in alarm. He had killed the camp robber. Together, the partners picked up the bird. Seeing its eyes were not glazed with the film of death, they fanned it with their hats and forced water into its beak. The camp robber soon recovered, and as they released it, flew away. It had learned its lesson and did not come back.

Pinky and Bear Grease had been working the claim for some time without success. They were getting discouraged, and when a passing miner told them of good colors farther down, they decided that the departure of the whisky jack had brought them bad luck, that the place was cursed, and they should move. So the two partners packed their gear and once again moved to a new location. A year later another miner took over the abandoned claim and made one of the rich strikes of the area two feet below where Pinky and Bear Grease had left off. The whiskey jack cost the two partners about $200,000 apiece.

Another version attributes the Livengood stampede to chance, rather than superstition. Jay Livengood and Teddy Hudson headed for the Tolovana in 1914, but as the country was still unmapped, they ended up on an unnamed tributary of the Tolovana. Here they found gold, but it was fine stuff. Jay Livengood was for pushing on to see if they couldn't find the Tolovana, but Teddy was of the opinion that what they had was pretty good. Since they were operating under a grubstake agreement, they returned to Fairbanks in the fall and reported what they had found. They perhaps gilded their prospects to impress the person who grubstaked them. When word got out of the find, there was a stampede into the area.[12]

People did not find much immediately and accused Livengood of having started the stampede for personal reasons. But the gold was there and it was found. The following year Dave Cascaden, taking a page from Klondike experiences, went up on the bench above the stream and located bench gold. A town soon developed named after Jay Livengood. In its heyday, it was a lively place. The commissioner, a Southerner by the name of Charles Laboyteau, was called Alabam after his state of origin since few people could pronounce his last name. As the principal official, he set the tone of Livengood with his pronouncement that "Anything goes here, except we sort of frown on murder." Today Livengood, a pleasant eighty-two-mile drive from Fairbanks, has some twenty or more houses and two residents.

Fairbanks outlived the towns it grew to service. Livengood, Olnes, Fox, Cleary—all are ghost towns. Even Chena, where the riverboats discharged their cargo and the only railroad in Alaska started and which should easily have outstripped Barnette's Cache, is gone. Today there is no sign of this onetime rival just eight miles from Fairbanks. The docks, the rail lines, the buildings have vanished. Chena is a public campground used mostly by local residents who find camping in rustic surroundings pleasanter in the heat of summer than living in town.

Only Fairbanks remains a thriving city, a cross between a family town and a mining camp. It is a complex, many-faceted town of prospectors, fishermen, hunters, rivermen, skiers—outdoor people with a mania for automatic transportation. Those who don't have cars have boats, and those who don't have boats have airplanes; and those who can, have all three with a snowmobile thrown in for good measure. Everywhere are boats and planes.

The plumber, the butcher, or the policeman on the beat has his own plane to fly off to nameless lakes on the weekends to fish or hunt or just to find gold.

Fairbanks was always a great drinking town. It still is. The streets are lined with saloons extending through the block. Typical of the city's split personality, each has two entrances. For the tourists and checchakos there are more sedate entrances along respectable Second Street. Sourdoughs, Indians, and servicemen use the rowdier, more boisterous entrances along the honky-tonk First Street. Inside it is all the same. Tourist and Indian, chee-chako and sourdough—they all belly up to the one bar running from street to street.

Fairbanks also has its lovely residential areas and a little Disneyland replica of an old mining town called Alaskaland. Here Clara Rust and Eva McGowan, who have lived in Fairbanks since its boom days, meet visitors, giving a solid authenticity to the near history that no masquerading college youngsters can achieve.

Clara Rust, whose father started the *Klondike Nugget* in Dawson before coming to Fairbanks, arrived in the lusty young mining town by steamer from St. Michael with the first two automobiles to appear in central Alaska. When she arrived, it was a solidly established city of five thousand, and she watched it fade away, as towns based on placer gold have a way of doing, until by 1920 there were barely more than one thousand people left in Fairbanks. She lived through its slow struggle to survive until World War II, when the arrival of military forces provided the impetus for a second boom. She is a knowledgeable part of the past forming an active continuity with the present. She was a part of that era when water was sold from house to house by the gallon from sleds with stoves built into the center of the water tanks to keep the vendor's assets from freezing. Her husband's mother had been a fortuneteller in Dawson, where she was tried for witchcraft, but the evidence of her successful predictions regarding mining ventures only gave her favorable publicity. She remembers the intriguing glitter of the strip in the long snow-cold nights with the music and bright lights hidden from innocent eyes by the zigzag entrance to the street of sin in the days when love and sex were not recognized by polite society.

Eva McGowan came from a refined family background in

Ireland to frontier Fairbanks to be married. Charming, vibrant, she never stops talking in a flood of delightful non sequiturs, throwing off sparks of history like flakes of gold in a pan of black sand. Buried under furs, she came from Valdez to Fairbanks by sled in midwinter and has never left, nor seems likely ever to leave, but will go on and on talking to anyone and everyone about any vagrant thought that touches her mind.

History still lives around Fairbanks as well as in it. There is Frank Miller, who runs Miller House between Circle and Fairbanks on the Steese Highway. With his wife, he maintains a little store, manages the post office under contract, both being retired postmasters now too old to hold government office, and, without help, keeps cabins for hunters. He met Amundsen at Eagle. He was in Dawson during the days of its glamor, and he knew the short, ebullient Swiftwater Bill, whose ambitions seemed to be to marry the most women and be the biggest spender in Dawson. In contrast to the licentious name that golden city has acquired, his recollection is of blue laws when no man could work on Sunday without a permit from the Mounties; no smut was permitted in public, no funny business; and women had to be decorous in dress and manner. Boredom, not gayety, was the norm of Dawson during the interminable winter nights. Partners would get irritable and cranky penned up together in their cabins. Peevish, they would argue about anything. A fellow would go outside and on coming back, if he said, "I saw the sun," the other would say, "You're a damn liar."

The Wackowitz brothers, Charley and Fred, live out on Chatham Creek at Cleary Mill. Charley is over one hundred and hasn't been to town for a quarter of a century. They live literally surrounded by gold. The small plot of vegetables they raise for themselves is outlined in gold, and the paths about their two houses (living together was too trying, so they built separate cabins) are paved with gold. It is not pure gold, true. To lick the problem of mud, they paved their paths with crushed gold-bearing quartz, the only rock they had. They needed a dry path and they made it with what was available.

While Fairbanks has the superficial appearance of a standard-gauge, mail-order modern city with its hotels, motels, fine restaurants, supermarkets, government buildings, department stores, and parking meters, it is still a frontier mining town. Gold is in its blood. The night clerk at a hotel has his own claim about twenty-five miles from town. During the summer, he goes out every afternoon and works a bulldozer on the hoped for vein until nearly midnight, when it is time to report for duty. It doesn't cost much, he says, it gets him out of doors, and it is fun. And maybe, his eyes light up, the faraway hope comes into his voice, and maybe this is it. There is gold everywhere around here. It is only a matter of time before someone finds quartz gold in quantities, and that is the real money, not this placer stuff. Drive into a service station, and conversation turns to gold. The young fellow who runs the station is importing scuba gear, not for sport but for gold prospecting.

Gold is luck, a gamble in which the only ante is time, and the stakes, wealth. People forget the tragedies, the hardships, and the bitter disappointments; instead they remember stories like that of Joe Butler. Joe was a cheechako, a real greenhorn. He carried field glasses and a geologist's small hand pick ax, and he talked in an odd, precise way that invited ridicule. From his first day in the North, he tried to be one of the boys, but he tried to do it fastidiously. There was about him that serious eagerness to belong that made him a natural to be taken on snipe hunts or sent for left-handed screwdrivers.

After studying maps and some old government bulletins he had brought with him, Joe Butler decided to try Barker Creek. The Barker had been pretty well mined over and the few good places staked. But no one thought to tell Joe that, rather they encouraged him in what everyone knew would be a wild-goose chase. He had to learn sometime. He put together an outfit and started. The third day out he met up with Charley Graham, who had a fair claim which he was working with a hydraulic. Charley was a real old sourdough who had been around the country since Adam was kicked out of Eden and had been running hydraulics since Noah was a kid. It was around two o'clock and hotter than the hinges on the gates of a well-known place, as it can be in the Tanana in midsummer.

Joe was eager to learn and did not mind asking questions. He came right to the point, asking where to find gold. Charley shut down his rig long enough to give serious consideration to the question.

"Now, let's see," he said, sizing up Butler for the obvious

cheechako he was, "there's some chestnut size nuggets up the creek a piece, but they don't mint much more than a thousand plunks a pound. Then, over that ridge," he pointed to a steep cliff in the distance, "there's a small tributary to the Barker where there's some fine slab gold; but it makes for a lot of work breaking it up so as you can tote it out."

While Charley was talking, Joe Butler took out his field glasses and studied the surrounding country. About a half mile up the creek, there was a bench a third of the way up the hillside. It was a fair piece from the stream bed but it did have a nice stand of timber that looked welcome to a person who had been hiking up the heat-reflecting bottom land. So he thanked Charley polite like and headed for the bench and the shade, leaving Charley chuckling over the stupidity of cheechakos. But damn if Butler didn't find gold up there that ran two dollars a pan.[13]

13

The Tailings

THE GOLDEN YEARS OF THE LAST STAMPEDE were from 1873 to 1915. These were the years of the opening up of the Far North, the peak of the individual drive when private fortunes were made at personal sacrifice, when the lone prospector could have a singular dream. From the arrival of McQuesten and Harper in the Yukon to the final stampede to the Koyukuk, the pioneering prospectors came first in small groups, then by the hundreds, and finally by the thousands. They fanned out into the immense wilderness from the Arctic Circle to the Gulf of Alaska, from the Bering Sea to the Mackenzie Mountains. Gold seemed to be everywhere, not just along the Stewart River and Forty Mile, Birch Creek, the Klondike, the Seward Peninsula, around Valdez and along the Copper River, and in the Tanana Valley.

The major stampedes were to Forty Mile, Circle, Dawson, Nome, Valdez, and Fairbanks, but there were secondary stampedes which appeared to be just as important at the time. On the Yukon between Eagle and Circle City, there was a populous complex of towns and camps with hundreds of mines before Barnette's Cache was established. Along this short stretch of the Upper Ramparts are Charley Creek, Fourth of July Creek, and Sam Creek. There are Michigan, Lucky Gulch, and Independence Gulch, all meeting at Nation, and the Nation River itself with

Hard Luck Creek. There are Washington, Boston, Woodchopper, and Thanksgiving. To service these gold-bearing streams were the towns of Star City, Nation, and Seventy Mile, as well as Fish Camp, Slaven's Cabin, and Woodchopper Roadhouse.

According to the April 1898 edition of *The Klondike News*, Star City was destined to be one of the leading towns on the Yukon. It never exceeded a half-dozen log cabins, straggling along the path a mile above Seventy Mile River. The same edition rhapsodized about the Seventy Mile: "It is supposed to be about 300 miles in length, but has never been prospected for more than fifty miles from its mouth. It lies directly in the Gold Belt and has numerous tributaries leading high up in the rugged mountains adjacent."

The *News* may have thought it was printing news, but the Forty Mile sourdoughs knew about Seventy Mile before there was a newspaper or a Dawson. Three miners, whose names have survived only as Froelich, Beam, and Rundell, were there before Carmack filed his discovery claim. They found pay dirt on Crooked Creek, a tributary of the Seventy Mile. For a year they averaged better than $20 a day apiece. Dissatisfied, they moved on to Mogul Creek, another tributary of the Seventy Mile. Again they found good paying gravel and again moved on, to Broken Neck Creek. This time they believed they had a real strike. In two weeks they shoveled $3,500 worth of coarse gold. They built a cabin and prepared to dig a fortune each, but the pay dirt petered out. At the mouth of Sonnickson Creek, still another tributary, a young Swede panned out $54 in dust and picked up a nugget worth $26.32 in one afternoon. It was up the Seventy Mile, on Barney Creek, that the miner for whom the stream was named reputedly found a rich claim and died of scurvy before he could develop it or tell of its location.

In two decades or less, communities were established, flourished, and were abandoned. But there was gold in the area, and the streams between Eagle and Circle were more thoroughly prospected than any similar area in Alaska. Miller's Camp on the Tatonduk River had delusions of greatness for a year or two. Nation rivaled Star City. A. D. Reynolds and his wife arrived in Circle City on July 3, 1907. After inquiring about prospects in the area, he decided on Nation as the likeliest place to make his fortune. He built a one-room cabin, and Reynolds' Roadhouse was in business. It did so well, a second room had to be added. Japanese, Frenchmen, Dutchmen, ladies, and women stopped for meals or spent the night with the Reynolds. The distinction between ladies and women was nicely drawn, apparently depending upon her companion. A Mrs. McVicar arrived on December 24, and it was noted in the register, "Mrs. McVicar, a lady, and a Lt. came from Dawson." The next day she departed with a different companion, so the entry for December 25 notes, "Mrs. McVicar, a woman, and a Dutchman left for Fairbanks."[1]

Between Eagle and Circle was the poor man's gold country. No big strikes were ever made, but gold was on every stream. For reasonable labor, a miner could anticipate reasonable wages. The small communities, the cluster of cabins here and there along the river, gave up hoping to rival Dawson. People were content with a living and the quiet life, for this stretch of the Yukon is the river country in its most attractive and amiable aspect. There are mountains and streams with an abundance of timber, fish, and game. As the river approaches Circle City, the close-pressing mountains recede until, at Circle, the Yukon enters what are called the Yukon Flats. From there to the Lower Ramparts, over two hundred miles, the land is like a puddle of shattered quicksilver. The Yukon is a congeries of rivers. Islands, sandbars, channels, sloughs, lakes, ponds, swamps, and meandering currents make it impossible for the novice to tell what is and what is not the Yukon. Lieutenant Schwatka, trying to reach Fort Yukon, eighty miles below the Upper Ramparts, would have drifted by without seeing it except for the help of Joe Ladue, who guided him into the correct channel. During the days of the steamboats, no captain would venture the trip between Fort Yukon and Circle City without a pilot. Great sections of the banks are continuously falling into the river, sudden bars are deposited, and channels shift overnight. Only an experienced pilot familiar with this particular stretch of water can detect the transient currents.

The Porcupine River enters the Yukon at the latter's northernmost point. Here Alexander Hunter Murray in 1847 established the westernmost Hudson's Bay Company post. Before deciding on a site, he called a meeting with the *gens de large* Indians to discuss possible fur trade and the political problems that might arise from doing business this far west. He smeared his face with tobacco juice to keep the mosquitos at bay and lit up his pipe as a smudge pot. The Indians told him they had seen Russians the previous summer and expected them back. The Russians had promised to return with two boats, not only to trade but to explore the Yukon to its source. Murray was not happy with this information. He realized he was in Russian territory and did not relish a confrontation before he was established. Despite this report, he was determined to establish a post as instructed. Because of the fear of trouble with the Russians, he not only erected a trading post but built a great stockade around it, making it the strongest fort on the Yukon.

It was to this remote outpost that Archdeacon Robert McDonald came, the first white man to find gold on the Yukon. Traveling at all seasons of the year, living off the country, he became ill. He was not expected to live, and the Reverend Bompas was sent out to replace him. By the time Bompas arrived, MacDonald had recovered, thanks to a plant the Indians found beneficial in cases of lung troubles, a plant by the descriptive name of "It cured his uncle." He stayed on for most of the century, translating the complete Bible, the prayer book, the hymnbook, and several other volumes into Takudh.[2] These translations are still used on the Yukon and the Porcupine, and by Chief Charley Moosehide when he conducts services in Dawson.

The Russians did not return, however, except for Ivan Simonsen Lukeen, who traveled alone to Fort Yukon in 1863. Feigning disgust with the Russian-American Company in St. Michael, he remained at Fort Yukon for several weeks. As a trader, he showed keen interest in the way the British conducted their fur trading. As a free agent who was considering establishing his own station, he made a detailed study of the construction of the post. Having gathered all the intelligence he could, he slipped away in the night and returned to report to his employers. This knowledge might have been of interest to the Russians, but there was little they could do about the British infringement. Russian strength in mainland Alaska was inadequate to contest any encroachment, let alone one as remote from Russian influence as Fort Yukon.

Two years before Lukeen's visit, Robert Kennicott, the first American to visit the Yukon, spent most of 1861 at Fort Yukon. He was later to return to the Yukon as head of the Western Union expedition, which included William Dall, Frederick Whymper, Frank Ketchum, and Mike Labarge, all of whom visited Fort Yukon in 1867. These men definitely established that the Kwikpak River of the Russians and the Yukon of the British were the same river. Prior to this time, some believed the Kwikpak flowed into the Pacific and the Yukon continued north to join the Colville River and empty into the Arctic Ocean.

In 1869 a fifty-foot steamer was brought from San Francisco to St. Michael for commercial use on the Yukon. The inaugural voyage of this first steamer on the Yukon had a dual mission. Primarily, the steamer was to establish American trading posts along the river for Parrott and Company, and at the same time it took Captain C. W. Raymond of the United States Army to Fort Yukon for the purpose of determining whether that post was in American territory and, if so, to advise the Hudson's Bay Company traders they must vacate. At 4 P.M. on July 31, after a trip of more than one thousand miles in twenty-three days, the steamer arrived at Fort Yukon with its military and commercial passengers.

For a week, weather made stellar observations impossible. Then the skies cleared. At midnight it was just barely dark enough for Captain Raymond to make his observations; on August 9, Captain Raymond notified John Wilson, the Hudson's Bay agent in charge of the post, that Fort Yukon was in United States territory,[3] that the trade by foreigners with natives was illegal, and that accordingly Hudson's Bay Company must vacate the post as soon as practicable.

Captain Raymond in his report noted that the procedure of the Hudson's Bay Company was to take furs each year up the Porcupine to its headwaters and over the pass to Rat River and LaPierre House, where they exchanged furs for trading goods and supplies. At the trading station, there were the chief trader and two or three clerks. The chief trader received £100 a year and the clerks £5. All supplies and equipment and clothing had to be purchased from the company. The chief trader received an allowance of tea for a year and sugar and flour sufficient to last two months at the most. The clerks received only a tea allowance and nothing more. Nor could they buy any clothing or supplies until the trading with the Indians was completed; only then could they make selections from what remained.

An inventory of trading goods at Fort Yukon showed: guns, double and single barrel; pocket knives, 1 and 2 blades; pants, ordinary and fine; white flannel shirts; red same; calico shirts;

prints; heavy cloth; blue-striped drugget; white same; shawls, large and small; cotton drill; bullets; shot; butcher knives; tin pans; tin cups; metal buttons; pearl same; linen thread; silk and cotton handkerchiefs; rings; overcoats; black neck handkerchiefs; Paris neckties; belts; gunpowder; ribbon, wide and narrow.[4] There is no mention of beads.

Parrott and Company took over the trading post, putting Moses Mercier in charge. It was here that McQuesten, Harper, and Mayo first entered the Yukon country, and McQuesten became the chief trader of the post three years later.

For twenty-five years under American occupation Fort Yukon had a desultory existence; then, with the beginning of the stampede to the Yukon, it became an active post. The advent of regular steamer service on the river gave it increased significance as a pilot station. River pilots, trappers, traders, travelers, and Indians gathered at Fort Yukon. Although not a gold town, it had its rough element, its majority of ordinary people, and its misfits. Among the latter must be listed a young girl from New York who resented every hour she had to stay in the town. She was there only because of misrepresentation, deceit, and downright fraud.

Her story begins on a sweltering summer day in New York. She was clerking in the millinery department of a store when a faultlessly attired man with coal black hair and neatly trimmed black beard entered and started buying in a lavish manner. He engaged the young salesgirl in conversation. The oppressive climate of New York was naturally a subject of discussion. From this, the man went on to tell of his home on the Yukon and of the fresh breezes and the cool, clear days and nights of the Far North country. As he talked, he waxed more and more eloquent. He took her to dinner and his description of Fort Yukon made it sound like a big city on the banks of a beautiful river. His home was painted with plush, palatial brush strokes. The more he told of life on the Yukon, the more intrigued became the young milliner already imbued with the mystique of the North from stories she had read of the Klondike. With the romantic myopia of youth, she saw in the stranger only the essence of stampede adventure. The haze of gold filmed her vision. Within a week they were married and left for Seattle. From there they took a ship to St. Michael, where they transferred to a river steamer.

Long before she reached Fort Yukon, she began to realize the country was not as she had pictured it. With no experience except her home environment, she had imagined the Yukon was like the Hudson with rolling hills, green trees, lovely homes, and sweeping lawns. Instead, she found a muddy river with meager trees along the banks and towns hardly more than collections of hovels. By the time she reached Fort Yukon, she expected little. But even so, since it was to be her home, she was horrified at the sight of the mudbank, the flats stretching away from the river, the few scraggly spruce, and the mean log cabins. The palatial home she had been promised was hardly more than a shack. Furthermore, during the long trip, her husband's hair had grown, revealing the dye job that had been done. His hair was almost snow-white and his beard completely white. He was not the vigorous, romantic figure she had seen through a girlish haze of romance in New York. He was an old man of seventy. And the shanty was filled with children by a former marriage, some older than herself. To help support the family, since her husband had spent most of his savings on his trip to New York, she took a job as a waitress in a restaurant serving meals to filthy, disreputable travelers. Disillusioned, heartsick, she saved what little money she could conceal from her husband, and one day while he was away, she boarded a steamer and fled Alaska.[5]

Fort Yukon could also be a happy, exciting place; at least, two young miners found it so. They were on their way to St. Michael on the steamer *Arctic* when they got frozen in at Fort Yukon and had to spend the winter there. Each had made his fortune—not great fortunes, but adequate for young men—and they were meeting their fiancées in St. Michael to get married. They saw Fort Yukon in a haze of anticipation, and in comparison to the lonely cabins they had been occupying for the past two years, Fort Yukon was a populous town, vital and pulsing with a social life they had not known for many months.

The young miners met their fiancées the next spring when the ice went out. The girls were waiting on the ship *Bertha,* lying off the mouth of the Yukon. Being of a romantic inclination, the girls had connived with Captain Hayes of the ship to take the wedding party out to sea, beyond the three-mile limit, where he performed the double wedding ceremony, before the ship returned to St. Michael. As one of the guests on the occasion wrote: "Such a supper and such a reception at Mr. Neumann's parlors. Gazing on

At the turn of the century Rampart was a thriving town
on the Yukon. Now only one person, Ira Weisner,
lives there. (E. A. HEGG)

An Indian fish camp near Beaver. The
fisherman sells smoked salmon to bush
pilots from Fairbanks. (PHILLIP HYDE)

The home of Silas Alexander, Indian
guide and boatman, at Fort Yukon.
(PHILLIP HYDE)

The Yukon Flats are between Circle and Rampart. Tens of thousands of ponds, sloughs, and old river channels provide nesting grounds for most of North America's waterfowl. (PHILIP HYDE)

serene and luxurious rooms filled with merry dancers, richly dressed women and gallant men and listening to the sweet strains of the professor's violin, I could hardly realize I was on a little island way up in the Bering Sea hundreds and hundreds of miles beyond the supposed limits of civilization."[6] This was written about St. Michael, a primitive collection of cabins no more pretentious than Fort Yukon. But the North was a mirror, reflecting the horror or beauty a person brought with him.

Although reports of gold, as well as furs, had attracted McQuesten and Harper to Fort Yukon in 1873, it alone of the towns of the upper Yukon had no direct connection with gold. No gold was discovered in its vicinity; it experienced no stampede. It grew and declined alternately as trading post, Indian village, supply depot for Circle and Dawson, pilot post, and missionary center. It was a part of the last stampede, however, and except for the stabilizing influence of a large Indian population, it would have gone the way of the other Yukon towns at the end of the golden years. Instead it is the largest town on the Alaskan Yukon. It has several stores, a post office, a school, three churches, a council meeting hall, an airport, and a 4-H club. The young boys hang around the stores, listening to the latest records. The young girls lounge through the streets in stretch pants and pink curlers. The adults are politically conscious. When there was an attempt to obtain a multi-billion-dollar appropriation to build a dam in the Lower Ramparts that would flood the Yukon valley all the way to the Canadian border, the Indians formed the GGG (*Gwitchya Gwitchin Ginkhye,* Yukon Flats People Speak) to fight for their homes and hunting lands. Their spokesman said, "If dam built, no salmon; no salmon, no food for dogs; no dogs, no trap lines; no trap lines, no living."

It is a bleak, desolate town crouched on the forever-eroding banks of the Yukon at its widest point. Schwatka gave the width of the river at this point as twenty miles. It may be at least five miles. No one knows, as it is constantly changing. Whatever the appearance of the country, the people are anything but bleak or desolate. The girls are extremely attractive, their mothers delightful conversationalists. The men fish for their salmon, shoot the caribou needed for the winter's meat supply, and make the most vicious home brew in the interior of Alaska.

Halfway between Fort Yukon and the lower end of the Flats

is the town of Beaver. It was the closest point on the river to the gold diggings on the Chandalar River. A glowing future was predicted for Beaver when quartz gold was found on the upper Chandalar, and a trail was built from the mines to the Yukon at Beaver. A townsite was staked out; cabins were hastily erected. Beaver readied itself for the stampede and inevitable boom. It never developed. The Chandalar quartz did not prove productive, so the stampede town that almost was never came into being. Still, it must be considered a stampede town. The umbilical trail connecting it with the interior gold area is there; a mile of road points a tentative finger hopefully into the wilderness, ready to be pushed farther if the need should arise. A few men are yet on the Chandalar hoping for a rich quartz find.

There is another and more romantic story of the beginning of Beaver. According to this version, a Japanese cabin boy jumped ship at Point Barrow and married an Eskimo girl. Rather than risk being discovered and returned to the ship, he set off across the northern slope with his wife and all her relatives. In the dark of winter, the small band fled across the vast wasteland, crossed the Brooks Range, and descended the southern slopes to the banks of the Yukon. Here, safe from pursuit, they established an Eskimo community which they called Beaver, either from the great number of those fur-bearing animals in the vicinity, or for the Japanese symbol of fertility. Credence is given this account by the fact that the present population is predominantly Eskimo, although the people native to the Yukon flats are Kutchin.

Typical of their Eskimo origin, the people of Beaver are friendly, warm, more outgoing than the other river people. Toorak, proprietor of a small store, who had come to Beaver in 1912 with his father and mother, needs no prompting to recall hearing about the great days of the Yukon, with its frenetic stampeders in search of gold. But the history of Beaver, as he knew it, was associated with fishing and trapping when there had been good money in otter, beaver, marten, and fox pelts—before imitation furs and new materials ruined the fur market. Money, however, was never an important factor in trapping. No matter how much money trappers made when the fur market was good, they never thought of leaving the Yukon for an easier life. When winter came, it was the trap lines and the bone-numbing nights of cooking a piece of frozen meat over an open fire in the snow. It was the solitude of a frozen river in the heart of a spruce forest. The arctic wind sifting snow off the mountain ridges, the chilling howl of the wolf, the pitting of human skill against animal cunning, and the substantial comfort of a dingy cabin with its stove and woodpile waiting beside it, and a dry bunk after days on the open trail—these were reasons enough for trapping.

Beaver has an air of independence and enterprise that is missing in the other towns. The people have organized for civic improvement. They have put in drains, brought in gravel, and built raised walks to defeat the mud. It is a drab, wilderness-cramped settlement of only one hundred, but alive with a singular energy.

Beyond Beaver are Purgatory and Victor's Landing. It was at Victor's Landing that one of the great unsolved gold robberies of Alaska occurred.[7] A steamer heading for the outside with a shipment of gold had a night watchman on guard at Fort Yukon, and at Beaver all was well. When the steamer reached Victor's Landing, the night watchman was gone and so was the gold. The steamer tied up and a search was instituted for the night watchman. He was found, after a few hours, hiding in a cache behind Victor's cabin. He was arrested and taken to Fairbanks. He insisted on his innocence. The prosecution pointing to the facts—one, that the gold was on board at Fort Yukon and Beaver; two, so was the night watchman; three, both were gone at Victor's Landing—concluded that the night watchman must have thrown the gold overboard with some form of markers and then jumped overboard himself with the intention of returning for the gold later. To the last, the watchman insisted on his innocence, but on the circumstantial evidence, he was convicted and sent to jail. Furthermore, since the watchman had been found at Victor's Landing and the loss had occurred near there, it was assumed that Victor was privy to the theft. It was known that Victor had developed some placer deposits, and it was thought he might be working them with the plan of appearing after a few years with the stolen gold, claiming it was from his own diggings. This did not happen. Victor was found dead in his cabin two years later and the gold was not recovered. This story has never been authenticated, but if true, there is a rich cache of gold in the Yukon somewhere near Victor's Landing.

A few miles downriver is Purgatory. It is not a town, nor has it anything to do with gold. And yet it is typical of the originality and individualism of the last stampede. It was the home of Sergeant William Yanert, who came to Alaska in 1897, and for five years was detailed to different survey parties. The esteem in which his superiors held him is suggested by the fact that they gave his name to several places on the maps he helped to develop.

In 1903, when Fairbanks was just getting started, he retired from the army; and like so many who fell in love with the North, he did not move into a town but selected a remote site on the Yukon between Beaver and the Lower Ramparts. Here he built a home and named it Purgatory after Dante's depiction of the icy depths of hell.

A self-styled philosopher, poet, and artist, he was really more of a prankster. When his cabin was robbed, rather than putting a padlock on the door, a thing repugnant to any old Yukoner, he shot a camp robber. He then dug a grave six by three and buried the bird. Piling the dirt in a mound over the small corpse, he placed a board at the head with the inscription: "Here lies a camp robber. I caught him at it and shot him. Yanert." His cabin was never again molested.

In later years, when people would stop by to visit and Purgatory became a tourist stop, he erected a huge devil along the path to his house, which he could operate by wires from his cabin. He did this not to scare people away—because he liked visitors—but just for the prank.

Where the Yukon Flats end and the thousands of channels gather together into one main stream, where the Lower Ramparts begin, is the old gold town of Rampart. In the same month that Carmack and Skookum Jim and Tagish Charlie found gold on the Bonanza, Minook Ivanov, a brother of Pitka and brother-in-law of Cherosky, found gold near Rampart. From a hole eight feet square by fifteen feet deep, he took out $3,000 worth of gold, and by the next year there were over a thousand people in Rampart.[8]

Al Mayo moved to Rampart, was mayor in 1897, and a booster of the town for many years. While he was mayor, an indignant minister accosted him concerning the sinful conditions in Rampart. The white men should be ashamed of setting so terrible an example for the Indians. Rampart is a veritable hell on earth, he proclaimed. At which Al Mayo rejoined, "Take your gawdamned Indians across the river where they can see hell and not be in it."

This exchange of words had an echo of the Russian days

when, in translating the Bible, all references to hell were omitted.[9] The Russian priests had felt the Indians suffered enough in this world, without being threatened with punishment in the next. Indeed, the priests could imagine no punishment greater than that which the Indians already endured in this life. Such a life made threats of retribution impossible, as a group of miners found in at least one reported case.

A white man having been killed by an Indian, a posse of miners descended on the Indian village and demanded the culprit. The miners came prepared for trouble and so were surprised to have a young man step forward immediately and give himself up. "I shot white man," he volunteered.

When the miners wanted to know why, he explained: "Preacher man shot by white man. They take white man outside. Two Indians they go with white man as witness. Two Indians return. Got much money. Got fine clothes. Man who shot Preacher man, he put in big house, fine skookum house with much food and fine clothing. I like to go skookum house. Get fine food and fine clothing." He wanted to go to prison. To him, it seemed a life preferable to a brush hut on the Yukon with inadequate clothing and winter months with barely enough food to stay alive. But the young Indian did not get a free trip to San Francisco or lodging in skookum house. He was hung on the spot to discourage such practical thinking.

The Indians were then second-class citizens, if even that. Except for a few like Carmack, McQuesten, Harper, Mayo, and Archdeacon McDonald, the white men who came to the Yukon made no attempt to understand the Indians and their way of life. They were siwashes, and siwash became a word of contempt in the lexicon of Alaska. A man who went siwash was outside the limits of society. When Dan Carolan, who had married an Indian and gone siwash, shot N. A. T. Joe for raping his wife, the populace was indignant. Carolan was seized and held on a charge of murder. An army officer in Rampart at the time wrote, "Carolan's wife was a squaw and according to Alaskan morality fair game."

Although Indians might not be first-class citizens in terms of white man's justice, Rampart considered itself a law-abiding, respectable community. It had its mayor and commissioner and enforced municipal regulations with vigor and strictness. A property owner who failed to comply with the law that trees be cut

and weeds burned within a reasonable time had his property con-
fiscated and sold at auction. Justice was enforced, but with an
appreciation of the practical realities of life. In appointing a new
commissioner at Rampart in 1900, Judge Wickersham instructed
the appointee: "In cases other than serious ones do not hold a
person over for grand jury. Mete out punishment immediately. A
fine is better than a jail sentence. The one brings the fine and costs
into the treasury, while the other compels the government to support a man in jail in idleness at a great expense."[10]

At its peak, Rampart had a population of between one and two
thousand. In addition to its permanent population, it housed a
sizable number of transients. Steamers unable to reach Dawson
or St. Michael found Rampart a good wintering place. Novelist
Rex Beach lived here and used the town and its people as background for *The Barrier*. Jack London stopped over at Rampart on
his way down the Yukon from Stewart River and Dawson. A
hard-eyed drifter by the name of Wyatt Earp pushed drinks in a
bar all winter to get enough money to keep going.

Today the permanent population of Rampart is one, but that
one is a community in himself. Known throughout the interior of
Alaska simply as Weisner, he is postmaster, miner, lawyer, doctor,
cannery operator, bookkeeper, storekeeper, and trader. He is a
voluble complainer who takes a self-pitying delight in the exigen-
cies of life. "A trading post," he will gladly explain, "is not like a
city store. It isn't as simple as just buying and selling. If there's a
profit, it's only at the end of a maze of trades and bookkeeping.
Take, for example, salmon. I buy salmon from the Indians. But the
Fish and Wildlife officer tells me I cannot buy fish from the
Indians unless they have licenses. If I do, I will be liable to a large
fine. Now, none of the Indians have licenses. Where would they
get them out here? So before I buy salmon, I must buy a lot of
licenses and give them to the Indians from whom I buy the
salmon. That's money I have to pay out. I have a cannery to can
the salmon. That costs money to operate. I hire Indian women to
work in the cannery. They come and go. They work a few days
and then quit. I can't keep track. They tell me later how much
time they work. I give them credit for the work. That takes bookkeeping. I also give credit to the Indians I get the salmon from,
since I don't have any money yet. That takes more bookkeeping. I
send the salmon to Fairbanks and trade it for supplies—food,

clothing, liquor, stuff the people of the Yukon want. These supplies I give to the Indians against the credit they have from the salmon or from working in the cannery, and I extend them credit for what they take in addition to what they have earned. More bookkeeping. Later, they bring in furs and pelts from the trap lines, which I take to balance their credit position. I then sell the furs in Fairbanks and finally get some money. It's all trade and bookkeeping. I guess you could call me a sourdough, a real sourdough. You hear a lot of smartass definitions of sourdough, but what it really means is a man who is sour on the country but hasn't got the dough to leave. That's me. The Government has been talking about putting a dam here in the Lower Rampart, and I sure as hell wish they would. They would have to buy me out before flooding my property, and then I could get the hell out of here."

He had liked the Yukon, but the life was for a young man facing a challenge and trying to beat it. The fun was gone for him. Now he was nothing but a bookkeeper. He hired an Indian to manage the store. He had two men and a cook up the creek operating a mine. He hired from five to twenty women during the canning season. This meant accounting for a dozen different taxes and social security for each, in addition to running the mine, overseeing the store, balancing barter arrangements, caring for the sick, adjudicating disputes. "Sure, I think the Rampart Dam is good. For me. For the Indians, no. They might get new houses and jobs for a few years on the project, but this is not their life. They fish, hunt, trap, cut some logs. They don't care about new houses and jobs. The dam would stop the fish run and ruin their lives."

He pointed to a jumble of huge log houses. "Two springs ago," he said, "the ice jammed up in the Ramparts. It didn't break up fast enough. The water rose thirty feet here where we are standing and cakes of ice as big as houses were pushed up on land like driftwood. Boats, trees, and houses were smashed. What about this force behind a dam? Maybe they have thought about it. I guess they have smart engineers, but sometimes people who have not lived in this country cannot fully appreciate the power of a river and how angry the old man gets when something tries to stop him from his natural flow. I don't know," he shook his head. "It would be good for me, but I don't think I would like to see it. This just wouldn't be the Yukon any more. There wouldn't be a river, just a big lake that wouldn't do anybody any good. The fish wouldn't be here. The timber would all be under water. The meandering sloughs and shallows, the millions of small lakes and ponds which are the natural nesting place for the wild fowl of western America would be gone, and I guess the ducks and geese would vanish. The beaver waters, the marten country, the feeding grounds for moose and caribou would be wiped out. These things you can't put a money tag on or call them progress or civilization, but I got a feeling they have value or God wouldn't have put them there."

Liquor posed a particular problem to Weisner. Although a good item on that remote stretch of the Yukon, it could not be sold in the store. Liquor had to be sold in a separate store, which, for personnel reasons, was impossible. Weisner resolved the dilemma in typical Weisner fashion. He blocked off a corner of his store for the liquor supply, installed a counter, and knocked a new door in the wall. Customers could enter from the outside and he could serve both stores from the inside.

"This is what I don't like about the Yukon now," he said. "When Wyatt Earp was pushing rotgut whiskey across the counter, there was no one to tell him how to run his business. Now, I can't sell liquor in the trading post. Liquor sales got to be in a separate place, only they don't tell me how to be in two places at once, so I sort of figured this up. You're in the liquor store now and you can't buy anything but liquor here. If you want any other supplies, you go back out and come in the other door. Had no complaints yet, but one of these days some darned fool with a badge is going to fly in and tell me I am not complying with the law. It's all laws and bookkeeping now. Perhaps the Rampart Dam is the best solution, wipe out the entire Yukon valley with all the history of the past that was free and all the Indians and animals and birds and fish. They could just put a bookkeeper up on the dam to figure the kilowatts, and there would be no need for any laws or regulations because there wouldn't be anyone here or anything to attract people."[11]

Does it ever get lonesome, living here like this?

"Hell yes. I'm human."

In fact, Weisner may be something more than human. Annually, with varying success, he advertises for a cook, female, blonde, attractive. In the Fairbanks *Daily News-Miner* of August 22, 1968,

Sam John, the newspaper's Rampart correspondent, reported, "There is no blonde in Rampart. There was an ad in paper for a blonde for Weisner, but she didn't show up."

In Alaska there are no secrets. Along the Yukon where communication is by radiotelephone, even the strictest confidences are public. The radio circuit is open for anyone to listen in. Sitting in a restaurant in Circle City, you can hear conversations between Rampart and the outside. A young man who was wintering in Rampart telephoned his girl in Seattle and proposed. The girl demurred. She wasn't sure. Her parents wanted her to wait. The young man, unfamiliar with how public he was making his intentions, urged the girl, if she had doubts about their compatibility, to come up and spend a month with him and find out.

This is Rampart, the end or the beginning of the Yukon gold country, depending on whether a person is descending or ascending the river. But some two hundred miles west the Koyokuk enters the Yukon, and up the Koyokuk there was gold. From almost the earliest days of prospecting in Alaska, there were men on the Koyokuk. Here was the most remote, the most inhospitable gold country in Alaska. Far north of the Arctic Circle, deep into the Brooks Range prospectors forced their way. The town of Coldfoot separated the men from the boys. It was named in derision of those who, reaching this point, got cold feet and turned back. Nellie Cashman, who had been in Dawson during its great days, was there. She mined so far north that she always referred to Fairbanks as the southland. And Swedes were there, as everywhere. Anderson and John and Gus Oleson took out $105,000 in three months, but they had to drive a shaft one hundred and twenty feet to bedrock to do it.

It was difficult country to mine. There was little wood to burn holes to bedrock, but such problems never stopped gold prospectors. They worked the benches of Archibald Creek, north of Weisman, which is north of Coldfoot. A nugget worth $1,100 was found on the Hammond River near the summit of the Brooks Range. Gold was taken from the Smith and Tramway Bar and Frying Pan Bar.

The tail end of the last stampede, the dying gasps, were the rushes to the Innoko and Kuskokwim. By 1910 Forty Mile was a quiet river post. The Klondike had been turned over to the dredges and hydraulics. Circle was a hoarse whisper of its boisterous heyday. Nome and Fairbanks were still prospering, but production was primarily from company mining. Valdez was content to be a port town for Fairbanks. The shipping companies and suppliers were eager to blow the slightest rumor into a major stampede. Old-timers, forgetting the hardships and disappointments and recalling only the thrills, excitement, and easy companionship of the old stampede days, were ripe for a last fling. Young men, who had been raised on the heady pap of sourdough tales, were eager to try their fathers' course. In this atmosphere, the slightest spark was sufficient to set off a stampede. With a report of good gold findings on Long Creek, the newspapers and magazines sounded the call for a stampede. The *Alaska-Yukon Magazine*, in October 1908, touting the riches of the new diggings, told from the comfort of an editorial room in Seattle how anyone could take out ten thousand dollars in a summer, working alone without machinery. This is what old-timers and new-timers alike wanted to hear. To hell with the companies, the dredges, and the deep mines. Here was country for a man with a pan, a shovel, and a little gumption.

Iditarod, Bethel, Flat, McGrath, and, of course, Ophir blossomed into sizable communities. Speculators swarmed up the rivers and staked out land. The instant saloon came back into its own—a tent, a plank laid across two boxes for a bar, and a man was in business. Stores, hotels, restaurants followed the stampede. A general store with the brave name of the Golden North Emporium was opened in Iditarod by Moses, who acted as a banker on the side. It was to Moses that Stub Dorgan, a gambler, came when he went broke, according to the *Alaska-Yukon Magazine* in June 1910 (page 40). Dorgan signed a promissory note for the amount he needed and headed back to the gaming tables with his new roll. But his luck was on the ebb. He lost all that he had borrowed. When the note came due, Moses asked Dorgan about repayment.

Stub shrugged. "I don't have it."

"So you don't pay," Moses asked, "what am I doing with this note?"

Stub Dorgan was a short-tempered man and a bully. He flipped a gun in Moses' face and said, "You're going to eat it, and eat it now, damn you."

That night Dorgan's luck turned. He won. He apologized to

Moses and paid the note, plus interest. But he was a gambler; sometimes he had money, and sometimes he was broke. Six months later, on the downswing, he had occasion once again to borrow from Moses. As Moses counted out the money, Stub started to write out the note on a blank form. Moses stopped him. "Here," he said, and handed Stub a large soda cracker, "write on this. It is more digestible."

These rushes did not generate the rich claims that made Dawson, Nome, and Fairbanks. A few did take out $10,000 in a summer, but not many. The last stampede was over. When men tried to reconstruct the flamboyant days, the gold was not there to support them. The stampeders straggled back to their homes and to the petty jobs they had left.

The last stampede is now only an exciting memory. Although Alaska and the Yukon Territory are on the verge of mineral development greater than any ever dreamed of in gold, the gold standard is still the only reality of the country. The Clinton asbestos mines on the Forty Mile River, with over three hundred employees, have built a new town. Japanese interests have committed themselves to spend $500 million developing the mineral resources north of Whitehorse. The White Pass and Yukon Railroad into Skagway is being reinforced and rebuilt to haul ore. New docks are planned for Skagway. Oil companies are planning a mass invasion of the North Slope to tap what is possibly the richest oil reserve in the world. But the new stampeders will be employees working on contract. The prospectors are hired hands of a board of directors carefully estimating costs against possible profits in air-conditioned offices in Los Angeles, New York, Toronto, and Tokyo.

The Alaskans and Yukoners hope some of the exploited wealth will rub off on them, but they will never believe in anything but gold. If some drunken bum should stumble into a bar with a hundred dollar poke, he would generate more excitement than an outsider with a wallet full of credit cards and an unlimited expense account. The one is luck that could be shared by anyone. The other is establishment-oriented reality, an anathema to a society dedicated to the gut individualism of the last stampede, which they know can never be repeated.

14

Now: Alaska and the Yukon

H OW MUCH GOLD CAME FROM THE LAST STAMPEDE? Comparatively speaking, not much. Canada, as a whole, produced
fifteen times as much gold as came from the Klondike. The
California gold mines yielded five times as much as came
from the Alaskan gold fields. South Africa in one year produces
nearly as much as Alaska and the Yukon Territory produced in
eighty-five years.

The quantity of gold is not the important factor in the last
stampede. Eleven million ounces came out of the Klondike. An
equal amount came from the beaches of Nome. The Tanana
mines around Fairbanks produced as much as the Klondike and
the Nome beaches combined. But it is the qualitative, not the
quantitative, values that make the last stampede unique. This
was the last frontier. Here frontier spontaneity had not yet been
smothered by the proprieties of civilization. The people were
bigger than life-size—the people like Leroy Napoleon McQuesten,
Arthur Harper, George Washington Carmack, Joseph Ladue,
Robert Henderson, "Ma" Pullen, Mollie Walsh, Big Alex Mc-
Donald, the Lucky Swedes, the Diggers, and Felix Pedro. So
were the primitive city-towns like Skagway, Dawson, Circle City,
and Nome. Even the criminals like "Soapy" Smith and Noyes
were of heroic stature. And all were epitomized by the uncontrolled, unregulated, ungoverned, self-willed Yukon River, an-

nually freezing and flooding from its source to its mouth, each year the ice breaking up unpredictably, gouging out new channels, laying down new sandbars, forming new ponds, lakes, and sloughs. Here, at the end of the nineteenth century were the people, the places, the country of which epics are made. Ulysses and Aeneas would not have been out of place on the Yukon.

These attributes were not peculiar to the end of the nineteenth century nor to Alaska and the Yukon. They combined in other places and other times, but this was the last time in history they were to exist. The vastness of the country, its remoteness, the slowness of communications, the lack of law—all these combined to develop a psychology of freedom, independence, and self-reliance, which marked the last stampede, traces of which still persist in Alaska. The sense of a free frontier, the quiet tempo, the uncluttered quality of life, these are still found in the North country among its scattered people.

Paradoxically, this psychology of independence persists in the Yukon and Alaska because of the company mines, which tended to destroy the individualism of the prospectors. With the advent of the company mines, gold lost its excitement and individual character. Men working for wages on the barges never experienced the thrill of color at the bottom of a pan or of nuggets in the riffles of a sluice box. They operated levers and throttles. They oiled machinery and drew their salaries. Or they worked in frozen ore beds more than one hundred feet underground. In the winter, they never saw the sun, going below while it was still dark and coming up long after the last gray light had faded from the sky. Men who had come north to avoid industrial bondage soon fled what they had come to escape. The companies did not care. Machines replaced men. Hundreds, then thousands, drifted south. The hard-core sourdoughs turned to trapping or prospecting on the fringe streams back against the Brooks Range or in the untracked country around Denali. Company mining drove out the labor pool that might have attracted other industry. Like a lost continent, Alaska and the Yukon drifted backward in time. Thus, the principal threat to the free life of the North, the big mining companies, in the end made it possible for that life to continue. It forced back into wilderness what it had torn from wilderness It recreated frontier conditions after frontier conditions had ended.

Now: Alaska and the Yukon

Between Whitehorse and the mouth of the Yukon two thousand miles of river reverted to a state more primitive than that during the height of the last stampede. In 1899 the river traffic was heavy. People were never out of sight of each other for long. New arrivals landed at Dawson on the average of one boatload every eight minutes. There were Indian fishing camps, trading posts, and soon roadhouses and woodchoppers' camps. Today the Yukon is deserted. The trading posts are closed, the Indian fishing camps abandoned, the roadhouses and woodchopper's camps lie along the banks like outgrown hellgrammite cocoons— Big Salmon, Little Salmon, Frickson's Wood Camp, Minto, Fort Selkirk, Thistle Creek Roadhouse, Moosehide, Fort Reliance, Forty Mile, Star City, Nation, and Woodchopper's Camp. The Yukon has reverted to a true primitive area, an open-air museum. Moss-chinked log cabins with sod roofs rise among shoulder-high fireweed like freshly sprouted mushrooms with the dirt still clinging to the caps. Sleds, wagons, tubs, and a few simple tools on the walls spell out the simple life that was there. The hulls of derelict steamers between Whitehorse and Dawson mark the end of a civilization that died. There are at least two *Cascas* wrecked along the shores, and the *Donvell* just below U. S. Bend. The steamer *Evelyn Norcom Dawson* sits in its decaying entirety in the middle of Shipyard Island just below Hootalinqua, as do three or four others across from Moosehide.

The first white men on the upper Yukon found Indians along the river. Today they may be seen only in the few towns. At the turn of the century sternwheelers churned the shallow waters of the Yukon from its mouth to Whitehorse, serving the populous communities along the way. Roadhouses, mail carrier's posts, woodchoppers' cabins, miners' and trappers' cabins marked the high-water line of man's northern thrust. Trading posts and missions once furnished physical and spiritual sustenance to the river folk. They are gone, leaving their mute trappings to give voiceless evidence of what was. At Little Salmon, Minto, Fort Selkirk, Moosehide, and Forty Mile mission churches still stand in good repair. Pews, lecterns, hymnbooks, stained-glass windows, and organs that still play may be found in deserted villages. One-roomed schoolhouses with desks, blackboards, and simple textbooks stand partially hidden among the wild roses. Abandoned boats, sleds, washing machines, mangles, and barber chairs footnote the domestic life of the departed. There are vacant habitable cabins and derelicts warped by floods and freezing and made a shambles by marauding bears.

With the termination of steamboat travel in 1955, Fort Selkirk was abandoned for a second time. A single trading post at Stewart River is the only one left to recall the stampede days when roadhouses and accommodations were to be found within a day's travel all along the river. Dawson is a tourist town of a few hundred. Fort Reliance is unmarked by any sign to recall that here McQuesten ran the trading post which first provided for miners who led to the last stampede. Forty Mile has been specified as a national monument, but there is no caretaker or a single resident living in any of the cabins of the first town on the Yukon. Eagle and Circle with only a few-score inhabitants give little evidence of the exciting stampede cities they once were.

The only town on the Yukon which grew rather than withered was Whitehorse, and it was not really a stampede town. It was a railroad town, an expanded depot where the trains and riverboats met. It developed only after the first rush was expended. It was the epilogue of the stampede, symbolic of the influence of New York and London, the railroad, the steamers, the dredges, and the hydraulic mining. It represented capital investment, not private initiative. As much as it tries today to play the Klondike tunes for tourists, the notes are false. It was only Dawson's greengrocer, its bumboat. Although a delightful town with a fresh frontier air, it is now more closely related to the Alcan Highway, the Clinton asbestos mines, and the multi-million-dollar Japanese mineral development than it is to gold and sourdoughs.

Of the stampede towns, only Fairbanks survived, and it could well have suffered the fate of Dawson and become a small company town servicing a few company-operated mines, but World War II, a military base, and a strong infusion of federal government money reversed a steady decline which had set in around 1911. It could still become a ghost town with the withdrawal of government subsidies, for there is no reason for its existence. The gold mines have closed. There is little agriculture, no timber industry, no fishing, no adjacent small communities requiring a central service point to justify its size. Only the prospects of an oil pipeline from the north and tourist flights from the south threaten not only to preserve it, but to stimulate additional growth in a country which should support few.

With the discovery of oil along the shores of the Arctic Ocean, on what is called the North Slope, and with the rush of oil companies to participate in the development of the richest oil pool in America, a new chapter may be written in Alaskan history reversing the drift backward in time. With the infusion of development capital, already exceeding the value of all the gold mined in Alaska, the state may become an industrial colony subject to the customs of exploitation, controlled by absentee landlords demanding rights in return for the money poured into the state. Already Alaska has had a taste of the dangers connected with the economic pendulum of industrial development. Stores greatly increased their inventories to meet the boom of what was widely heralded as a new stampede. It did not develop. Thousands of underemployed in the Lower Forty-eight, their hopes fired by the catch phrase, "stampede," were warned by Alaska not to come north. This was not a stampede. The last stampede ended with Fairbanks and Kuskokwim. The days of Forty Mile, Circle, Dawson, Nome, and Valdez would not be repeated. This strike was for stockholders, not for adventurers. The boys on the Kuak and the members of the Batavia party would find nothing for them in the North Slope. They would find little excitement or pleasure in a steam-heated life, housed, clothed, and fed by company transportation that leaves no margin of chance. The sourdough individualism and independence that developed the gold fields are not required. There is no place for the miners' law that promulgated rules and codes to fit the times and conditions.

What is happening in Alaska today, the struggle between conservation and development, is a reflection of long-existing conflicting views. The May 1910 issue of the *Alaska-Yukon Magazine* editorialized what many thought then, and still do: "We don't believe in conservation in a new and virtually unexplored country. We don't believe that the public domain belongs to all the people. It belongs to those who have the initiative to develop it."

An alternative view was espoused, thirty years before the discovery of oil on the North Slope, by Robert Marshall, one-time chief of the Division of Recreation and Lands, U. S. Forest Service, in testifying before a Congressional committee on national resources. He recommended "that all of Alaska north of the Yukon River, with the exception of a small area immediately adjacent to Nome, should be zoned as a region where the federal government will contribute no funds for road building and permit no leases for industrial development. . . .

"In the name of a balanced use of American resources, let's keep northern Alaska largely a wilderness!"

But leases have been sold, a road has been carved out of the land from the oil fields to Fairbanks. Fairbanks, as a natural base for the oil fields, now appears doomed to grow. The noxious smog which blankets the city during the winter months may spread to blight the surrounding valley. It may be too late to keep northern Alaska a wilderness or to save the Eskimos from the loss of lands historically theirs. The caribou may be forced from their natural pastures and migration routes by pipelines, the fragile tundra disturbed beyond redemption.

However grave the impact of this new strike, it is doubtful if it can seriously affect the Alaskan way of life, the heritage of the last stampede. In a country with a population, outside of Anchorage and Fairbanks, of only a few thousand people scattered over a half-million square miles, the shackling codes of urbanized society are not yet necessary. Self-reliant independence is endemic. From Nome to Eagle, from Fort Yukon to Valdez, everyone seemingly knows everyone else. State legislatures are accordingly intimately responsive to the wishes and moods of their constituencies. No one is pushed around by a remote government. The miners' law is gone, but the miner's spirit of independence is still all-pervasive, and the humanistic codes of the stampeders are still the rule—hospitality, the acceptance of a person for what he is, the inviolability of a cache.

BIBLIOGRAPHY

BOOKS

Alaska Northwest Publishing Company. *The Milepost.* 20th ed. Edmonds, Wash., 1968.

Amundsen, Roald. *The Northwest Passage.* 2 vols. London, 1908.

Andrews, Clarence Leroy. *The Story of Alaska.* Caldwell, Idaho, 1940.

Baird, Andrew. *Sixty Years on the Klondike.* Vancouver, 1965.

Barbeau, Marius. *Alaska Beckons.* Caldwell, Idaho, 1947.

Berton, Laura Beatrice. *I Married the Klondike.* Boston, 1954.

Berton, Pierre. *The Klondike Fever.* New York, 1958.

Brooks, Alfred Hulse. *Blazing Alaska's Trails.* Caldwell, Idaho, 1953.

Carroll, James A. *The First Ten Years in Alaska: Memoirs of a Fort Yukon Trapper, 1911–1922.* New York, 1957.

Caughey, John Walton. *Gold Is the Cornerstone.* Berkeley, Calif., 1948.

Chevigny, Hector. *Russian America: The Great Alaskan Venture, 1741–1867.* New York, 1965.

Clark, M. *Roadhouse Tales.* Girard, Kans., 1902.

Cody, H. A. *An Apostle of the North.* Toronto, n.d. [1908?].

Curtin, Walter R. *Yukon Voyage.* Caldwell, Idaho, 1938.

Darling, Esther Birdsall. *Baldy of Nome.* San Francisco, 1913.

Fraser, J. D. *The Gold Fever.* N.p., 1923.

Golder, F. A. *Bering's Voyages.* 2 vols. New York, 1922.

———. "Mining in Alaska before 1867," in *Alaska and Its History,* edited by M. B. Sherwood. Seattle, 1967.

Granburg, W. J. *Voyage into Darkness.* New York, 1960.

Gruening, Ernest. *The State of Alaska.* New York, 1954.

Hamilton, Walter R. *The Yukon Story.* Vancouver: Mitchell Press Ltd., 1964.

Harman, Eleanor, and Marsh Jeanneret. *A Story Workbook in Canadian History.* Toronto, 1950.

Harris, A. C. *Alaska and the Klondike Gold Fields,* N.p., 1897.

Haskell, William B. *Two Years in the Klondike and the Alaskan Gold Fields.* Hartford, Conn., 1898.

Heller, Christine. *Wild Flowers of Alaska.* Portland, Ore., 1966.

Heller, Herbert L. *Sourdough Sagas.* Cleveland, 1967.

Henderson, Lester Dale. *Alaska.* Juneau, 1939.

Heyerdahl, Thor, Soren Richter, and Hj Riiser-Larsen. *Great Norwegian Expeditions.* Oslo, n.d.

Hinton, A. Cherry. *The Yukon.* Toronto, 1954.

Hulley, Clarence C. *Alaska, 1741–1953.* Portland, Ore., 1953.

———. *Alaska: Past and Present.* Portland, Ore., 1958.

Ingersoll, Ernest. *Golden Alaska.* Chicago, 1897.

Krause, Aurel. *The Tlingit Indians: Results of a Trip to the Northwest Coast of America and the Bering Straits.* Translated by Erna Gunther. Seattle, 1956.

Lanks, Herbert C. *Highway to Alaska.* New York, 1944.

Lazell, J. Arthur. *Alaskan Apostle.* New York, 1960.

Leonard, John W. *The Gold Fields of the Klondike.* Chicago, 1897.

Marshall, Robert. *Arctic Wilderness.* Berkeley and Los Angeles, 1956. (2nd ed.; *Alaska Wilderness: Exploring the Central Brooks Range,* 1970.)

Mathews, Richard. *The Yukon. Rivers of America Series.* New York, 1968.

McKeown, Martha Ferguson. *The Trail Led North.* New York, 1948.

McQuesten, Leroy N. *Recollections of Leroy N. McQuesten of Life in the Yukon, 1871–1885.* Dawson City, Y.T., n.d. [June 1952?].

O'Connor, Richard. *High Jinks on the Klondike.* New York, 1954.

Okun, S.B. *The Russian-American Company.* Translated by Carl Ginsburg. Cambridge, Mass., 1951.

Place, Marian T. *The Yukon.* New York, 1967.

Price, Elizabeth Bailey. *My Seventy Years,* as told by Mrs. George Black. London, 1938.

Pringle, George C.F. *Adventures in Service.* Toronto, 1929.

Rickard, T.A. *Through the Yukon and Alaska.* San Francisco, 1909.

Robertson, Frank C., and Beth Kay Harris. *Soapy Smith, King of the Frontier Con Men.* New York, 1961.

Sanchez, Nellie van de Grift. *Stories of the States.* New York, 1931.

Schooling, Sir William. *The Hudson's Bay Company, 1670–1920.* London, 1920.

Schwatka, Frederick. *Along Alaska's Great River.* 2nd ed. Chicago, 1898. (A section on the Klondike was added to the 1885 edition.)

Sherwood, Morgan B. *Exploration of Alaska, 1865–1900.* New Haven, Conn., 1965.

———, ed. *Alaska and Its History.* Seattle, 1967.

Shiels, Archie W. *The Purchase of Alaska.* College, Alaska, 1967.

Smith, William Henry. *The Life and Speeches of the Honorable Charles Warren Fairbanks.* Indianapolis, 1904.

Spurr, Josiah Edward. *Through the Yukon Gold Diggings.* Boston, 1900.

Stewart, Elihu. *Down the Mackenzie and up the Yukon in 1906.* London, 1913.

Stuck, Hudson. *Voyages on the Yukon and Its Tributaries*. New York, 1925.

Taylor, H. West. *The Pioneers of the Klondike*, as told by M. H. E. Hayne. London, 1897.

Tollemache, Stratford. *Reminiscences of the Yukon*. London, 1912.

Tompkins, Stuart Ramsay. *Alaska: Promyshlennik and Sourdough*. Norman, Okla., 1945.

Wickersham, James. *Old Yukon*. Washington, 1938.

Willoughby, Barrett. *Alaska Holiday*. Boston, 1940.

———. *Alaskans All*. New York and Boston, 1933.

Winslow, Kathryn. *Big Pan-Out*. New York, 1951.

Wolle, Muriel Sibell. *The Bonanza Trail*. Bloomington, Ind., 1953.

Young, S. Hall. *Alaska Days with John Muir*. New York, 1915.

UNPUBLISHED MATERIAL

Manuscripts

Berkeley. Bancroft Library, University of California.

Berry, Major N. P., "Developments in Alaska." A recorded conversation between Berry and Mr. Petrov, February 3, 1879.

"Statement of Charles Kruger." Remarks regarding the transfer of Sitka made by Kruger, September 17, 1885.

Mizony, Paul T., "Gold Rush: A Boy's Impression of the Stampede into the Klondike during the Days of 1898."

Schieffelin, Edward, "Trip to Alaska, 1882–1883."

College, Alaska. Library and Archives, University of Alaska.

Frank Buteau Papers. Letters and notes, 1900–1935.

Douglas, Sir James, "Journal, 1835," and "Journal, 1840–41."

"Edwards' Track Chart of the Yukon River, Alaska." A navigational map of the Yukon drawn in 1898 by W. B. Edwards for his own use.

Major General C. S. Farnsworth Papers. Collected letters, articles, and photographs from 1898 to 1901.

Hartnett, Maurice A., "Dairy of Trip to Kotzebue Sound, 1898–99."

Correspondence of the Honorable James Wickersham with A. J. Balliet of Rampart, 1900–1901.

Historical Record of the Fairbanks Order of Pioneers of Alaska, Igloo No. 4. A bound collection of autobiographies of members, bits of Alaskan history, club news, verse, and dates and names of first arrivals on the Yukon.

Pilz, George E., "Pioneer Days in Alaska."

Dawson, Yukon Territory. Dawson Museum.
  Diary of H. H. Scott, 1898–1899.
  Diary and Letters of Alden R. Smith, 1898–1899.
  Taylor, A. Innes, "The Early History of Forty Mile and the Yukon." Mimeographed.
  Turenne, Father Edmont, "A Monument to a Man of God."
  "Reports of Royal North-West Mounted Police, Forty Mile, Yukon Territory." Daily log kept at Forty Mile from 1909 to 1912.
Eagle, Alaska. Museum.
  Diary of A. D. Reynolds, 1902–1915.
Juneau. Alaska Historical Library.
  Benedict, Neal D., "The Valdes and Copper River Trail," 1899.
Juneau. Alaska Territorial Archives.
  Records of the Proceedings of the City Council, Sitka, Alaska, 1867–1875.
Seattle. Special Collections Division, University of Washington Library.
  Mr. and Mrs. George W. (Marguerite) Carmack folder in the Meany file.
Stewart Island, Yukon Territory.
  John D. Lawrence manuscript about early days at Stewart Island, 1900–1910, in the possession of Mrs. Yvonne Burian.

Dissertations, theses

McLean, Dora Elizabeth. "Early Newspapers on the Upper Yukon Watershed, 1894–1907." Master's thesis, University of Alaska, 1963.
Monahan, Robert Leonard. "The Development of Settlement in the Fairbanks Area, Alaska." Ph.D. dissertation, McGill University, 1959.

TAPED INTERVIEWS

Circle, Alaska
  Helen Callahan, the daughter of Cherosky, whose strike on Mastodon Creek started Circle City, August 10, 1968, Fairbanks, Alaska.
  Mary Warren, July 28, 1968, Circle City.
Dawson, Yukon Territory
  Don Donnell, July 14, 1968, Dawson.
  Frank Miller, July 28, 1968, Miller House, Alaska.
  Taffy Williams, July 13, 1968, Dawson.
Eagle, Alaska
  Barney and Borghild Hansen, July 23, 1968, Eagle City.

Fairbanks, Alaska
  Fabian Carey, August 23, 1968, Fairbanks.
  Clara Rust, August 9, 1968, Fairbanks.
Forty Mile, Yukon Territory
  Crystal McQuesten Morgan, born in Forty Mile, the daughter of
  Leroy N. McQuesten, May 12, 1969, Berkeley, California.
Livengood, Alaska
  Carl Clark, August 11, 1968, Livengood.
Nome, Alaska
  Laura Johnsen, August 19, 1968, Nome.
  Carric McLain, August 19, 1968, Nome.
Rampart, Alaska
  Ira Weisner, August 28, 1964, Rampart.
Sitka, Alaska
  Zela Doig, 1968, Sitka.
Skagway, Alaska
  George Rapuzzi, June 26, 1968, Skagway.
Stewart Island, Yukon Territory
  Yvonne Burian, July 11, 1968, Stewart Island.
Valdez, Alaska
  Billy Quitch, August 29, 1968, Valdez.

Pamphlets

Adams, C. W. *A Cheechako Goes to the Klondike*. Privately published: n.p., n.d.
Balcom, Mary G. *Ghost Towns of Alaska*. Chicago: Adams Press, 1965.
Boericke, William F. *Prospecting and Operating Small Gold Placers*. New York, 1960.
Carmack, George. *My Experiences in the Yukon*. Privately published by Marguerite Carmack, 1933.
Fairbanks Commercial Club. *Description of Fairbanks*. Fairbanks, April 1916.
Farrar, Victor J. *An Elementary Syllabus of Alaskan History*. Seattle: Library, University of Washington, n.d.

Government Documents

United States

Abercrombie, Captain W. R. *Copper River Exploring Expedition, Alaska, 1899*. Senate Document No. 1023, 56th Cong., 1st sess., 1900.
Baker, Marcus. *Geographic Dictionary of Alaska*. House Documents,

vol. 78. Geological Survey *Bulletin* No. 299. Washington, D. C.: U. S. Government Printing Office, 1906.

Dunham, Samuel C. "The Yukon and Nome Gold Fields," Department of Labor *Bulletin* No. 29. Washington, D. C.: U. S. Government Printing Office, 1900.

Herron, Lieutenant Joseph S. *Explorations in Alaska, 1899, for an All-American Overland Route from Cook Inlet, Pacific Ocean, to the Yukon.* Washington, D. C.: U. S. Government Printing Office, 1901.

Jackson, Sheldon. *Report on Education in Alaska.* Washington, D. C.: U. S. Government Printing Office, 1886.

Mertie, J. B. *A Geologic Reconnaissance of the Dennison Fork District, Alaska.* Department of Interior, Geological Survey *Bulletin* 827. Washington, D. C.: U. S. Government Printing Office, 1931.

Orth, Donald J. *Dictionary of Alaska Place Names.* Geological Survey Professional Paper 567. Washington, D. C.: U. S. Government Printing Office, 1967.

Petroff, Ivan. *Report on Population and Resources of Alaska at the Eleventh Census: 1890.* Washington, D. C.: U. S. Government Printing Office, 1893.

Ray, Captain P. H., and Lieutenant W. P. Richardson. Letters to the Adjutant General, U. S. Army, Washington, D. C., September 15, 1897–November 2, 1899. Records of U. S. Army Command, Department of the Columbia, Record Group No. 393, The National Archives, Washington, D. C.

Raymond, Captain Charles W. *Report of a Reconnaissance of the Yukon River, Alaska Territory, July to September 1869.* Senate Executive Document No. 12, 42nd Cong., 1st sess., 1871.

Schrader, Frank Charles. *Preliminary Report on a Reconnaissance along the Chandalar and Koyukuk Rivers, Alaska, in 1899.* U. S. Geological Survey. Washington, D. C.: U. S. Government Printing Office, 1900.

Canada

An Act Respecting Placer Mining in the Yukon Territory, *Canadian Revised Statutes* chapter 300 (1952).

Murray, Alexander Hunter. *Journal of the Yukon.* Canadian Archives Publication No. 4. Ottawa, 1910.

Ogilvie, William, *Early Days on the Yukon.* Ottawa, 1913.

PERIODICALS

Alaska Journal, I, nos. 10, 28, 32 (May 6, September 9, October 7, 1893), Juneau.

· BIBLIOGRAPHY ·

Alaska Review, II, no. 4 (Spring and Summer 1967). Alaska Methodist University, Anchorage.
Alaska Sportsman, 1934-1970. Alaska Northwest Publishing Company, Edmonds, Washington.
Alaska-Yukon Gold Book, 1930. Sourdough Stampede Association, Inc., Seattle.
Alaska-Yukon Magazine, III, no. 6–XI, no. 9 (August 1907–July 1911). Harrison Publishing Company, Seattle.
Appleton's Booklovers Magazine, VII, nos. 1, 2, 3, 4 (January 1906).
The Beaver, Summer, Autumn, Winter 1969, and Spring 1970. Hudson's Bay Company, Winnipeg, Manitoba.
California Historical Society Quarterly, XXXV, no. 4 (December 1956).
Church Missionary Intelligencer, XLV, no. 554, or n.s. XIX, no. 222 (June 1894). The Religious Tract Society, London.
Harper's New Monthly Magazine, LV, no. CCCXXX (November 1877).
The Pacific Historical Review, December 1934 and November 1959.
Political Science Quarterly, XXVII, no. 3 (1912).
The Tanana Magazine, Quartz Edition—The Fairbanks *Daily Times,* December 1912. Times Publishing Company, Fairbanks.
World Traveler, XVIII, no. 7 (July 1926). World Traveler Magazine Corporation, New York.

NEWSPAPERS

Alaska Appeal, May 6, 1879, San Francisco.
Alaska Herald, October 15, November 1, 1868, San Francisco.
Dawson *Daily News,* August 15, 1924.
Fairbanks *Daily News-Miner,* April 3, May 5, 1909.
———, Annual Edition, XXI (July 1923).
———, Alaska Progress Edition, 1967.
Fairbanks *Daily Times,* February 11, 1910–March 14, 1911.
Jessen's Weekly, July 17, 1952, Fairbanks.
———, annual edition, *Jessen's Historical Edition,* Fairbanks, 1968.
The Klondike News, April 1, 1898, San Francisco and Dawson. (Reproduced in 1966 by Shorey Bookstore, Seattle).
The Ninety-Eighter, July 1, 2, 3, 4, 1948, Fairbanks. Souvenir publication of the "Days of '98" by the Dorman H. Baker Post of the American Legion.
Nome *News,* February 20, 1903.
Seattle *Times,* December 25, 1949.
The Sitka Times, September 19, October 24, 31, November 7, 1868. Handwritten copies. Bancroft Library, University of California at Berkeley.

NOTES

1. *Alaska and Its History*, ed. M. B. Sherwood (Seattle, 1967), pp. 150–155.

2. William A. Dunning, "Paying for Alaska," *Political Science Quarterly*, XXVII, no. 3 (1912). Accusations of bribery, payoffs, and political scandals cloud the actual facts of the transfer of title and payment in 1867–68. Since 1917 the Russian archives have been closed to western scholars, so that a definitive study of the sale of Alaska cannot yet be made.

3. S. B. Okun, *The Russian-American Company*, trans. Carl Ginsburg (Cambridge, Mass., 1951), p. 248.

4. *Alaska Herald*, October 15, 1868, San Francisco. This newspaper and its reporting may not be too reliable, but the article does reflect the then current interest in gold and in reports or rumors of gold in Alaska.

5. George Pilz, "Pioneer Days in Alaska," a manuscript in the archives of the University of Alaska library. Pilz claims that he was responsible for the discovery of gold in Auke Bay, which led to the founding of Juneau. Juneau and Harris, acting as his agents, took advantage of his trust in them. However, the general tone of Pilz's account is so paranoiac that it is difficult to give it full credence. He saw himself as being persecuted by the Alaska Commercial Company. Naval officers who expected to share in the development of gold mines turned against him as the result of malicious lies spread by enemies. People he befriended used his very home to work against him during his absence. Embittered by failures, he distrusted everyone.

6. Captain W. R. Abercrombie, *Copper River Exploring Expedition, Alaska, 1899*, Senate Document No. 1023, 56th Cong., 1st session, 1900.

7. The author has not followed the Edmonton Trail and so cannot speak about it firsthand, as he can about the Chilkoot or Dyea Trail, Valdez, and the Yukon. Nearly all books about the Klondike made some reference to the Edmonton Trail and its horrors. One book states that only two out of ten thousand who started completed the route. No doubt it was a long, difficult route considered reasonable only by the Edmonton merchants who profited by it. Even to an experienced woodsman it might have been a long summer's trip. From Edmonton

it was across country to the headwaters of the Athabasca River. From there, it was downhill for about a thousand miles—down the Athabasca River to Lake Athabasca, down the Slave River to Great Slave Lake, across the lake to the Mackenzie River and down the Mackenize to the Peel River. From there, it was uphill to the headwaters of the Peel, then overland portage across the Ogilvie Range to Dawson. It would seem that only the most benighted or obstinate Canadian wishing to avoid American customs would consider such a route, and yet many did.

CHAPTER 2

1. Marius Barbeau, *Alaska Beckons* (Caldwell, Idaho, 1947), p. 320.

2. Donald J. Orth, *Dictionary of Alaska Place Names* (Geological Survey Professional Paper 567; Washington, D. C.: U. S. Government Printing Office, 1967), p. 61.

3. As late as 1865 members of the Western Union survey party in Russian America were unsure as to whether the Kwikpak and the Yukon were the same. Even today so prestigious an organization as the United States Air Force is apparently ignorant of the Yukon's course. An Air Force map on the wall of the airport at Nome has a thirty-mile gap in the river. About two hundred twenty miles from its source, the Yukon enters Lake Labarge. Between Lake Labarge and the Teslin River, the Air Force map shows no river. To the early miners, this stretch was known as the Thirty Mile River. It is a very real river with superb grayling fishing and marked by several wrecks of steamers that once navigated between Dawson and Whitehorse. Early cartographers divided the upper Yukon into several parts. Above Whitehorse it was called the Fifty Mile River. From the Whitehorse Rapids to Lake Labarge was the Twenty Mile River. From there to the Teslin was the Thirty Mile River. Between the Teslin and the Pelly River, which enters at Fort Selkirk, was the Lewes River. With the confluence of the Pelly and Lewes, the Yukon started. Although these popularly accepted divisions persisted for many years and still show up on some modern maps, the accepted course of the Yukon River now includes the Lewes, the Thirty Mile, the Twenty Mile, the Fifty Mile, and beyond to Crater Lake.

4. There is some question as to whether Fort Selkirk was destroyed by the Chilkoot or Chilkat Indians. Both tribes traded with the interior Indians and were instrumental in denying white traders ingress from the coast to the Yukon. The Chilkoots used the pass bearing their name, while the neighboring Chilkats followed a much longer overland route to the north reaching the Yukon farther downriver. Either or both tribes could have been involved in the destruction of Fort

Selkirk, but since determination of which tribe was responsible is not germane to the last stampede, the point has not been researched.

5. Frederick `Schwatka, *Along Alaska's Great River* (Chicago, 1898), p. 204. When he reached Fort Selkirk, Schwatka thought his original exploration of the Yukon was finished since men had charted the river beyond that point. Rather crude mapping of the Yukon had been made of that portion between Fort Selkirk and Fort Yukon. Below Fort Yukon, Captain Raymond had made a survey in 1869. Although Schwatka considered this chart to be excellent, he continued his own survey to the mouth of the river.

6. McQuesten and Harper started the communities of Selkirk, Stewart, and Forty Mile. Ladue and Harper founded Dawson. McQuesten probably started Eagle. He had a post there for over a decade before it became a military post and the center for civil authority in the interior of Alaska. McQuesten is responsible for Circle City, Fort Yukon, and Tanana. Al Mayo started Rampart. Beaver is the only community in this thousand-(approximate)-mile stretch of river for which one of these four men is not responsible at least in part.

7. Leroy N. McQuesten, *Recollections of Leroy N. McQuesten of Life in the Yukon, 1871–1885* (Dawson City, June 1952). Richard Mathews, *The Yukon* (New York, 1968), p. 68, gives the third member of the party as George Wilkenson. However, McQuesten says it was McKrieff. No first name is given.

8. McQuesten in his *Recollections* speaks of the Peace River instead of the Peel River. I have used Peel, as I am sure use of Peace River was error on the part of the copyist in compiling the *Recollections* from the original source. The Peel River enters the Mackenzie near its mouth and forms the natural route to the Rat River portage taken by McQuesten and Mayo on their way to Fort Yukon.

9. McQuesten calls the LaPierre House, LaPear House.

10. According to the historical record of the Fairbanks Order of Pioneers of Alaska, the unpublished record of Igloo No. 4, twenty-three men who accompanied Lieutenant McClelland on the U. S. cutter *Jamestown* crossed the Chilkoot that year. The usual story is that a couple of rounds from the cutter convinced the Chilkoot Indians that the white men had a right to use the trail. However, diplomacy and Indian authority may have played a part.

According to Mrs. Zela Doig, Librarian of the Sheldon Jackson College, interviewed in Sitka in 1968, when General Davis and his troops were withdrawn from Sitka in 1873, a warlike faction of the Tlingit Indians wanted to take advantage of the absence of troops to erase all vestiges of white people in the area. A second faction was opposed to attacking the white settlers. Knowing of the danger, the whites sent an appeal to the United States Navy for help. The appeal was ignored. As danger seemed increasingly imminent, the British in Vancouver were asked for help, and a British warship was dispatched to Sitka. By the time it arrived, the danger had receded. The pacific element among the Indians had prevailed; the hostile chief, however, continued to be a concern. When Lieutenant Beardslee arrived with an American ship with instructions to maintain peace, he deputized the former hostile chief to keep order among the Indians. The stratagem was highly successful. The chief took his duties seriously, even doing the seemingly impossible task of controlling the use of liquor among the Indians. Since Tlingit authority extended throughout the Lynn Canal area, he was taken along on the cutter *Jamestown* to Dyea. It might have been his authority that convinced the Chilkoots rather than a cannonade.

11. Alaska Progress Edition, 1967, of *Daily News-Miner*, Northern Commercial Company 100th Anniversary Section, Fairbanks, Alaska.

Chapter 3

1. T. A. Rickard, *Through the Yukon and Alaska* (San Francisco: Mining and Scientific Press, 1909), p. 131. "Home of the north wind," rather than "cruel wind," is the translation of Skagway given in Orth, *Dictionary of Alaska Place Names*, p. 883. However, a northerly is a cold, harsh wind so that either "cruel" or "north" would be an appropriate translation of the Indian word.

2. A note apparently written by A. E. Hegg and filed with his collection of photographs in the University of Washington library says, "Ben Moore, son of Capt. Moore, was 31 July 26, 1897, when Skaguay was deluged with stampeders. For 40 years his family had lived here unmolested. His 160 acre homestead was taken by the stampeders without question or by your leave. His daughter had a moose drawn cart." A. E. Hegg photographed the last stampede from Skagway to Nome.

3. *Alaska-Yukon Magazine*, VII, no. 1 (October 1908), 385–386.

4. *Ibid.*, 385.

5. Skagway *News*, July 8, 1898, reprinted in *Jessen's Historical Edition* (Fairbanks, 1968), p. 23.

6. Martha Ferguson McKeown, *The Trail Led North* (New York, 1948), p. 111.

7. Barrett Willoughby, *Alaskans All* (New York, 1933), pp. 163–198, and Bud Branham, "Gold Rush Mother," *The Alaska Sportsman* (August 1940), pp. 26, 30, 32.

8. In the newspapers at the time of her murder the spelling of her first name is invariably "Molly." However, the inscription on the bust in Skagway is "Mollie Walsh." For uniformity, I have used this spelling.

CHAPTER 4

1. Aurel Krause, *The Tlingit Indians*, translated by Erna Gunther (Seattle: University of Washington Press, 1956), p. 5.

2. Orth, *Dictionary of Alaska Place Names*, p. 210.

3. Alden R. Smith, letter posted in Sheep Camp, but undated. Letters of Alden R. Smith, copied from original letters, by Clayton Scoins, East Pembroke, New York; mimeographed copy of this collection is in the Dawson Museum, Dawson, Y. T.

4. *Ibid.*

5. Harry L. Grow, his personal account of life on the Dyea Trail in 1898, prepared for The Order of Yukon Pioneers, Igloo No. 4, Fairbanks, in the private collection of David Wharton, Ojai, California. Grow packed from Dyea over the Chilkoot Pass during the same period as the Batavia party.

6. Diary of H. H. Scott, 1898, Batavia party of New York (copy in Dawson Museum, Dawson, Y. T., of document in Public Archives of Canada), April 3, 1898. The price no doubt fluctuated with the season and the demand, but this was the price quoted by H. H. Scott on April 1, 1898.

7. Grow, pages are unnumbered.

8. This story was told by my grandfather, Eugene Cady, who was on Lake Bennett in 1898. Unfortunately his account of the stampede was meager, as he returned to his family only briefly after his Klondike experience.

9. Robert D. Jones, "A Municipal Farmer," *Alaska-Yukon Magazine*, III, no. 6 (1907), 488.

10. A wooden sign on the church relates its brief history. Also, Paul T. Mizony, "Gold Rush, A Boy's Impression of the Stampede into the Klondike During the Days of 1898" (ms. in Bancroft Library, University of California at Berkeley), mentions late 1899 as the time the church was completed.

CHAPTER 5

1. *The Klondike News*, April 1, 1898, published at San Francisco and Dawson. (Reproduced, Seattle: Shorey Bookstore, 1966), p. 9.

2. *Recollections of McQuesten*, p. 13. The four miners were R. Poplin, G. Marks, C. McCoskey, and Wm. Checking these names against the Historical Record of the Fairbanks Order of Pioneers of Alaska, the complete names are probably, Richard (Dick) Poplin, John Marks, Jim McClusky, and William Hayes.

3. *Ibid.*, p. 14; and Historical Record of the Fairbanks Order of Pioneers of Alaska.

4. This account is taken from a description of early days at Stewart Island from 1900 to 1910, written by John D. Lawrence, an undated document belonging to Mrs. Yvonne Burian of Stewart Island.

CHAPTER 6

1. Marcus Baker, *Geographic Dictionary of Alaska* (Geological Survey *Bulletin* No. 299; Washington, D. C.: U. S. Government Printing Office, 1906), p. 372, "This river was named Deer River by the Western Union Telegraph expedition in 1867. It has also been called Clondyke and Chandik or Deer." However, according to William Ogilvie, the official Canadian surveyor on the Yukon when Dawson was founded, Klondike is an adaptation of the Indian word *Trondiuck*, meaning hammerwater, because the Indians trapped salmon by hammering stakes into the streambed. The Reverend Robert McDonald, who understood the Indian dialects better than any other person on the Yukon, concurred with Ogilvie's explanation, but with some refinements. According to McDonald, Klondike came from *Trurkhndik* or *Trhokhndik*, meaning Driftwood River. The base word "trurh" means stone hammer. The stone hammer was used to drive the stakes made from driftwood which formed the sides of the fish traps. (Bishop Stringer, Reverend Brenno, Reverend Seymour, and Captain Baynton, "The Churches in the Yukon," *Alaska-Yukon Magazine*, V, no. 6 [1909], 422–429.) At the time that Fort Reliance was built in 1874, McQuesten referred to the Klondike as the Tondeg.

2. "How Gold was Discovered in the Yukon, From an old newspaper." No author, date, or source is given on this tourist sheet given away by the Dawson Museum, Dawson, Yukon Territory.

3. George Pilz, "Pioneer Days in Alaska," p. 43.

4. Affidavit given to the Yukon Order of Pioneers at Forty Mile, February 1895. The original document has been lost, but the making of the affidavit was reported by several persons in the area at the time.

5. Frank Buteau, "A paper on the Yukon," November 1, 1935, Frank Buteau Papers, Archives, University of Alaska.

6. George W. Carmack, *My Experiences in the Yukon* (privately published, 1933), p. 9. According to Carmack's version of the meeting with Henderson, Henderson did tell him there were claims left but he did not want any siwashes around. The siwashes were Skookum (an Indian word meaning large or powerful, a common nickname in the Yukon) Jim, Carmack's closest friend, and Tagish Charlie, his brother-in-law. Skookum Jim, angry at Henderson's words, asked Carmack after Henderson left, "What's matter dat white man? Him killet Inchun moose, Inchun cariboo, catchit gold Inchun country. No likit Inchun stakit claim. Whyfo no good?"

"Never mind, Jim," Carmack told him. "This is big country. We need not bother our heads about Bob Henderson or his creek."

7. Carmack, Mr. and Mrs. George W. (Marguerite), Meany file, Special Collections Division, University of Washington Library, Seattle. A photograph in this file of the original recording of Carmack's claim shows the discovery date to be August 17, 1896, but the application date, September 24, 1896. Why the September date? It is known that Carmack wasted no time in going to Forty Mile to file his claim. Possibly Carmack had to rerecord his claim because of measurement discrepancies discovered after his original filing. There was considerable overlapping of claims in the original staking. A subsequent government survey was necessary to establish legal ownership.

8. H. West Taylor, *The Pioneers of the Klondike,* as told by M. H. E. Hayne (London, 1897), pp. 134–136.

9. *Ibid.,* p. 143.

10. An unidentified, undated newspaper clipping, Carmack file, University of Washington.

11. According to a conversation May 12, 1969, in Berkeley, California, with Mrs. Crystal McQuesten Morgan, a daughter of L. N. McQuesten, Bob Henderson did very well from his claim and left the Yukon a wealthy man. He and Carmack visited the McQuesten home in Berkeley when she was a child. She recalls them both as well-off and as good friends.

12. Dr. Clarence C. Hulley, *Alaska, 1741–1953* (Portland, Oregon, 1953), p. 250, says Ladue moved his store and sawmill from Forty Mile to the mouth of the Klondike. This is doubtful as there is no mention in any reliable accounts of Ladue's having a store at Forty Mile. Harper, as a partner of Ladue, might have moved from there.

13. Fairbanks *Daily News-Miner,* May 5, 1909.

14. Laura Beatrice Berton, *I Married the Klondike* (Boston, 1954).

15. Interview with Don Donnell, Dawson, July 14, 1968.

16. Interview with Frank Miller at Miller House, July 28, 1968.

17. "Jonking Miller" is Scott's spelling for Joaquin Miller, the California poet, who had been sent to Dawson by the *San Francisco Examiner* to report on the gold rush. "Loas town" is his spelling for Louse Town, the suburb across the Klondike River from Dawson where the prostitutes lived.

18. Wallace M. Craigie, a letter to Farnsworth, June 13, 1900, Farnsworth Papers, Archives, University of Alaska.

19. Walter R. Hamilton, *The Yukon Story* (Vancouver: Mitchell Press Ltd., 1964), p. 83.

20. George C. F. Pringle, *Adventures in Service* (Toronto, 1929), pp. 39–49.

21. Alden R. Smith, letter dated October 2, 1898, Dawson Museum.

22. Alden R. Smith, letter dated December 18, 1898.

23. *Ibid.*

24. Diaries of Alden R. Smith and H. H. Scott, Dawson Museum.

CHAPTER 7

1. Father Edmont Turenne, "A Monument to a Man of God," an undated paper in the Dawson Museum, Dawson, Yukon Territory.

2. James Wickersham, *Old Yukon* (Washington, D. C., 1938), p. 155.

3. The birth certificate of McQuesten's daughter, Mrs. Crystal McQuesten Morgan, who was born at Forty Mile in 1891, reads, "Forty Mile, Alaska."

4. An incidental, unmarked, unfiled paper in the Dawson Museum.

5. Farnsworth, letter dated January 26, 1901, Farnsworth Papers, University of Alaska Library.

6. McQuesten, *Recollections*, p. 10.

7. *Ibid.*, p. 11.

8. *Ibid.*, pp. 11–12.

9. Josiah Edward Spurr, *Through the Yukon Gold Diggings* (Boston, 1900), p. 109; and Hulley, *Alaska: Past and Present*, p. 227.

10. The founding of Forty Mile is variously given as 1886 and 1887. The latter date is probably correct. The trading post, which was the beginning of the town, was established by McQuesten and Harper. But McQuesten had gone to San Francisco for supplies in 1886 before the first good strike on the Forty Mile River was reported. He did not return to the Yukon until the breakup of ice in 1887. The two men then closed up the posts at Fort Reliance and Stewart River and established themselves at the mouth of the Forty Mile River. A report by William Ogilvie in the Dawson Museum gives 1887 as the year McQuesten moved his post from Stewart River to Forty Mile.

11. Interview with Helen Callahan in Fairbanks, August 10, 1968. She attended the mission school at Forty Mile.

12. Interview, Crystal McQuesten Morgan, Berkeley, California, May 12, 1969.

13. H. A. Cody, *An Apostle of the North* (Toronto, 1908), p. 267.

14. Frank Buteau, A paper on the Yukon.

15. Taylor, *The Pioneers of the Klondike*, p. 2. The first North-West Mounted Police post was set up at Fort Cudahy on a small island across from the town of Forty Mile. A large sign on the island states it to be the site of Fort Constantine. Actually, the post was not called Fort Constantine, after its first commanding officer, until it was moved to the Forty Mile townsite a few years later.

16. *Ibid.*, p. 68.

17. *Ibid.*, p. 122.

18. *Ibid.*, p. 91.

19. Spurr, pp. 116–117.

20. *Ibid.*, p. 142.

21. Dawson *Daily News*, Friday, August 15, 1924.

22. Pioneers of Alaska, Igloo No. 4, University of Alaska Library.

23. These accounts are developed from the weekly reports made by the Royal North-West Mounted Police, Yukon Territory, Forty Mile, to headquarters in Dawson, March 14, 1909–August 19, 1912. They are in the Dawson Museum.

CHAPTER 8

1. Orth, *Dictionary of Alaska Place Names*, p. 291.

2. Mrs. Crystal McQuesten Morgan recalls that her father had a post at Eagle. She is not certain of the date, but she does remember his talking about a post he had there, and she thinks it was about 1886.

3. Schwatka, *Along Alaska's Great River*, p. 251.

4. *The Klondike News*, April 1, 1898, 33.

5. Dora Elizabeth McLean, "Early Newspapers on the Upper Yukon Watershed, 1894–1907," Master's thesis, University of Alaska, 1963, p. 40.

6. Samuel C. Dunham, "The Yukon and Nome Gold Fields," Department of Labor *Bulletin* No. 29 (Washington, D. C.: U.S. Government Printing Office, 1900), p. 840.

7. Records of the U. S. Army Commands, Department of the Columbia, Letters Received, no. 650 (1899), The National Archives, Washington, D. C., Record Group No. 393.

8. Records of the U. S. Army Commands, Department of the Columbia, Letters Received, no. 3498 (1899), Record Group No. 393. This is a petition from the Chamber of Commerce of Eagle, dated November 1, 1899, and forwarded to the Secretary of War by Major P. H. Ray with his endorsement, subject to efficient civil government being established at once and maintained, "as the reservation, as now defined, gives protection to all property owners within its limits in the absence of any form of civil government."

9. Farnsworth Papers, diary entry dated December 23, 1900. University of Alaska Library.

10. Records of the U. S. Army Commands, Department of the Columbia, Letters Received, no. 2292 (1899), Record Group No. 393.

11. James Wickersham, *Old Yukon*, p. 164.

12. Roald Amundsen, *The North West Passage*, II (London, 1908), 212–249.

13. Interview with Barney Hansen, former mayor of Eagle, in Eagle City, Alaska, July 23, 1968.

14. Interview with Mrs. Borghild Hansen, Eagle City, Alaska, July 23, 1968.

15. Farnsworth Papers, "Address by C. S. Farnsworth, C. O., Fort Egbert, upon the occasion of the opening of a reading room at Eagle, October 31, 1900."

CHAPTER 9

1. Orth, *Dictionary of Alaska Place Names*, p. 219, gives the beginning of Circle City as 1887, "when L. N. McQuesten located a trading post here." Dora Elizabeth McLean has McQuesten establishing a post at Fish Camp in 1891 prior to moving to Circle. Helen Callahan, who lived in Circle before the turn of the century and whose father, Cherosky, with his partner, Pitka, made the first big strike in the Circle district, recalls that in moving to Circle, her family first stopped at a site about thirty miles upriver from Circle City. This site she remembers by its Indian name of "Manny Hills," or "Many Hills." This could be the same as Fish Camp; her recollection is not clear. She does recall that her uncle Pitka made the gold discovery which led to the founding of Circle City. Frank Buteau in his papers refers to the founding of the Circle City mining district as 1892, as does Lester Dale Henderson, *Alaska* (Juneau, 1939), p. 216. However, Marian T. Place, *The Yukon* (New York, 1967), p. 109, and Dr. Clarence C. Hulley, *Alaska: Past and Present*, p. 228, give 1893 as the date for the beginning of Circle City. Marcus Baker does not give a date for the founding of the town, but he does give 1899 for the establishing of a post office at Circle. Conversations with Helen Callahan and all other sources would seem to make 1893 the most logical year for the beginning of Circle. Certainly 1887 is much too early, as that is when McQuesten moved his trading post to Forty Mile, described by Spurr as the oldest mining camp on the Yukon.

2. Wickersham, *Old Yukon*, p. 118.

3. According to "The Churches in the Yukon," *Alaska-Yukon Magazine*, VI, no. 1 (October 1908), the Reverend McDonald found gold on Birch Creek and at other places on the Yukon. He sent samples to London, where *The Times* published an account of his gold findings. Later, according to the same article, when the Klondike came into the news, *The Times* published another article on the gold discoveries made by McDonald. However, a search through *Palmer's Index to The Times* from 1860 through February 1898, reveals no reference to the part played by Archdeacon McDonald in the various discoveries of gold along the Yukon, according to J. Gordon Phillips, Archivist for *The Times*. Despite this indication of the unreliability of the *Alaska-Yukon Magazine*, or at least of the specific article, McDonald is generally credited with the first report of finding gold along the tributaries of the Yukon around 1863–64.

4. A. Cherry Hinton, *The Yukon* (Toronto, 1954), p. 47.

5. The names are variously spelled by different writers as Poitka and Sonoiska or Pitka and Sarosky. Helen Callahan, the daughter of one and the niece of the other, says their names were Pitka and Cherosky. Pitka was the brother of her mother, whose father's name was Pavlov. This would make Pitka's name, Pitka Pavlov. As for her father, she is not sure of his last name. She does not recall him well,

as he left her mother while Helen Callahan was a small child, and her mother married Dan Callahan. According to Helen Callahan, family names did not mean much to the Indians. They knew people by relationship to a person who had done something to merit a significant nickname. A hunter who killed a bear with only a knife might be known by the name of Man-who-kill-bear-with-knife. His father would then become known as the Father-of-man-who-kill-bear-with-knife. His sons and daughters would similarly be known by relationship to Man-who-kill-bear-with-knife. Or a family might be known by relationship to Woman-who-sew-beautiful-mukluks. For this reason, it is difficult to establish Indian genealogy. A man upon becoming the Father-of-man-who-kill-bear-with-knife would lose any name connecting him with his parents.

6. This description of Tanana gives an improperly pretentious impression of a town which was not much of a settlement in 1893. It was, however, the largest community on the Yukon, excepting Forty Mile. The Indians met annually at the confluence of the Yukon and the Tanana rivers to trade before the coming of the Russians. Both the Russians and the British traded here with the Indians before the United States purchased Alaska. From 1869 on there were American trading posts at different sites in this area. The Alaska Commercial Company, the Northern Commercial Company, and the North American Trading and Transportation Company had trading posts, as did private traders. McQuesten had, in 1876, what he referred to as the Tanana Station. In 1891 the St. James Episcopal Mission located at Tanana.

7. McKeown, *The Trail Led North*, p. 188.

8. Wickersham, p. 24.

9. *Ibid.*, p. 125.

10. "Order of Pioneers of Alaska" lists "Dutch" Kate as the first white woman to cross the Chilkoot (1888). Hulley, *Alaska: Past and Present*, p. 229, has "Dutch" Kate arriving in Circle City in 1888. This date is obviously in error and may be a typographical mistake, since Hulley accepts 1893 as the founding of Circle City.

11. J. Arthur Lazell, *Alaskan Apostle* (New York, 1960), p. 152.

12. *Ibid.*, p. 93.

13. Subject: P. H. Ray on Alaska, order of President for Captain Ray to proceed to Alaska without troops to investigate and report condition of affairs, August 6, 1897, The National Archives and Records Service, Washington, D. C.

14. Summary of letters written by Captain Ray during October and November 1897, contained in telegram to the Adjutant General of the Army, Washington, D. C., from Robinson, Quartermaster, Seattle, Washington, January 31, 1898, Record Group No. 393, The National Archives, Washington, D. C.

15. *Ibid.*, Letters Received, no. 1569, 1898.

16. *Ibid.*, AGO 74786, 1897.

17. *Ibid.*, Letters Received, no. 1593, 1898.
18. *Ibid.*, AGO 70224, February 1, 1898.
19. *Ibid.*, AGO 70224, December 18, 1897.
20. *Ibid.*, Letters Received, no. 1709, 1898.
21. *Ibid.*, Letters Received, no. 440, 1899.
22. Dora Elizabeth McLean, "Early Newspapers on the Upper Yukon," p. 33.
23. The Honorable Stratford Tollemache, *Reminiscences of the Yukon* (London, 1912), p. 148.
24. Don Donnell, interview in Dawson, Yukon Territory, July 14, 1968. Herbert L. Heller, *Sourdough Sagas* (Cleveland, 1967), p. 90, gives a version of this story. Stovepipe was a valuable commodity; but more important, the incident illustrates the way stampeders leavened justice with humor, and the form of humor that appealed to them.
25. Spurr, *Through the Yukon Gold Diggings*, p. 203.
26. *Ibid.*, p. 167.
27. "Order of Pioneers of Alaska," autobiography of Thomas Davis.
28. Mary Warren, interview in Circle City, Alaska, July 28, 1968.
29. Dora Elizabeth McLean, p. 33.
30. Curtin, *Yukon Voyage*, p. 239.

CHAPTER 10

1. "Journal of George Russell Adams," edited by Harold F. Taggart, *California Historical Society Quarterly*, XXXV, no. 4 (December 1956).
2. Curtin, *Yukon Voyage*, p. 135. Neil Vawter, United States Marshal at St. Michael, thought the reported strike a fake because, as he said, there was no means of prospecting at this season, there being no coal to thaw the ground. However, the newspaper, *Aurora Borealis*, Healy, Alaska, December 31, 1898, reported a gold strike at Cape Nome. It said three men panned about $76 worth of gold dust on Snow Creek in late October. They panned out $163 the next day, and on October 31, took $624 in five hours.
3. Farnsworth papers, letters from Wallace M. Craigie, September 3, 1899, Library, University of Alaska.
4. Maurice A. Hartnett, "Diary of Trip to Kotzebue Sound, 1898–99," Archives, University of Alaska Library.
5. The story of the three Australian miners is a fictionalized composite of facts. The facts are that finding gold was a combination of hard work and luck; men of many nations were involved in the Nome stampede; there were old beaches deep underground which, if located, yielded rich placer gold; the frozen muck and gravel had to be thawed with steam points; men leased mines or worked them on

a share basis; there were boisterous episodes to leaven months of dreary work—all the details of the story are facts. Facts alone, however, lack the deeper truth which comes from relating them to people with human values and drives. This must be done to develop the emotional atmosphere in which the stampeders lived, and that atmosphere is as much a part of history as the factual details.

6. *Alaska-Yukon Magazine*, IV, no. 4 (December 1907), 396, 508–511.

7. Rickard, *Through the Yukon and Alaska*, p. 334.

8. *Alaska-Yukon Magazine*, IX, no. 2 (December 1909), 116–117.

9. Rickard, p. 350.

10. Lecture by Mrs. Ruth Allman, House of Wickersham, Juneau, 1968.

11. *The Klondike News*, April 1, 1898, p. 12.

12. John A. St. Clair, "Seward Peninsula, 1907," *Alaska-Yukon Magazine*, III, no. 6 (August 1907), 513.

CHAPTER 11

1. Orth, *Dictionary of Alaska Place Names*, p. 1016.

2. *Ibid.*, p. 6.

3. Captain W. R. Abercrombie, *Copper River Exploring Expedition, Alaska, 1899*, Senate Document No. 1023, 56th Cong., 1st sess., 1900.

4. Neal D. Benedict, "The Valdes and Copper River Trail," 1899, manuscript in Alaska Historical Library, Juneau.

CHAPTER 12

1. *Recollections of McQuesten*, p. 5.

2. *Jessen's Weekly*, Fairbanks, Alaska, July 17, 1952, p. 2.

3. *Recollections of McQuesten*, p. 10.

4. Frank Buteau papers, University of Alaska Library.

5. *The Ninety-Eighter*, Fairbanks, July 1, 2, 3, 4, 1948, p. 8.

6. Interview with Fabian Carey, Fairbanks, August 23, 1968.

7. C. W. Adams, A *Cheechako Goes to the Klondike* (n.p., n.d.), p. 56.

8. *The Ninety-Eighter*, July 1, 2, 3, 4, 1948, p. 8. Jujira Wada, according to C. W. Adams, was cook aboard the *Lavelle Young* when the Barnette party was taken upriver. However, he is generally associated with Fairbanks and the spreading of the news of the Fairbanks strike in Dawson. An early picture shows him as a husky young Japanese in running costume.

9. Department of Interior, *Minerals Year Book* (Washington, D.C.: U.S. Government Printing Office, 1946), p. 221.

10. Letter from George Anderson to Alden Smith dated November 23, 1905, Letters of Alden R. Smith, Dawson Museum.

11. Fairbanks *Daily Times*, January 11, 31, and February 1, 1911.

12. Interview with Carl Clark, Livengood, Alaska, August 11, 1968.

13. Fairbanks *Daily News-Miner*, April 3, 1909.

CHAPTER 13

1. A. D. Reynolds, Diary, December 24, 1908, Museum, Eagle, Alaska.

2. *Alaska-Yukon Magazine*, V., no. 6 (September 1908), 422–429. Archdeacon McDonald worked mostly with the Tinjizyoo Indians, taking a Tinjizyoo woman for his wife. The French-Canadians called these people the *loucheux* or "crooked-eyed" Indians. However, the Indian name, Tinjizyoo, translates more delightfully into "the kind men."

3. Clifford Wilson, "The Surrender of Fort Yukon One Hundred Years Ago," *The Beaver* (Autumn 1969), p. 47.

4. Captain Charles W. Raymond, *Report of a Reconnaissance of the Yukon River, Alaska Territory, July to September 1869* (Senate Executive Document No. 12, 42nd Cong., 1st sess., 1871), p. 36.

5. Helen Callahan, interview, August 10, 1968.

6. *Alaska Journal*, I, no. 32 (October 7, 1893), 16.

7. Stuck, *Voyages*, p. 119.

8. William B. Haskell, *Two Years in the Klondike and the Alaskan Gold Fields* (Hartford, Conn., 1898), p. 499.

9. Willoughby, *Alaskans All*, p. 60.

10. Wickersham, correspondence with A. J. Balliet of Rampart, 1900–1901, Archives, University of Alaska Library.

11. Ira Weisner, interview, August 28, 1964, Rampart, Alaska.

NAME AND PLACE INDEX

Index

Fort Yukon, 12, 249; American troops in, 18–19, Alaska Commercial Co. at, 19; lack of supplies in, 64; founded, 249–50; early history of, 250–51; 1869 inventory of, 251–52; Parrott and Co. take over, 252; New York girl lured to, 252–53; social life in, 253; today, 256
Fourth of July Creek, 247
Fox (town), 224, 235, 242
Franklin, Sir John, 14
Freiherz, Frau, 218
Frickson's Wood Camp, 269
Froelich (miner), 248
Frying Pan Bar, 264

Gerstle, Lewis: letter of, 23–24; principles ignored, 162
Gestler (miner), 19
Gold Bottom (river), 79
Golden City, 235
Golovin, 196
Glacier Creek, 187, 240
Globe, 240
Graham, Charley, 245–46
Graphie Grace, 83
Gregor, Jack, 151, 153–54
Grow, Harry, 55–56

Hammond River, 264
Hansen, Borghild: youth of, 141; journey to Eagle, 142; as teacher in Eagle, 143–45
Hard Luck Creek, 224, 248
Harper, Arthur: prospects Yukon, 3, 17, 20; at Fort Yukon, 19, 252; at Fort Reliance, 20; prospects Klondike, 78; at Dawson, 84; Forty Mile R. Strike of, 106; at Forty Mile, 108, 109, 287n10; prospects Tanana R., 226; at Tanana Station, 226; communities founded by, 282n6
Harris, Fred, 3
Hart, Fred, 19
Hartnett, Maurice: winters on Kuak R., 189–90; trip to Nome, 191, 192; prospects Snake R., 193; leaves Nome, 195
Haven, 196
Healy, Capt. John: forms N. A. T. & T. Co., 117; Forty Mile post of, 117 18, unpopularity of, 118, on stampede conditions, 165
Hegg, E. A., 5, 283n2
Henderson, Robert: credited with

Klondike gold discovery, 77, 79; and Joe Ladue, 78–79; Gold Bottom strike of, 79; abandons claim, 83; and Carmack, 285n6
Hertzer, Frank, 191
Hesy: in railroad dispute, 221-22
Holt, George, 3, 22
Hootalinqua (river), 64
Hudson, Teddy, 242
Hudson's Bay Company: on Yukon R., 3, 14, 18; on Porcupine R., 249; at Fort Yukon, 249–51 passim; vacates Fort Yukon, 251
Hughes, John, 66
Hultberg, Nels C., 186
Hunker, Andy, 103
Hunt River, 191

Iditarod, 265
Independence Gulch, 247
Innoko (river), 264
Iowa John, 120
Iron Creek, 196
Ivanov, Minook, 259

Jackson, Sheldon, 162
Jamestown, U. S. cutter: fires on Chilkoot Indians, 22, 282n10; at Dyea, 43
Jock. See Diggers, the
Johnsen, Laura, 209–10
Johnston, Capt. E. W., 202, 203
Judge, Father William H.: builds Dawson hospital, 8, 92, 103
Juneau, Joe, 3
Juneau (city), 11

Kearns, Jack. See McLernan, John
Kenai River, 2
Kennaley, Pat, 151, 153–54
Kennicott, Robert, 250
Ketchum, Frank, 17, 250
King, Whistling, 22
Klatt, Emile, 59–60
Klondike News, The, 211, 248
Klondike River, 4, 5, 6, 11; machinery on, 9, 264; early prospecting on, 77–80 passim; known as Trundeck, 77; gold from tributaries of, 85; world hears of, 86; quantity of gold from, 267; origin of name, 285n1
Klowosinak River, 219
Klutena City, 218
Klutena, Lake, 117
Kotzebue Sound, 192
Koyukuk (river), 8, 264
Krause, Arthur, 43

298

Index

Mogul Creek, 248
Moran, Bernard H. "Casey," 92–93
Morgan, Blackie, 73–75
Moses: lends money to gambler, 265–66
Mt. Drum, 219
Mt. Sanford, 219
Mounties. See North-West Mounted Police
Mulrooney, Belinda, 90
Mulrooney, Margaret, 236–37

Nation (town), 12, 247, 248, 269
Nation River, 134, 247
Nelson, John, 78
Nelson, Peter, 78
Nenana, 235
Newman, Hannah, 39, 40
Newman, "Packer" Jack: kills faro dealer, 37; as protector of Mollie Walsh, 36–37; commissions bust of Mollie, 39–40
Niukluk River, 179
Nome, 4, 11, 12, 265; Noyes gang fraud in, 8, 205–6; compared with Dawson, 179; stampede to, 188, 191; name changed, 194; as tent city, 194–95; first car in, 203–4; lawlessness in, 204; incorporation of, 207; fighting in, 207–8; gold wealth of, 208, 267; today, 208–10; mining in, 291n5
Nome News, 207–8
Nordale, Oscar, 236
Northern American Transportation and Trading Company (N. A. T. & T. Co.), 117, 133, 165
North Slope, the, 223, 271
North-West Mounted Police: poundage checks made by, 52; at Forty Mile, 114–17, 126–27; and miners' law, 116; first post of, 287n15
Northwest Trading Company, 43
Norton Sound, 17
Not River, 196
Noyes, Arthur E.: judge in Nome, 205; arrested, 206
Nulato (trading post), 14, 15

O'Brien, Pinky, 240–41
O'Brien Creek, 241
Ogilvie, William, 110, 287n10, 285n1
Ogilvie (trading post), 78
Olnes (town), 224, 235, 242
Omoluk, 196

Ophir (town), 265; Diggers in vicinity of, 196, 197; Carlson claim at, 203

Packtrain Saloon, 42
Parrott and Company, 251
Pavlov, Pitka: and Cherosky at Forty Mile, 149, 150; on the Mastodon, 151; in Tanana, 151; and the three Bostonians, 153–54; as recalled by Helen Callahan 289n5
Pedro, Felix: prospects Tanana R., 227, 231; early life, 230; meets Barnette, 231; strike of, 232
Pedro Camp, 224, 235
Pedroni, Felice. See Pedro, Felix
Peel River, 15, 19, 282n8
Pelly River, 4, 15, 22
Pemberton, Jonathan, 151; seeks Preacher's Creek, 152; on journey to Birch Creek, 153–54; heeds McQuesten's advice, 156
Peninsula City, 218
Pilz, George, 78, 280
Pinney, George M., 165
Pitka. See Pavlov, Pitka
Poplin, Dick, 64, 65
Porcupine River, 15, 249
Powers, Isaac, 66
Preacher's Creek, 152
Pullen, "Ma": arrival in Skagway, 33; businesses of, 33–34; opens inn, 34–35; inn of, today, 40
Purgatory, 258, 259

Quitch, Billy, 220, 221

Rabbit Creek, 4, 79, 80. See also Bonanza
Rampart, 12; founded, 259; Indians in, 260; law in, 260–61; today, 261–64 passim
Rapuzzi, George, 42
Rathe Brothers, 22
Rat River, 15, 251
Ray, Col. P. H.: at Fort Egbert, 134; on mining camp conditions, 163, 164, 165; and Eagle petition, 288n8
Raymond, Capt. C. W., 251, 282n5
Reid, Frank H., 32
Reynolds, A. D., 248–49
Richardson, Capt. W. P.: at Eagle, 132, 176; at Fort Egbert, 134, 135; at Circle City, 166, 167–68

300

Index

Index

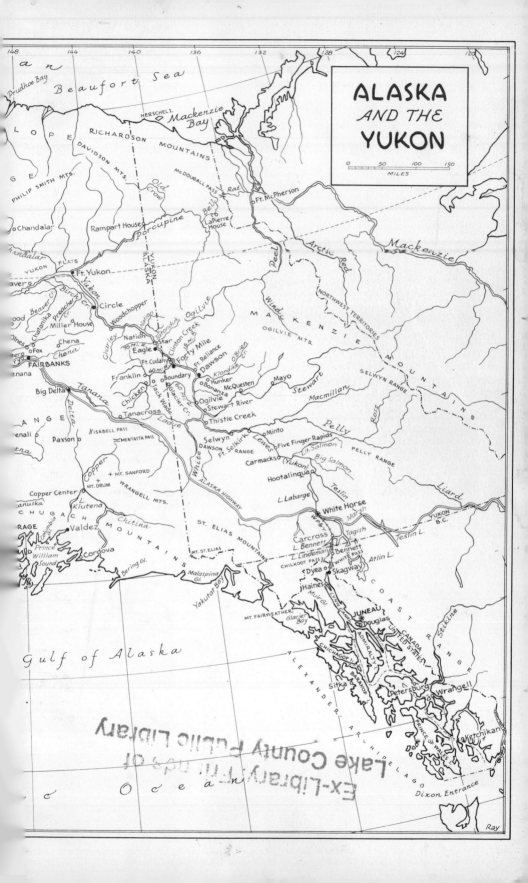

ALASKA
AND THE
YUKON

0   50   100   150
MILES

Beaufort Sea

Prudhoe Bay

Herschel I.   *Mackenzie Bay*

RICHARDSON

SLOPE   DAVIDSON MTS.   MOUNTAINS

McDOUGALL PASS

PHILIP SMITH MTS.   *Old Crow*   Rat   Ft. McPherson

Chandalar   Rampart House   *Porcupine*   LaPierre House   Bell   Peel

Chandalar   YUKON FLATS   Ft. Yukon   ALASKA/YUKON   Arctic Red   *Mackenzie*

avero   Beaver Cr.   Circle   Woodchopper   NORTHWEST TERRITORIES

wood   Chatanika   Preacher Cr.   Birch Cr.   Charley   Nation   Kandik   Ogilvie   WINDY   M A C K E N Z I E   MOUNTAINS

Olnes   Fox   Chena   Miller House   Nation   Tatonduk   Clinton Creek   OGILVIE MTS.

ery   Chena   Chena   Tol. R.   Eagle   Star   Forty Mile   SELWYN RANGE   Ross

FAIRBANKS   Ft. Cudahy   Ft. Reliance   O'Brien Cr.

nena   Franklin   40 Mi.   Boundary   Dawson   McQuesten   Mayo   Stewart   Ogilvie MTS.   M O U N T A I N S

Big Delta   Tanana   Chicken   60 Mi.   Hunker   Klondike   Macmillan

Jack Wade   Glacier Cr.   Bonanza

Tanacross   Ladue   Ogilvie

ISABELL PASS   White   Stewart River   Pelly

RANGE   Thistle Creek   SELWYN   Minto   Five Finger Rapids   PELLY RANGE   Liard

enali   Paxson   MENTASTA PASS   DAWSON   Ft. Selkirk   RANGE   Lewes   Lit. Salmon   Big Salmon

tna   Copper   MT. SANFORD   Carmacks   (Yukon)

Copper Center   MT. DRUM   WRANGELL MTS.   ALASKA HIGHWAY   Hootalinqua

anuska   Klutena   Chitina   Teslin

CHUGACH   Columbia   Valdez   MOUNTAINS   ST. ELIAS MOUNTAINS   L. Labarge   White Horse   Marsh   YUKON B.C.

RAGE   Prince   Cordova   MT. ST. ELIAS   Carcross   Wye.   Tagish   Teslin L.

William Sound   Bering Gl.   L. Bennett   COAST

Malaspina Gl.   L. Lindeman   Bennett   Atlin L.

Yakutat Bay   CHILKOOT PASS   Dyea   WHITE PASS   Skagway

MT. FAIRWEATHER   Haines   RANGE

Gulf of Alaska   Glacier   Muir Gl.   Glacier Bay   JUNEAU   Douglas   CANADA   Stikine   RANGE   UNITED STATES

CHICHAGOF I.   ADMIRALTY   UNITED STATES

Sitka   BARANOF   A L E X A N D E R   Petersburg   Wrangell

ARCHIPELAGO   PRINCE OF WALES   Ketchikan

O c e a n   Dixon Entrance

Ray